37,50
60B

Harvesting Change

Laura J. Enríquez

Harvesting
CHANGE

Labor and Agrarian Reform in Nicaragua,

1979–1990

The University of North Carolina Press

Chapel Hill and London

The paper in this book meets the guidelines for permanence and du-
rability of the Committee on Production Guidelines for Book Longevity of
the Council on Library Resources.

95 94 93 92 91   5 4 3 2 1

Library of Congress Cataloging-in-Publication Data

Enríquez, Laura J.
  Harvesting change : labor and agrarian reform in Nicaragua,
1979–1990 / by Laura J. Enríquez.
      p.   cm.
  Includes bibliographical references and index.
  ISBN 0-8078-1957-3. — ISBN 0-8078-4315-6 (pbk.)
  1. Land reform—Nicaragua.   2. Agricultural laborers—Nicaragua—
Supply and demand.   3. Agriculture—Economic aspects—Nicaragua.
I. Title.
HD1333.N5E57   1991
333.3'17285—dc20   90-50715
                                                                        CIP

A Maurizio, Margarita, Gladys

y tantos otros

quienes han comprometido sus vidas

para que el futuro de su pueblo sea mejor

Contents

Tables

Figures and Map

Figures

Map

Preface

When I arrived in Nicaragua in 1982 to begin the fieldwork for what was later to become this book, the major question guiding my research was the role played by internal structural obstacles, inherited from the past, in conditioning the options open to Nicaragua's new policy makers. Nicaragua's heritage of dependent development, such as the incomplete nature of its economy and its consequent trade dependence, would certainly affect efforts to transform it.

I went prepared to study this process of change in either industry or agriculture, being particularly interested in the dilemmas that would confront policy makers and their responses to these dilemmas. It quickly became apparent, however, that to understand the essence of the transformation process, I had to examine what was taking place in the countryside. I knew that the dilemma that I ultimately chose to study, the tension between agroexport production and agrarian reform, had arisen in other countries that had experienced structural changes in agriculture. It was for precisely this reason that the study seemed like a worthwhile endeavor. Given the dependence on the production of a few export crops that characterizes many small Third World countries, efforts to change the nature of agricultural production so as to improve the standard of living of the rural population and promote more balanced development would inevitably threaten to undermine the system of production that had heretofore been the basis of their economies. My hope was that an examination of the process of agrarian reform in Nicaragua would shed light on one of the many such problems that were likely to be encountered by these countries' planners in their efforts to find an alternative course of development.

Eight years later (in the autumn of 1990), as I write this preface, it appears that most of the objectives held by Sandinista policy makers when this study was begun have been replaced in the agenda set forth by the new UNO (Unión Nacional Opositora) government. Although UNO has adopted an official posture of promoting reformist capitalism, a number of the government's early initiatives point to the goal of reshaping agricultural policy in ways reminiscent of not-so-progressive, dependent capitalism. For example, the announcement of decrees 10-90 and 11-90 paved the way for the return of (or the provision of compensation for) property confiscated during the Sandinista administration. And although the decrees were officially suspended in July 1990, they have been partially implemented. The state sector (in agriculture, the state farm sector) would be most affected by this policy. In addition, the restructuring of agricultural credit policy along much more traditional lines suggests the inevitable outcome of once again excluding small farmers from the resources that can improve their production and their standard of living, to say nothing of the potential the policies represent for the loss of peasant property through indebtedness.

Regardless of the threats to the achievements of Sandinista agrarian policy inherent in the UNO government's first policy initiatives, however, the strength of the FSLN and the peasants' and workers' organizations make a complete "return to the past" impossible. Thus, even though many of the redistributive policies described in this book are being, or will be, altered by the UNO government, the tensions that the Sandinista agrarian reform generated will not disappear. The economy will continue to be dependent on agroexport production to ensure its stability. Yet the Nicaraguan peasantry, which has been largely released from the toils of agroexport harvest labor, will undoubtedly be loathe to return to the pattern of leaving their *minifundios* to work on the coffee and cotton estates part of each year. In sum, the numerous dilemmas encountered by the Sandinista government as it attempted to restructure Nicaraguan society will not miraculously be resolved, even with the ascendance of a new program with capitalist coloring.

The time frame for this case study was the period between 1979 and the completion of the 1983/84 agroexport harvest. This four-year period was chosen so as to ensure that the data would not simply reflect the dislocation caused by the war against Anastasio Somoza Debayle but would also show a pattern over time, corresponding to the advancement of the agrarian reform. The completion of the 1983/84 harvest was chosen as the end of the study because by that time the Contra war was beginning to endanger agricultural production. The effects of the war on coffee in particular made any discussion of the impact of other factors on its production irrelevant. Consequently, I chose to end the study before the war overshadowed the relationship between the agrarian reform and agroexport production. Yet it was not enough to describe the problem of labor shortages in this four-year period because the process of agrarian reform continued unabated after that time and subsequently underwent some significant changes. The modification of the Agrarian Reform Law in 1986, for example, opened the way for a major expansion in land redistribution. Thus the Postscript attempts to bring the study up to the present time, touching on later occurrences related to the key issues that emerged in the early years of transformation.

A variety of methods were used to conduct the research. They included participant observation, formal and informal interviews, and archival research. In-depth interviews were conducted with a cross section of the population connected with agricultural production. Interviews were held with high-level officials from the ministries of Agricultural Development and Agrarian Reform, Planning (later the Secretariat of Planning and Budget), and Labor, the National Development Bank, and the Central Bank; those conducting research on the agrarian reform; small-, medium-, and large-sized agricultural producers and members of cooperatives; representatives from the agricultural workers' union, the union of small- and medium-sized farmers, and private sector organizations; both volunteer and traditional harvest workers; agrarian reform technicians; and representatives from a multinational agricultural inputs corporation. These interviewees reflected a range of political perspectives.

I was based in Nicaragua's capital, Managua, throughout the years 1982 to 1989 while I collected information for this study. Interviews were conducted in five of the country's six regions (excluding Region I, the North and South Autonomous Regions, and Special Zone III); in Managua; in some of the provincial capitals, including Matagalpa, León, Chinandega, Jinotepe, and Granada; in several small towns in the coffee- and cotton-growing regions; and on a number of *fincas*.

The completion of this project was made possible by the cooperation and support of more people than it is possible to name. My first thanks must go to the numerous informants who shared their thoughts, concerns, and hopes with me, seeking nothing in return. Without their generosity in devoting precious time to converse with me when all else must have seemed more urgent—the war, the economic crisis, and the never-ending changes that one confronts constantly in a revolutionary society, to say nothing of the trials and tribulations of daily life—this study would have remained nothing more than an idea. Because of the highly politicized environment in which I conducted my interviews, the identities of those I interviewed will remain anonymous. Interviews are referred to by number and general category of the informant.

This study evolved over an eight-year period, during which many people contributed to its conceptual development. In its formative period, Richard R. Fagen challenged me to push on in my thinking and make the linkages between the externally imposed constraints implied in dependent development and the internal class relations that characterize most Third World societies. Paul M. Lubeck was very helpful in the selection of the problem I ultimately chose to study. William H. Friedland generously shared his expertise in the areas of agricultural development and the transition to socialism.

At a later stage, several colleagues provided comments and criticisms that I found extremely useful in addressing the weaknesses of my arguments and data base. Carmen Diana Deere, Rose J. Spalding, Richard Stahler-Sholk, and Peter Utting read drafts of various chapters, and their suggestions were greatly appreciated. Conversations I had with David Kaimowitz, Francisco Mayorga, Kent Norsworthy, and Michael Zalkin also proved beneficial in the development of my analysis. Martín Sánchez-Jankowski gave me helpful suggestions as well. Moreover, Michael Burawoy and Carlos M. Vilas offered insights at critical moments that enabled me to overcome what seemed to be insurmountable obstacles. The two anonymous reviewers for the University of North Carolina Press also stimulated me to strengthen the manuscript in innumerable ways. Finally, my editor, David Perry, demonstrated patience without limits and much appreciated sympathy at several traumatic moments, both of which facilitated the success of our joint endeavor.

In addition, three people provided me with research assistance as this project drew to a close. Nahela Becerril and Marlen I. Llanes scouted out minute pieces of information that must have seemed to them just one more example of the obsessive nature of North American social scientists yet were essential for documenting my assertions. Marta Parajon typed and retyped and retyped this manuscript more times than she wants to remember, as well as contributing to the research effort.

The Centro de Investigación y Asesoría Socio-Económica (CINASE) and the Ministerio de Desarrollo Agropecuario y Reforma Agraria (MIDINRA) provided me with essential institutional support during my seven-year stay in Nicaragua. My association with CINASE (1982–85) facilitated my study of the agrarian reform from outside of the process, and my tenure with MIDINRA (where I was a consultant in MIDINRA's Programa Alimentario Nicaragüense from 1985 to 1989) gave me an insider's understanding of the difficulties entailed in implementing social change–oriented policies. Neither institution, however, nor any of those who gave their time to read and comment on my work bears any responsibility for its final expression.

Several others collaborated with this project by offering me support at crucial moments. Maxine R. White, Robert Marotto, and Beth Stephens deserve my gratitude for coming through when I needed them. Douglas L. Murray contributed greatly in the early stages of the project's conceptualization and my first attempts to put my findings on paper. Maurizio tolerated my many moments of frustration, as well as sharing in the joy of the breakthroughs. He and Edith made my daily life bearable during what seemed like a never-ending endeavor.

Finally, I wish to acknowledge the important role my parents, Jean and Eduardo Enríquez, played in this long process. Without their love and support, this undertaking would have been impossible.

Harvesting Change

I

The Problem of
Breaking Out of Dependent
Capitalist Development

The overthrow of Nicaraguan dictator Anastasio Somoza Debayle on July 19, 1979, marked a turning point for all of Latin America. Not since the overthrow of Fulgencio Batista in Cuba in January 1959 and the ill-fated Chilean experiment in the early 1970s had any country in the hemisphere experienced such a fundamental break with its heritage of extreme under-development, inequality, and dependence on its northern neighbor, the United States. Nicaragua suddenly became the latest in a series of Third World countries seeking to escape the constraints of dependent capitalist development. Ranging from Tanzania, Mozambique, and Angola, to Viet-nam and Cuba, these countries had begun the process of transforming their socioeconomic structures. Although the process has varied widely in form, each country expressly sought to bring about a more just distribution of its national resources and increased independence in the international arena.

All of these Third World revolutions, however, had to contend with hos-tility and intervention from the advanced capitalist nations. Ironically, the same capitalist countries that threatened these nascent socialist societies were those that Marx (1966) had argued would lead the world in revolu-tionary change. Instead, capitalism in the Western industrialized world adapted to each new crisis and remained hegemonic. Rather, it was in the Third World that revolutionary movements gained strength after World War II. The most powerful of the advanced capitalist countries (particularly, but not only, the United States) responded with strong opposition to these efforts to promote revolutionary change.

In addition to contending with intervention by the Western industrialized nations, each of these revolutions has been faced with an array of obstacles arising from its location in the international economy. That location was a product of the historical development of the capitalist world system. Class dynamics internal to each country interacted with the expansion of international capitalism in forming the social structures that characterize the Third World today. This process of development affected all of the Third World nations that attempted to break out of dependent capitalism. Although these nations were tremendously varied, they had some important features in common: they were "all . . . small, open, under-developed primary export economies on the periphery of the world market system" (FitzGerald, 1984a:30). These shared features became formidable obstacles to social transformation for all of the countries in transition. Moreover, they compounded the constraints imposed by the advanced capitalist countries and served to limit the scope and options of revolutionary programs.

This study examines the role of internal structural obstacles in the process of revolutionary transformation in the case of Nicaragua. In addition to external aggression, the Nicaraguan revolution had to contend with the constraints placed on it by the country's own history of dependent development. Its continued dependence on agroexport production conditioned the process of agrarian transformation so central to the revolution. As the transformation progressed, conflicts arose between the peasant/food crop and the agroexport sectors over the use of certain resources.

One example of these conflicts, the tension that arose from competing labor requirements between the peasant/food crop and agroexport sectors, is the subject of this book. New employment possibilities that opened up through the agrarian reform threatened to upset the delicate balance developed in prerevolution years to meet the labor requirements of the agroexport sector. The labor shortages Nicaragua experienced in the agroexport harvests beginning in 1979 were the clearest expression of the threat posed by the agrarian reform. These shortages worsened as the various programs that composed the agrarian reform advanced. *Campesinos*, who in the past were driven to the harvest out of sheer economic necessity, found new options through the agrarian reform and became less willing to seek employment in the harvests.

Moving to a more theoretical level, the agroexport model has been dependent upon an agricultural work force that is characterized for its cheap labor.[1] The relative advantage that agroexport countries like Nicaragua have in the capitalist world market comes from their low labor costs.[2] This aspect of agroexport dependency has implications for those undertaking revolutionary transformation. The primary goal of revolutionary change is the development of a more just society. A critical element in working toward this goal is the attempt to raise the standard of living of the impoverished majorities through a redistribution of these countries' resources. But revolutionary policy makers must come to terms with the fact that continued participation in the international capitalist economy on the basis of agroexport production implies the maintenance of an exploitative system of labor relations. Herein lies a major dilemma for those attempting fundamental social transformation. This is the dilemma that underlies the following case study.

Before analyzing the problem in detail, however, it is necessary to describe several of the defining features of Nicaragua's dependent capitalism that gave rise to and conditioned this dilemma. Nicaragua shares these general characteristics with numerous Third World countries, although its development has most closely paralleled that of the other Central American republics. Therefore, though the focus in this chapter will be on the Nicaraguan case, the model of dependent capitalist development described below can easily be found elsewhere. Likewise, this discussion should suggest the difficulties of social transformation throughout the periphery of the world capitalist system.

Following this sketch of the structural legacy of dependent capitalism inherited by the Nicaraguan revolution, the remainder of the chapter looks at how dependent capitalism generated revolutionary social change in Nicaragua and, finally, touches on the dilemmas and contradictions this legacy has created for the transformation process in many Third World countries. All of these themes will be developed in greater detail and placed in their historical context in Chapters 2 through 5.

Dependent Capitalism in Nicaragua

The internal barriers conditioning social transformation in Nicaragua evolved over the four centuries since Spain began to colonize the New World.[3] Colonization began the irreversible process of Nicaragua's integration into the capitalist world economy. It became a supplier of raw materials, first for Spain and later for Europe and the United States. A domestic bourgeoisie gradually emerged that shared a common interest in the wealth generated by raw materials production. The dependent capitalism that developed as a result of these processes gave rise to certain structural features that posed obstacles to social transformation. These features included the incompleteness of the country's economy, the continued existence of a large peasant sector, and a less than fully consolidated state.[4] These structural elements were accompanied by certain social conditions that included extreme inequality and poverty. All of these elements taken together characterized Nicaragua's heritage of dependent development.

The Incompleteness of the Economy

The incompleteness of the economy was perhaps the most important barrier to Nicaragua's attempt to break away from dependent capitalism. In an incomplete economy one sector predominates in the accumulation of capital, a precondition for development. In Nicaragua this was the primary goods sector. Thus all other goods, including capital goods, had to be imported via the international market. A number of problems arose as a consequence of this situation.

In Nicaragua, primary goods production has largely taken the form of agroexport production. Its economy came to center on the production of coffee, cotton, sugarcane, and beef, geared almost exclusively to external markets. The agroexport sector gained predominance in the competition for land and labor over the production of crops destined for the domestic market. An important consequence of this dependence on primary goods production was the external orientation that came to characterize Nicaragua's economy. The essential dynamic component for capital accumulation and expansion came from without, instead of within.[5]

Dependence on primary goods production, however, did not preclude the development of industry in Nicaragua. During the 1960s, a limited process of industrialization was begun throughout the region under the auspices of the Central American Common Market (CACM). The CACM made possible the substitution of some locally produced consumer durables and nondurables for those that previously had been imported, but it did not promote the development of a capital goods sector. Instead, it instituted a system that depended on external sources for capital goods inputs.[6] Furthermore, though the CACM stimulated the development of some agroindustry, it did not bring about a significant increase in the vertical integration within Nicaragua's economy. To the contrary, this "industrial growth . . . produced an important differentiation in production, parallel to and superimposed upon the traditional axis of the system, the export agricultural economy" (Torres

Rivas, 1983:16). As a result, Nicaragua came into the 1970s still largely dependent on agroexport production—and remains so today.

Dependency on primary goods is more profound in Nicaragua than in some other Third World countries in part because of its small size. As one study concluded, "Though smallness need not necessarily be a constraint on development, it implies that the quantity and variety of resources available is limited and that the domestic market is narrow" (INIES/CRIES, 1983a:9).[7] A narrow market and limited resources typically cause a higher than usual level of trade dependence. That is, "trade is large in relation to total economic activity" (INIES/CRIES, 1983a:9). In Nicaragua, 34 percent of the Gross Domestic Product was generated by export earnings in 1975, compared to 10 percent for Latin America and the Caribbean as a whole (calculated from BID, n.d.:440, 443).

Another important aspect of Nicaragua's agroexport dependency is that its comparative advantage in this type of production stems largely from its low labor costs. Speaking of the Third World generally, José Luis Coraggio (1984:42) suggests that hidden behind the idea that the generation of surplus in these countries is based on geographical advantage lies its underpaid labor force. Nicaragua is characterized by a climate and geography that favor the production of coffee, cotton, and sugarcane, among other crops. Its exceptionally high yields in these crops result from natural attributes in the country (and indeed the region) that are advantageous to their production. The country's cheap labor is, however, more important in making it attractive for the agroexport production and limited industrial activities that take place there. Nicaragua's economic development has been based on the subjection of the majority of the population to an extremely low standard of living.[8]

Finally, Nicaragua's heritage of an incomplete economy meant that its agroexport production had to be maintained or it would be unable to import the innumerable goods it still did not produce. This condition held true even in the changed circumstances of the revolutionary transformation. Foreign exchange levels had to remain stable for the economy to function normally. Yet Nicaragua is among the world's "price-takers," not "price-setters."[9] Many factors combine to produce changes in international commodity prices,[10] most of them unrelated to the specific situation of any one of the numerous countries that produce agroexport commodities, although price fluctuations have a serious impact on all agroexport-dependent nations.[11] For Nicaragua, this impact is heightened by its specialization in only a few export crops. A drop in international prices for these export crops has disastrous consequences for the entire economy.

Constant vulnerability to the international market has been compounded in the past decade by a general worsening in the terms of trade for Nicaragua and other primary producing countries.[12] More and more agricultural goods are required to purchase the same quantity of manufactured goods and petroleum products. Nicaragua's former president Daniel Ortega (1982:68) captured the gravity of this tendency for all of Central America: "In 1977 our countries had to produce 338 bushels of cotton, or 1,394 bushels of sugar, or 98 bushels of coffee to buy one tractor. Four years later, in 1981, we must produce 476 bushels of cotton—an increase of 41 percent—to buy one tractor; or 2,143 bushels of sugar—an increase of 54 percent or more; or 248 bushels of coffee—an increase of 145 percent."[13] Nicaragua's foreign exchange balance has worsened, and prospects for a reversal are dim.[14] The pressure remains to produce ever-increasing amounts of export crops in order to improve, even slightly, the country's foreign exchange balance.

A dismal foreign exchange balance is only one symptom of an economic crisis that is affecting all of Latin America (CEPAL, 1985; 1986a). As prices for imported goods have increased over the past several decades, countries throughout the region have come to rely more heavily on foreign assistance to make ends meet from month to month. Nicaragua's effort to break out of dependent capitalism, however, closed the door to many sources of foreign assistance that were previously open to it (Maxfield and Stahler-Sholk, 1985; Conroy, 1984). While other countries in the region struggled with the difficulty of paying back the foreign debt they had accumulated through their dependence on foreign assistance,[15] Nicaragua was confronted by a foreign debt passed on from the Somoza regime, serious difficulty maintaining export earnings, and extremely limited access to new assistance. In sum, Nicaragua continued to share the consequences of its incomplete economic development with the rest of Latin America, even as it attempted to break with that heritage through revolutionary transformation.

The Existence of a Large Peasant Sector

The economic manifestations of Nicaragua's dependent capitalism interacted with its national class structure to condition the process of social transformation. The class structure that emerged in Nicaragua with the development of dependent capitalism did not disappear overnight following the overthrow of the old regime. Rather, it played a key role in shaping the new era, so that, for example, the continued existence of a large peasant sector was extremely important for the agrarian transformation promoted by the revolution.

The expansion of capitalism into Nicaraguan agriculture resulted in a growing emphasis on production of export crops, while leaving intact a sizable peasant sector whose production came to play a central role in Nicaragua's agroexport dependency. This relationship was stabilized in the rural class structure that emerged with the development of agrarian capitalism.[16] The three major class groupings in the rural social structure have been the bourgeoisie or large landowners, the peasant or *campesino* sector, and the agricultural proletariat. The bourgeoisie can be roughly divided into large- and medium-sized producers, differentiated primarily by the size of their landholdings and the extent to which they specialize in agroexport production. Large landowners are generally defined as those whose farms are greater than five hundred *manzanas* in size and are highly specialized in export crop production (and, to a lesser degree, in commercial food crop production). They composed less than 0.5 percent of the agricultural Economically Active Population (EAP) in 1978.[17] In contrast, medium-sized producers have between fifty and five hundred *manzanas* and cultivate some crops for the domestic market (especially corn and industrial sorghum), but still concentrate on export agriculture.[18] These latter producers composed approximately 4.5 percent of the agricultural EAP.

The largest grouping in the rural class structure is the peasant sector.[19] The peasant or *campesino* sector can be divided into the rich and middle peasantry, who own or have access to between ten and fifty *manzanas* of land, and the poor peasantry, who have access to fewer than ten *manzanas*. The former group composed 21.6 percent of the agricultural EAP in 1978 and produced most of the country's commercial crop of basic grains, as well as participating to a limited degree in export crop production (particularly coffee production). The latter group represented 36.4 percent of the agricultural EAP, and it produced primarily for its own consumption. A significant part of the peasant sector (the poor peasantry) has not had access to sufficient land to provide for its subsistence on a year-round basis and, therefore, has participated in the wage labor force for a few months of each year.

The last major class grouping in the rural social structure is the agricultural proletariat. This class includes both those who are employed in wage labor on a year-round basis (and composed 19.8 percent of the EAP in 1978) and those who participate in agricultural wage labor for only a few months of the year (17.3 percent). The key feature distinguishing the rural proletariat from the peasant sector is that the former has no access to the means of production (land in particular) to provide for its own subsistence. These workers have traditionally supported themselves by finding employment in processing facilities on the agroexport estates; composing the small group of maintenance workers on the plantations; participating in petty commodity production in the countryside and supplementing this income with harvest labor; or remaining in the reserve labor pool that provides the day-to-day labor needs of the large- and medium-sized capitalist growers. Their survival has been largely dependent on finding wage labor for at least several months of the year on the agroexport plantations.

The development of dependent capitalism in Nicaragua brought about a specialization within agriculture.[20] The emerging capitalist sector (both large and medium-sized) devoted itself primarily to the cultivation of export crops, which provided the real profits. This class identified with its counterpart in the advanced capitalist countries rather than with the traditional sectors within Nicaragua. The local bourgeoisie was concerned with improving its own position vis-à-vis the international market, not with promoting some form of integrated national development.[21] When this class did produce for the domestic market, its endeavors were characteristically capital-intensive and commercially oriented. It specialized in high-technology rice and industrial sorghum operations, leaving corn and bean production to the peasant sector.

As commercial agriculture expanded, it came into direct competition with peasant/food crop production for land and labor. The capitalist growers were able to push thousands of peasant farmers off the most fertile land and onto very small, marginal plots elsewhere. The first wave of dispossessions brought about by the expansion of capitalism occurred during the coffee boom of the nineteenth century. Half a century later, the cotton, beef, and sugarcane booms forced large numbers of *campesinos* further into the agricultural frontier and, to a lesser extent, into urban areas.

In addition to being geographically marginalized, the peasantry was excluded from the modernization process that accompanied the development of agroexport and commercial food crop production. Technical, infrastructural, and financial assistance offered by the government went almost exclusively to medium and large producers. Thus peasant production remained traditional in nature. The consequence was a stagnation in most food crop production and increased impoverishment of the *campesino* sector.[22]

Yet the expansion of capitalism into the Nicaraguan countryside was only partial. A relationship developed between the *campesino* and capitalist sectors that was essential for the expansion of agroexport production. This relationship has come to be known as "functional dualism,"[23] a situation in which "the capitalist sector . . . produces commodities (on capitalist *latifundio* and commercial farms) on the basis of hired semiproletarian labor, and the peasant sector . . . produces use values and petty commodities on the basis of family labor and delivers cheap wage labor to the capitalist sector" (de Janvry, 1981:84).[24]

The agroexport sector needed large numbers of workers during several months of the year for the harvest. Only a small part of the work force was employed year-round. Over time, a complementary relationship developed whereby poor peasants fulfilled the temporary labor requirements of the agroexport growers. Although a sizable part of the *campesinado* had been able to resist the process of proletarianization that was engendered by agroexport capitalism and continued to farm their own small plots of land, the marginal quality of that land and the traditional production techniques they used made it increasingly difficult for them to support themselves throughout the year solely from what was produced on their *minifundios*. Thus during the critical months of the agroexport harvests, these peasants offered their labor for wages. This relationship eliminated the need for agroexport growers to support a large labor force on a permanent basis and enabled the *campesinos* to supplement the income earned on their own farms.

The expansion of agricultural capitalism in Nicaragua greatly weakened the position of the peasantry, yet this expansion would not have been possible without the continued existence of a peasant sector. Complete proletarianization of the labor force ran contrary to the interests of agroexport capitalism, which requires a semiproletarianized population. Thus a relationship developed between the capitalist, agroexport sector and the more traditional peasant sector. The "disarticulated accumulation" characterizing Nicaragua's economy gave rise to this relationship (see de Janvry, 1981), which continued to condition the country's development even as its new government pushed forth changes designed to facilitate a break out of dependent capitalism.

A Less Than Fully Consolidated State

The final structural legacy affecting the process of social transformation in Nicaragua is the state structure that developed alongside dependent capitalism. It both established the conditions for and was strengthened by the expansion of agroexport capitalism.

The development of the Nicaraguan state was defined first by colonialism and later by the expansion of capitalism and postindependence imperialism. The state structure implanted by Spain and Portugal throughout Latin America during the colonial era expressed their primary interest in the region, which was to exploit Latin America's natural resources to the fullest in order to finance the economic development and wars of the motherland. The colonial state was clearly designed to administer the wealth of the crown rather than to address the concerns of those living under its authority. The Latin American wars of independence were an expression of resentment against the foreign orientation of the colonial state. Yet freedom from Spain's domination did not immediately produce strong, individual nation-states.[25]

Formal independence came to Central America in 1821. In Nicaragua, independence was followed by a period of anarchy. Different landowning families established political fiefdoms, and the national state reflected the shifting strength among competing oligarchical groups.[26] Several imperial powers (England and later the United States) played these interoligarchical conflicts to their advantage in machinations that would continue until the overthrow of Somoza in 1979. Their explicit interest in Nicaragua derived from its potential as a location for an interoceanic canal. Their implicit interest, however, was much broader—to gain hegemony over the region through this strategic foothold. The continuous intervention of these powers in Nicaragua's political and economic affairs profoundly influenced the country's course of development.

The landowning class, which coalesced to promote the expansion of coffee production during the late nineteenth century, initiated the first stage of consolidation of the Nicaraguan state and began the intimate relationship between the state and agroexport production that still exists today. The state played a crucial role in the development of agroexport production and the marginalization of the peasantry.[27] It provided infrastructural, financial, and technical assistance to this budding capitalist class and legitimated the concentration of land and labor essential for the expansion of export-crop production. The strength of the state grew as this sector developed.

In contrast, the state interacted with the subsistence goods sector only insofar as its promotion of agroexport production affected these small producers. The state contributed to the marginalization of the peasantry by opening up land to the agroexport sector. It also facilitated the development of the relations of production that came to characterize agroexport production.[28] Labor regulations enacted by the state beginning in the late 1800s were designed to ensure a sufficient labor supply for cash crop producers (Torres Rivas, 1980b). These laws were reinforced by the state's exclusion of subsistence producers from government assistance, which forced the *campesinos* to supplement their incomes on the agroexport estates. In sum, "toward the end of the nineteenth century, the interests of the coffee oligarchy became the interests of the entire society. Coffee was a symbol of progress. These interests were represented by the emerging State" (Torres Rivas, 1980b:85).

The pattern of the state as representative of agroexport interests strengthened as export crop production developed.[29] Because this sector was the state's principal constituency, the guiding logic behind policy making, both that related to specific issues and its general vision of development for Nicaragua, was that of capital, or profit. Development was seen as the means by which the private accumulation of the capitalist class could be expanded. Policy making related to other sectors of society was relevant only insofar as it affected the interests of this small elite group and usually worked to the disadvantage of the better part of the population. Even in periods heralded as ones of dramatic (state-promoted) "growth" of the economy, the benefits of that development rarely "trickled down" to the "popular classes."

Yet the autonomy of the emerging Nicaraguan state was also limited by Nicaragua's position in the international market.[30] Regardless of the state's efforts to protect the agroexport sector, the country's economy remained subject to the vacillations of the world market, which could bring it wealth or ruin.[31]

The Social Conditions Resulting from Dependent Capitalism

The social conditions engendered by Nicaragua's dependent capitalism were crucial in the development of the revolutionary process. Extreme inequality and poverty were among the most important by-products of agroexport capitalism in Nicaragua. They were also a cause of its intrinsic instability.

Inequality had characterized social relations in Nicaragua since colonial times (Ayon, 1977). The development of agroexport capitalism, beginning with the coffee boom in the nineteenth century, heightened the unequal distribution of the nation's resources. The key resource affected was land.[32] Because agriculture was the principal generator of wealth in Nicaragua, the extreme concentration of agricultural land led to an equally extreme concentration in income.[33]

Economic inequality resulted in tremendous poverty. The landowning elite lived in luxurious homes and took frequent trips to the United States and Europe while the vast majority of Nicaraguans lived in conditions of abject poverty.[34] The wealth generated by agroexport production remained largely in the hands of the small class of capitalist landowners.[35] Furthermore, Nicaragua's reliance on the production of several export crops as the basis of its economy implied that the agricultural work force would have to be subjected to a low standard of living. Thus for the workers and *campesinos*, who formed the majority of the rural population, growth in the agroexport sector meant illiteracy, extremely limited access to medical care, and miserable living and working conditions.

In contrast to the deteriorating conditions of the rural poor, each wave of export-oriented expansion further consolidated the control of the small group of capitalists over Nicaragua's political and economic structure. The concentration of resources in agriculture was only one part of the process of consolidation, although the most important part. Establishment of the Central American Common Market gave this elite group a new, highly profitable project in which to invest their agroexport wealth. Increased control in the political arena accompanied the solidification of control in the economic arena. Following Nicaragua's historical pattern, those in positions of political power represented the interests of the upper class. Tensions did develop between the Somocista faction and other factions of the Nicaraguan upper class stemming from the former's "unfair" monopolization of the state apparatus in promoting its own interests (see Spalding, 1987). Yet the Somocista state also clearly represented the shared interests of this capitalist class.

Tensions Inherent in the Agroexport Model

The tremendous poverty and inequality that accompanied the expansion of Nicaragua's agroexport capitalism created a social tension that would become an inherent part of this model of development. At different moments this tension reached crisis proportions. The development of agroexport production resulted in a chain of peasant uprisings. In certain periods more coordinated efforts were made to overthrow the existing order. The rebellion waged by Augusto César Sandino during the Great Depression was an expression of growing opposition to the injustices fostered by Nicaragua's first coffee boom.

The social tension inherent in agroexport capitalism was heightened during periods of economic crisis. As falling prices in the international market wrought havoc on the economy, the rural poor bore the brunt of the burden. Under "normal" conditions this vast impoverished population was a time bomb waiting to explode. An awareness of the explosive nature of these social conditions lay behind the various agrarian reform programs launched in Nicaragua during the 1960s and 1970s,[36] but these programs were designed so as not to threaten the existing political and economic structure.

Instead, the old regime primarily relied on repression to eliminate social unrest. Reform was replaced by repression when the failure intrinsic to superficial reform became apparent.[37] When politics could no longer legitimate the social formation, the state's last line of defense was coercion.

Failed reform programs and government repression only aggravated the already strained social relations between the poor majority and Nicaragua's wealthy few. Repression was, ultimately, no more successful in eliminating unrest than cosmetic reforms had been. This delicate situation started to give way by the mid-1970s, as the non-Somocista bourgeoisie began to distance itself from the Somoza regime and the fruit of fifteen years of political organizing by the Frente Sandinista de Liberación Nacional (FSLN) was born. By 1979, the FSLN had succeeded in forming a united opposition, which together with increased hardship brought on the poor by the economic crisis that began in 1978 and the upsurge in repression employed by Somoza, lit the fuse, igniting the time bomb.[38]

Revolutionary Social Change

The scenario of political and economic crisis that characterized prerevolutionary Nicaragua was similarly experienced by a number of other Third World countries. In some of these countries, revolutionary movements developed in response to the crisis. When genuine reform proved impossible, profound social change came to be seen as the only alternative. During the past decade, this process affected three of the five Central American republics. A revolutionary government was established in Nicaragua. El Salvador and Guatemala were engulfed in civil wars between ruling factions and revolutionary movements. Even Costa Rica, the region's model of stability and social peace, felt the effects of the economic crisis. Strikes repeatedly threatened Costa Rica's banana production. The very essence of agroexport production was being questioned by Central America's poor majority, who had received little of the wealth their labor generated.

The course taken by revolutionary movements, where they arose, expressed both national specificities and similarities stemming from these countries' histories of dependent capitalist development. The revolutionary movements in Nicaragua, El Salvador, and Guatemala have had a number of common goals. They have all sought a redistribution of their nations' wealth in order to eliminate extreme inequality. The revolutionaries also shared an understanding of the roots of that inequality and poverty. Transformation of the previously existing economic and political structure was central to the platforms of those promoting revolutionary social change in the three countries. The revolutionaries believed that only through such fundamental social change could the basic needs of the majority of the region's population be met. It was believed that this transformation would also foster a more balanced model of development, which would improve the terms under which these economies operated in the international market.

Policy makers in all of the Third World countries that began the process of revolutionary transformation found that the social structure they had inherited continued to condition their course of development. Although it was relatively easy to begin the process of redistributing the national wealth, transforming an economy based on primary goods production proved to be very difficult.

The Dilemmas of Revolutionary Transformation

The overthrow of the old regime opens a new era for a revolutionary movement. The task of guiding the revolutionary transformation is significantly more complex than that of uniting forces against an unpopular government. The new regime faces competing sets of demands from the different class interests that have joined together in the revolutionary alliance. The stage is set for a renewed period of struggle as the process of modifying the nation's socioeconomic structure is begun.

Revolutionary governments are established with the express purpose of carrying out a fundamental restructuring of the society. The struggle against the old order involves more than replacing the particular person, or group of persons, in power. A redistribution of power and wealth aimed at reducing the extreme concentration of income and control over the means of production is central to the agenda of the new regime. The goals are to provide the poor majority with increased access to health care, education, and a higher standard of living, as well as participation in developing the policies that are supposed to bring about these goals.

Greater equity is to be achieved through what has come to be known as the "logic of the majority."[39] Following the logic of the majority requires that meeting the basic needs of the greatest part of the population be the top priority. This runs counter to the previously hegemonic "logic of private accumulation." It is the new government's mandate to reverse the priority system that guides policy making. Reliance on this alternative logic, however, represents more than a political orientation for policy makers. It also represents a political necessity. That is, for the new regime to maintain the legitimacy it was granted upon its establishment, it must fulfill the commitments that its leaders made during the earlier stage of struggle against the old order.

In addition to these political exigencies, the new government is confronted by another, often competing, set of exigencies based in the economy. The first of these is to reactivate the economy. If a long military struggle was waged against the previous regime, the country's infrastructural base may have sustained extensive damage, and the economy may have been weakened by capital flight and production stoppages. Once the reconstruction process has begun, a course of economic transformation must be set in motion. This may (and *will*, in all likelihood) entail the implementation of development projects that will strengthen the country's economic base. The concrete benefits produced by these projects will probably only be apparent over the medium to long term, yet they require major investments in the short term. At the same time, traditional sources of investment funding are frequently cut off, and the private capital that remains in the country is often reluctant to participate in the new government's development agenda. Many of those members of the capitalist class who remain to see it installed will resent their lack of control in the political arena and choose to withhold their cooperation from the new regime. All of these factors combine to complicate the task of maintaining the nation's financial solvency. Without

financial solvency, survival over the medium to long term, much less political and economic transformation, will be impossible.

In order to guarantee the nation's financial solvency while carrying out
the revolutionary transformation it is necessary to maintain a reasonable
foreign exchange balance. Yet because of the incompleteness characteristic
of the peripheral economy, these nations are extremely trade-dependent. To
continue importing the capital goods required for industry and the multi-
tude of inputs required for agricultural production (to say nothing of the
political need to import certain consumer goods for the middle class and, to
some extent, for the popular classes), requires maintenance of the country's
foreign exchange balance (see FitzGerald, 1986). Thus the activities that
previously generated foreign exchange earnings must be continued or replaced by others. The history of heavy reliance on export agriculture to bring
in foreign exchange, however, limits the options available at this stage. One
option is to diversify the country's agroexport dependency by producing
other crops in addition to, or instead of, the previously produced crops.
Another option is to stimulate the process of industrialization to reduce
imports, but this option is not open to many countries in transition because
it requires a significant infusion of capital (as well as a relatively large
market), which is not always readily available. The final option is to continue producing the same crop, or set of crops, that had formerly been the
basis of export-oriented production. Although some combination of these
options may be attempted, many small, peripheral countries in transition
have no choice but to remain dependent on one or several key crops.

Continued reliance on a few key crops for the generation of foreign
exchange earnings has implications for the course of transformation.[40] Nicaragua and other primary goods producers have the advantage in the international market that their labor costs are low. Without a major increase in
mechanization (requiring a large infusion of capital), cheap labor will remain the essence of agroexport production.

With the expansion of agroexport capitalism, the relationship between
the agroexport and peasant sectors guaranteed an adequate labor supply to
capitalist production through the marginalization of the peasant sector. The
revolutionary transformation of these fundamentally agricultural societies,
however, requires a major restructuring of the agrarian sector. The logic of
the majority necessitates a reorientation of agricultural production so that it
addresses the needs of the rural poor instead of those of agroexport elites.
The preservation of a system of production relations dependent on cheap

labor is inconsistent with this reorientation. Yet this political necessity comes into conflict with the economic necessity of maintaining agroexport production in order to guarantee the generation of foreign exchange earnings.[41] Thus the advancement of agrarian reform designed to improve the standard of living of the rural poor gradually undermines the delicate relationship that has been the basis of agrarian capitalism. The question that arises for revolutionary planners is, How can living standards be raised when the country's economic foundation is, and will continue to be for the foreseeable future, rooted in unjust relations of production?

The remainder of this book situates this question in the context of the revolutionary transformation that began in Nicaragua in 1979. The Nicaraguan revolution was confronted by many of the dilemmas raised above. It experienced a severe economic crisis and was unable to achieve the complete reactivation of the economy. At the same time, a profound process of transformation was initiated.

An agrarian reform program was at the center of this transformation. Because agriculture has been, and will continue to be, the key sector of the economy, its transformation was essential in restructuring the entire economy. The agrarian reform also played an important role in consolidating the power base of the regime and therefore was probably the most critical program to be implemented by the new government. The agrarian reform, however, was carried out within the context of Nicaragua's continuing dependence on agroexport production. Thus surfaces the dilemma that is the focus of this study.

This dilemma, however, is just one of many that arise in the process of revolutionary transformation. "The contradiction between structures and goals will rise to the surface and become [even] more intense as the transformation process continues" (Resnick, 1981:234). Overcoming the structural legacy of dependent development is the great challenge facing policy makers who participate in this endeavor, as they are reminded yet again that overthrowing the old regime is only the beginning of the struggle.

2

The Development of
Dependent Capitalism
in Nicaragua

Many of the difficulties confronted by the Nicaraguan revolution stemmed from the socioeconomic structure inherited by the new regime. That structure was a product of several hundred years of political and economic development that resulted in what could be characterized as dependent capitalism, which engendered the conditions that led to demands for revolutionary reform.

The development of capitalism in Nicaragua was first expressed and has remained concentrated in that country's agricultural sector and was based almost exclusively on the expansion of agroexport production. The social and economic development of the Central American region as a whole, from colonial times to the present, has been marked by its gradual integration into the international economy through the production of a succession of agroexport crops. This integration increasingly brought capitalist relations of production into heretofore precapitalist societies.[1]

In Nicaragua, the expansion of agricultural capitalism took place in stages marked by distinctly different types of agroexport production. Beef, cacao, and indigo were Nicaragua's first agroexport products. Their production began during the colonial era. Coffee followed these early export crops at the end of the nineteenth century. But it was not until the 1950s, with the full-scale adoption of cotton production for export, that the Nicaraguan economy became completely integrated into the international economy.

Each stage in the development of Nicaragua's export agriculture had repercussions on the rest of the economy. Cotton production, in particular, stimulated the growth of related industries and modernized the country's financial structure. Yet the economy remained overwhelmingly dependent on the production of a few agricultural products for sale in the international market. The discussion that follows traces this process of development that resulted in the socioeconomic structure that conditioned Nicaragua's revolutionary options.

The Colonial Period

Nicaragua's introduction to the world market began when Spain colonized Central America early in the sixteenth century. Unlike several of Spain's earlier conquests, this region did not offer the conquerors readily accessible riches, but the Spaniards did find a large indigenous population that soon proved useful in their plundering of South America.

Spain's initial interest in the New World lay in the tremendous wealth offered by the Incan and Aztec empires. The Indian population then inhabiting what is now Nicaragua was quickly incorporated through slave labor into Spanish efforts to secure Peru's silver for the mother country (Ayón, 1977). In the course of the next quarter of a century, the slave trade transformed one of the most highly populated regions in the world into an underpopulated colony (Las Casas, 1945; and Newson, 1982). Nicaragua's later development was conditioned by this depopulation. At the time of Spain's conquest of Nicaragua, the latter's population was estimated to be between 600,000 and 1 million people (Radell, 1969). By 1548 that number had been reduced to approximately 30,000. Within a decade after Spain's entry into the region, the slave trade was Nicaragua's primary economic activity.

The Spanish royal authorities outlawed slavery in the mid-1530s (Ayón, 1977). The prohibition proved difficult to enforce, however, because the slave trade was so lucrative. By this time other industries, including shipbuilding, had sprung up around the slave trade.[2] Ironically, the slave trade was largely responsible for its own demise. By the 1550s the indigenous population had been decimated. Slavery, forced labor and resistance to it, and diseases introduced during the Spanish conquest had killed off most of the indigenous population. The death of the slave trade brought a shift in Spain's interest in Nicaragua to its other key resource, land.

The Seeds of Export Agriculture

In addition to providing slave labor for Spain's conquest of the Incas, Nicaragua supplied agricultural goods to the conquerors. The *encomienda* system, established by the Spaniards upon their colonization of the region, facilitated the extraction of these agricultural goods from the indigenous population. In this system, "a nucleus of the native population was 'commended' or entrusted to a Conquistador who was to be responsible for ensuring that his 'wards' were instructed in the Roman Catholic faith and, in return, was given the right to use them as a labor force" (Furtado, 1976:17). Tomás Ayón (1977:227) described this commendation process less diplomatically: "The natives were [even] branded, just like slaves."[3] This relationship also required that the Indians pay a tribute to the Spaniards. Corn was the most important form of tribute, although the list of items offered as payment also included beans, cotton, salt, and chickens. After the abolition of the *encomienda* was decreed in 1543, colonial legislation set up a new system of forced labor to ensure the colonizers an adequate labor supply, *el repartimiento*. Under this latter system a certain percentage of Indians from each village were conscripted to work for landholders, miners, and government officials. Although they were supposed to be paid for their labor because of the "freer" nature of this system, a relationship of debt peonage normally evolved between the Indians and those for whom they worked (Woodward, 1976). Both of these systems arose in response to the decimation of the indigenous population and the need to ensure an adequate supply of labor for the *conquistadores*.

Nevertheless, by the mid-sixteenth century Nicaragua's small but growing agroexport sector began to encounter a serious obstacle—a shortage of laborers. As a consequence, labor-intensive crop cultivation had to be gradually abandoned. Labor shortages have periodically arisen since that time.[4] The response of those who first encountered the problem in the mid-1500s was to turn to less labor-intensive agricultural activities. Cattle raising, in particular, began to assume more importance at this time because its reduced labor requirements made it attractive to the landowning class.

The introduction of livestock to Nicaragua was authorized by the Spanish crown in 1527, but it was not until the end of the century that cattle raising became widespread. The increase in livestock production constituted a notable change in Spain's interest in Nicaragua. Previously, the country's agriculture had been significant only as a source of foodstuffs for those engaged in conquests elsewhere in Spanish America. Now, Nicaragua's agriculture began to be seen as a potential basis for commercial venture, that is, as a generator of export earnings.

Cattle raising rapidly consumed more and more of the land that had previously been used by the indigenous population for subsistence production. European demand for tallow and hides, in addition to the demand within the region for meat, stimulated the expansion of cattle raising. Southwestern and central Nicaragua were the areas most affected by this dramatic shift in priorities. The department of Chontales (in central Nicaragua) became the most important cattle region in Central America (Radell, 1969:155).

Cattle raising engendered extensive *hacienda*-type land tenure, which was complemented by subsistence production. The *hacienda*-type estate also ensured that the remaining indigenous population would be tied to the *hacienda*. As indigenous communal lands were broken up, the population was forced to farm on small, individual plots of land. Subsistence production predominated on these small plots, or *minifundios*. Tributes exacted from the indigenous population provided food and labor for the *hacienda*. This complementary relationship between *hacienda* (or *latifundio*) production and the *minifundio* characterized Nicaraguan agriculture through the mid-twentieth century.

The *latifundio-minifundio* relationship constituted the second form of articulation between the nascent capitalist sector and the precapitalist peasant sector. Peasant agriculture had heretofore been almost entirely geared toward subsistence, that is, production in this sector was motivated by its use value. Yet the peasantry's growing relationship with the capitalist sector gradually transformed its essential nature. The articulation between capitalist and precapitalist production had earlier been expressed in the slave laborer/*hacendado* relationship. The second phase of articulation was to be much more enduring.

Cattle raising and subsistence agriculture predominated throughout the colonial period. Several other agroexport commodities were introduced during this period, however, the most important of them being cacao and indigo. Cacao was Nicaragua's first major agroexport crop. The Spaniards found cacao under cultivation upon their conquest of the region. The indigenous population had used cacao as a beverage and as a medium of exchange,[5] but it was not until the mid- to late-1500s that it began to be grown on a commercial basis.

Large-scale cacao production became attractive to the *latifundistas* because the indigenous population was already acquainted with its cultivation practices, it required less labor than some other contemporary crops, it offered lucrative investment possibilities for Granada-based landholders, the cacao varieties produced in Nicaragua commanded high prices on the international market (primarily Mexico), and local demand was high (Radell, 1969:165).[6] Several long-lasting patterns were initiated with the spread of cacao production. The first was the boom-and-bust cycle typical of export agriculture throughout the world. The ramifications of this pattern are especially serious for those countries that are dependent on one or two export crops. Cacao was one such crop for Nicaragua. Its first boom occurred and was reversed by the end of the sixteenth century. Climatological conditions, market competition, and labor shortages combined to produce cacao's first bust (Biderman, 1982). The chronic shortage of labor became a key issue in agricultural production and has continued to have an impact since that time. British pirate raids were alleged to have compounded the other factors in causing the second production decline of cacao in the seventeenth century. Regardless of the "conjunctural" factors specific to each bust, this pattern was to characterize Nicaraguan agriculture, and therefore the country's economy, for the next three and a half centuries.

Cacao continued to be produced throughout the colonial period, but shortly after the first bust its importance was eclipsed by the next in a series of agroexport crops, indigo. Indigo cultivation was introduced to Nicaragua at the beginning of the seventeenth century, stimulated by the demand in Europe for natural dyes. The department of Rivas, in southwestern Nicaragua, was the key indigo-growing region, as it had been for cacao earlier.

Indigo production reinforced the agroexport model begun by cattle raising and cacao cultivation, but it differed from cacao in two important ways. First, indigo production was compatible with cattle raising. In fact, cattle played a role in the crop's cultivation: once the indigo seeds were planted, cattle were brought into the area to pack the seeds. Later in the production process, land planted with indigo could be used for grazing cattle because they did not eat the plant. The combination of extensive cattle raising with indigo cultivation proved profitable for *hacienda* owners. Second, indigo cultivation required less labor than cacao. The harvesting and processing of indigo required large numbers of laborers for two to three months of the year. During the rest of the year the laborers who worked in the *obrajes* (the indigo-processing facilities) tended their own subsistence crops or the landowner's cattle. Difficulty in meeting the labor requirements of the *obrajes* was one of several factors contributing to the first decline in indigo production in the 1620s and to its limited growth generally (Lanuza, 1976). Indigo production went through several more cycles of boom and bust before the invention of synthetic dyes brought about its final demise late in the nineteenth century. But the social relations to which indigo production gave rise have continued to be an integral part of Nicaraguan agriculture.

Independence

The struggle for independence from Spain was largely motivated by the desire of the landed classes throughout Latin America for more freedom in their relations with the international market. The Spanish crown had fiercely regulated commerce with its colonies, although with limited success. Spain's monopolization of the colonies' trade relations was seen by the burgeoning merchant class and certain sectors of the landed class as an unjust constraint.[7] But for Central America, independence from Spain did not resolve the question of what course to take in the future.

Independence came to Central America at a time when the oligarchy still had no unified definition of what course national development should take.[8] This lack of unity stemmed in part from the historical development of the ruling class. In keeping with the pattern of Latin American development, an oligarchy gradually emerged from the Creole descendants of the colonial order. This oligarchy increasingly found itself in conflict with elements from within its own ranks who represented the evolving bourgeoisie. In Nicaragua, this conflict was expressed in the struggle between the "conservatives" of Granada and the "liberals" of León. The *hacendados* symbolized conservatism, promoting a continuance of the order established during the colonial era, with close church-state relations and a preference for the isolation and stability inherent in *hacienda* production. The liberals were "a European influenced bourgeoisie that sought to wipe out by decree the pre-Columbian and colonial past and to integrate [the economy] . . . into the expanding flow of international trade" (Furtado, 1976:36). The two factions pulled together troops by pressing "their" peasants into service to fight each other (Levy, 1976:180).[9] Constant political turmoil left Nicaragua unable to define itself either politically or economically.

In the late 1850s a political peace was achieved between the liberals and the conservatives. The liberals had been totally discredited by this time because of their association with North American filibuster William Walker.[10] The consolidation of conservative power in Guatemala under Rafael Carrera also affected the political balance in Nicaragua (Lanuza, 1976). The influence Guatemala held over the region immediately following independence had still not entirely disappeared. After Walker's ouster from Nicaragua in 1857, the conservatives' reign was undisputed until 1893.

Temporary political peace did not produce any dramatic changes in the economic situation, however, and economic stagnation continued. In the several decades preceding independence deteriorating trade relations between Spain and the colonies caused a slowdown in the economic activity of the latter, which was compounded by the postindependence wars in Nicaragua. Scarce labor was taken out of agricultural production and forced into the various rival armies. Indigo and cacao production waned at this time. The ultimate result was a return to the cattle *hacienda* and subsistence production.

Nicaragua's independence from Spain did not greatly affect life in rural Nicaragua. The retreat to the cattle *hacienda* symbolized the constancy of this period and underlined the fact that the lives of peasants had not been fundamentally changed by independence.[11] Although forced labor was legally abolished in 1812, new forms were found to ensure an extraction of surplus from the peasantry. For example, the *colonato* system required that rent be paid to the landowner in the form of labor services. And rent in kind was the essence of the *medieria* or *aparceria* system. Moreover, these labor systems addressed the continuing preoccupation with tying scarce labor to the land. The state also attempted to reinforce the *latifundio/minifundio* relationship through legislation designed to make more land available to the *latifundistas* (Lanuza, 1976). Legislation enacted during this period also sought to legalize the communal holdings of the Indian population. Although the ostensible goal of this legislation was to secure, once and for all, the rights of this population, its primary goal was to facilitate taxation of this land, thus ultimately weakening the Indians' land tenure.[12] In sum, independence gave the oligarchy freedom to accumulate land. The peasantry won the guarantee of continued servility.

Freedom from Spain's colonial trade constraints did not significantly alter Nicaragua's relations with the world market. The revival of the cattle *hacienda* and the decline of cacao and indigo production signaled a slight retreat from interchange with the international economy. A shift did occur, however, in Nicaragua's key trading partners. Whereas during the colonial period Spain had monopolized trade relations, England now stepped in to take its place. Nicaragua's trading partners did not become more diversified; one simply replaced another. In the mid-1800s the United States began seriously competing with England for this privileged position.

Another factor that had drawn international interest to Nicaragua since the Spanish conquest was the country's unique geography. Its Pacific and Caribbean coasts and two large lakes with connecting rivers made it an ideal location for interoceanic travel. By the mid-nineteenth century a route had been established between the two coasts that was used extensively during the California gold rush. Nicaragua's importance as a potential site for an interoceanic canal had motivated the involvement of England and the United States in Walker's filibustering attempts. This potential was to play a strong role in international maneuvering around Nicaragua for the next fifty years (Wheelock, 1980).

The struggles between liberals and conservatives following independence and the subsequent intrigues of the imperialist powers blocked the unification of forces essential to promoting Nicaragua's development. Regional political and economic rivalries kept the oligarchy divided during the colonial period. These rivalries were heightened during the 1800s. The entrance of England and the United States as allies of one or the other faction only compounded this situation. Finally, thirty-six years of conservative rule reinforced the country's developmental stagnation. It took a change of regime to shake Nicaragua out of its slumber and plunge it irrevocably into the international economy. This change came during the last decade of the nineteenth century.

The Introduction of Coffee

The Liberal Party made a comeback in 1893 with the presidency of José Santos Zelaya, whose sixteen years as president of Nicaragua (1893–1909) brought major changes to the country. The economy took a critical step forward into the international market. Political power became more solidified than it had been since Nicaragua's independence from Spain. The Zelaya presidency marked the final break with the colonial era and the takeoff of agricultural capitalism in Nicaragua.

The initiation of large-scale coffee production in Nicaragua was at the center of the transformation that began during this period. Coffee cultivation was introduced to the region at the end of the eighteenth century.[13] By the mid-1800s it had become an important export crop for El Salvador, Guatemala, and Costa Rica.[14] The widespread adoption of coffee cultivation came later in Nicaragua. Varying accounts date its introduction to Nicaragua between 1840 and 1850 (Squier, 1972; Levy, 1976). But it was only in the last fifteen years of the nineteenth century that its cultivation became generalized. This delay was a result of the same conditions that had produced economic stagnation throughout the nineteenth century: oligarchical infighting and meddling by the imperialist powers. Zelaya's presidency was critical for coffee's emergence as Nicaragua's new key crop.

Zelaya's rise to the presidency was both an expression of and a necessary condition for Nicaragua's expanding agroexport capitalism. According to Jaime Wheelock (1980:26), "the liberal regime of José Santos Zelaya signaled the ascent to power of the Nicaraguan *latifundista* bourgeoisie and the overthrow of the traditional oligarchy, which had been incapable of bringing about a coherent solution to the demands of agroexport groups for structural reforms." Zelaya represented the liberal vision of development. This vision "based its reformist actions on the strategy of converting Central America into an export region of primary products destined for the industrialized countries—by which means they intended to overcome the chronic economic crisis and stagnation and thereby consolidate the new social order" (Torres Rivas, 1980b:51). Zelaya was to lay the groundwork for this new stage of Nicaragua's history.

A central element of this transformation was the government's more directive stance in guiding the development process. The earlier conservative regimes had been characterized by their passivity in determining the country's economic course. Zelaya's reformist government embodied the notion of the state playing an active role in the nation's economic development. During his regime, archaic legal and administrative institutions were modernized, thereby erecting a more flexible state structure that had the strength to push through reforms creating the necessary conditions for capitalist production.

The groundwork laid by the Zelaya regime in its promotion of agroexport production included the reorganization of landownership, development of economic infrastructure, and the strengthening of the state. The first of these changes had been initiated during the conservative regime, but Zelaya's government dramatically accelerated the process. Legislation passed by the conservatives facilitated the concentration of land into *latifundios* and promoted the spread of coffee production into the central mountain region (see map 2.1). Coffee cultivation had not reached this region until the 1870s, a quarter of a century after its introduction in the Pacific. Legislation enacted between 1857 and 1889 sought to further its expansion by granting conces-

HONDURAS

Atlantic Coast

**Northern
Interior**   **Agricultural Frontier**

Basic
grains

Sugarcane   Basic grains   *Atlantic
Ocean*

Coffee and   Basic grains

**North
Pacific**   basic grains

Cotton

**Pacific
Interior**

Dairy

Pacific Ocean   **Central
Pacific**   Cattle

Coffee

**South
Pacific**

Cattle
and sugar

Basic grains = corn, beans, sesame, rice, and sorghum   COSTA RICA

Source: FIDA (1980:vi).

Map 2.1
Macroregions of Nicaragua

sions and providing subsidies to those willing to migrate there and become coffee farmers (Radell, 1969). (Such significant incentives had not been necessary in the more highly populated Pacific highland region.) An effort had also been made to tie labor more closely to the land. Yet the state had never been strong enough to enforce this legislation.[15] Zelaya's liberal regime revolutionized the process of gradual transformation. The goal was to make coffee cultivation attractive to potential growers.

The means Zelaya's government employed included the breakup of indigenous, communal landholdings. Peasants who could not present land titles to prove their ownership of the land were subject to expropriation. Church property and public land were made available to would-be coffee producers. A 1902 agrarian law offered land grants to foreigners and nationals who were willing to use the land for "public utility," meaning coffee cultivation (Biderman, 1982:54). Many Europeans, particularly British and Germans, immigrated to Nicaragua at this time to try their fortune at coffee production. Through these measures the Zelaya regime opened the way for the increased concentration of land, which in turn facilitated the development of coffee production.

Nicaragua's economic infrastructure expanded dramatically during the Zelaya years. Large-scale coffee production had begun in Nicaragua's Pacific highland region because of its accessibility to the country's ports. During Zelaya's presidency, roads and railways were constructed and communications facilities were modernized. This infrastructural development laid the foundation for the later expansion of coffee growing in Nicaragua's central highlands. This infrastructure, which had not been necessary for *hacienda* and subsistence production, was essential for agroexport production. The resulting improvements in the connections between rural Nicaragua and the world market made coffee production more attractive. The end of the isolation inherent in *hacienda*/subsistence production had begun.

Integration into the International Economy

Coffee production dramatically changed Nicaragua's relationship with the international economy. The country's coffee exports doubled during the first decade of Zelaya's regime, from an average of 9 million pounds a year in the early 1890s to an average of 18 million pounds by the turn of the century (Torres Rivas, 1980b:Statistical Appendix, Table 1). Given the three-year lag between planting and the first coffee harvest, these figures illustrate the extent of the increase that occurred almost immediately following Zelaya's assumption of the presidency.

The most important buyer for Nicaragua's coffee crop at this time was Europe. During the first three decades of the twentieth century there was a gradual increase in the percent of Nicaraguan coffee imported by the United States. Later, this process was accelerated because of the difficulties of trade with Europe during World War II. Consequently, by 1943 the United States was purchasing 99.9 percent of Nicaragua's coffee exports.[16]

When Nicaragua's coffee production underwent its first major expansion at the end of the nineteenth century, the price of coffee on the world market was high. The beverage was in increasing demand in Europe. Coffee production, however, was soon to undergo the boom-and-bust pattern that had characterized cacao and indigo production earlier. Nicaragua's first experience with the volatility of the coffee market came with the downturn in prices that followed World War I.[17] The market was gradually recovering when the Great Depression caused prices to fall once again. This time the recovery was much slower. When the coffee market finally improved again, Nicaragua was beginning to produce several other agroexport crops.

The bust in Nicaragua's coffee production during the late 1920s and 1930s had a much greater impact on the national economy than the cacao and indigo busts had earlier in the country's history because more of the nation's agricultural production was devoted to that one export crop than had been the case at any previous time. The pitfalls of integration into the capitalist world economy as a primary goods producer would be experienced again as the Nicaraguan economy became increasingly dependent on agroexport production.

Latifundio/Minifundio Production

Coffee production made the process of Nicaragua's integration into the international economy irreversible. Much of the nation's economy, however, still remained outside of this process. The capitalist relations of production that coffee production introduced to the Nicaraguan countryside came to coexist with the precapitalist relations of production characteristic of the cattle *hacienda* and subsistence farming. The Nicaraguan coffee plantation was, in fact, dependent on the continued existence of subsistence production.

The legislation that led to an increased concentration of land also addressed the issue of labor for the developing plantations. Labor scarcity continued to be a problem and was exacerbated because coffee production required a large labor force for several months of the year (Cumberland, 1980). Two means were employed to ensure coffee producers an adequate labor supply. The first was a series of regulations legislated by the Zelaya government: "To facilitate labor recruitment, vagrancy laws were passed, including an 1894 law giving 'agricultural' judges the right to force anyone over 14 to work, and an 1898 law establishing 'libretas de obreros' (worker passes) and an 1899 'Ley de los Vagos' (vagrancy law)" (Biderman, 1982:54). The second, more long-lasting solution to the problem of labor scarcity was the continued coexistence of the *minifundio* with the *latifundio*.

The opening up of agricultural land to prospective coffee producers necessitated the removal of the many subsistence farmers who had previously worked the land. Once dispossessed of their farms, and therefore their livelihood, these small producers had several options left to them. One was to move further onto the agricultural frontier. Until this time subsistence farming still occupied the most productive land in the coffee-growing regions. If these small producers chose to move to the frontier, they would have to farm marginal land with little or no existing infrastructure, which made producing enough for themselves and their families more difficult. Mere survival increasingly required the sale of their labor power on the agroexport plantations to supplement earnings generated on the farm.

Another option taken by some of those pushed off the land in the coffee region was to rent, often in kind or labor services, a small plot on one of the newly formed plantations. Indebtedness inevitably accompanied this move.[18] Debt, combined with the inability of these tiny plots to produce enough to feed a peasant family on a year-round basis, usually forced one or more family members to sell their labor to the plantation owners. Coincidentally the labor requirements on the coffee plantation increased, especially during the harvest months. The solution to the problem of land was, therefore, also the solution to the problem of labor.

One final option open to this displaced population was to migrate to urban areas. Many who did so tried to eke out a living producing artisan goods. Migration to the cities was less popular at this point than it was later in Nicaragua's history, yet coffee production did initiate a process of proletarianization, however limited. This was a further expression of the expansion of capitalist relations of production into Nicaraguan society. Land and labor were becoming commodified. But that expansion was still partial.[19]

The coffee plantation tended to produce a semiproletarian rather than a proletarian class.[20] It depended on the continued existence of precapitalist production. Whether the harvest laborers came from rented plots on the plantation, *minifundios* in the area of the *finca*, or those further into the agricultural frontier, they were essential to meeting the labor requirements of the plantations during this peak season. Yet these workers remained largely outside capitalist production relations because they were employed only during the harvest months. Capitalism did not make another significant advance into the Nicaraguan rural economy for fifty years.

Zelaya's Nationalism and U.S. Intervention

The process of transformation initiated by Zelaya's assumption of the presidency came to an abrupt halt in 1909, when an alliance of conservative forces, backed by the United States, brought to an end this brief experiment in liberal reformism. Zelaya's overthrow began another series of liberal/conservative struggles, accompanied by a U.S. occupation that, with only a few brief interruptions, lasted for almost twenty-five years. The end of the Zelaya regime and the return to power of the Conservative Party marked the beginning of nearly a half-century of stagnation in the development of Nicaragua's agrarian capitalism.

A central component of Zelaya's governing platform was a strong nationalist ideology that defined the government's international relations. The adoption of this independent posture in Nicaraguan foreign policy coincided with the development of a new foreign policy position in the United States in the form of Theodore Roosevelt's reinterpretation of the Monroe Doctrine. This new policy aimed to place the United States in a position of unmitigated hegemony in the hemisphere (LaFeber, 1983). The Zelaya government chose not to bow to the pressure inherent in the foreign policy of its northern neighbor. It contracted loans with Europeans when their rates proved to be favorable and expropriated some property owned by North Americans. Zelaya even went so far as to discuss the possibility of constructing a canal through Nicaragua using European financing and technical assistance. Zelaya's independent foreign policy clearly went against the grain of this new interpretation of the Monroe Doctrine. These acts and others "persuaded the yankee government that Zelaya's impertinent nationalism represented a manifest risk for the strategic interests involved in the construction of the Panama Canal, where not only this incalculable investment was at stake, but more importantly, the destiny of this territorial axis, the monopoly of which was vital to the U.S. for the defense and expansion of its imperialist power" (Wheelock, 1980:108). The United

States responded by providing military backing to a conservative uprising. The conservatives reciprocated by placing a suitable representative of both conservative and U.S. interests in power, Adolfo Díaz.

Díaz's government had only a very small domestic base of support, which was primarily composed of the most backward part of the Nicaraguan oligarchy. U.S. intervention ultimately served "to strengthen the hand of the traditional oligarchy vis-à-vis the reform-minded coffee entrepreneurs. As a result, bourgeois reforms were much shallower in Nicaragua than they were in El Salvador, Costa Rica, and Guatemala" (Deere and Marchetti, 1981: 44). The Zelaya regime was the last expression the coffee bourgeoisie would have as an independent political actor. The capitalist interests represented by the coffee bourgeoisie did not again come to the forefront of the national agenda until another sector, the cotton bourgeoisie, evolved.

Díaz's government was extremely weak. It was subjected to repeated liberal rebellions.[21] The United States maintained an almost constant military presence in Nicaragua until 1933 in an attempt to sustain the series of weak conservative governments begun by Díaz. Before the U.S. Marines finally left in 1933, they created, equipped, and trained the Nicaraguan National Guard. The original conception of this force was that it would be a nonpartisan army that would maintain peace in spite of interparty bickering, but it began and remained until its demise a fierce partisan of U.S. interests in Nicaragua (see, e.g., Millett, 1977).

The last five years of U.S. occupation were distinguished from the previous eighteen by General Augusto César Sandino's war against the U.S. Marines and the Nicaraguan National Guard. Sandino refused to put down his arms when the rest of the liberal generals (who had heretofore been his allies) made a peace pact with the United States in 1927 that allowed for continued U.S. domination. Sandino's Pequeño Ejercito Loco (crazy little army) maintained its armed warfare until the marines left Nicaragua on January 1, 1933.

Sandino's army differed from the rest of the "liberal" forces in that it represented the class interests of the *campesinos*. Sandino's platform included the restoration of national independence (because Nicaragua remained subject to political and economic intervention), internationalism (particularly identified with the rest of Latin America), and an agrarian reform that would bring the benefits of the country's agricultural riches to all Nicaraguans.[22] The agrarian reorganization initiated by Sandino's army redistributed land in the northern coffee-growing region that was its base of operations. Land in the "liberated zones" was returned to those who had been displaced during the coffee boom at the end of the nineteenth century. It was then farmed collectively by the *campesinos*.

The threat Sandino's "revolutionary" program represented to coffee and mining interests located in this region was largely responsible for the persistence of efforts to destroy this movement.[23] During the last years of the marines' occupation, world attention focused on their war against Sandino's guerrilla army. Even after the marines left Nicaragua and Sandino's army had laid down its arms, National Guard Director Anastasio Somoza García remained determined to bring an end to this threat. In the midst of negotiations between the new Sacasa government and Sandino's army, Somoza had Sandino killed. The next target of the National Guard was the community of Sandino's followers in Wiwili (participants in his agrarian reform program), where the Guard killed more than three hundred people (Millett, 1977: 159). Although Somoza successfully eliminated this final obstacle to his rise to power, the legacy left by Sandino would haunt the Somoza family until its overthrow in 1979. Sandino's emphasis on agrarian reform and his adamant nationalist and anti-imperialist stances would find expression once again in the platform of the Frente Sandinista de Liberación Nacional.

Shortly after Sandino's assassination, Somoza maneuvered Juan Bautista Sacasa out of the presidency and assumed the position himself. This was the beginning of a reign of power by the Somoza family that was to last nearly half a century. Upon his elevation to the directorship of the National Guard, Anastasio Somoza García owned nothing more than a run-down coffee plantation. In the course of the next twenty years he became the wealthiest man in Central America (Weber, 1981). After eight years in office, Somoza owned fifty-one cattle ranches and forty-six coffee plantations. This was just one facet of the family's wealth, but it suggested the pattern of financial dealings the family was to follow in the years to come. In sum, the Somozas ran the country as if it were their private estate.[24]

The Somoza family's domination of Nicaragua's political and economic life was to condition the country's development. The formation of an independent capitalist class was suppressed until the rise of cotton production in the 1950s. The dynasty ran the country like a medieval fiefdom even at the time of its overthrow in 1979. The underdevelopment Nicaragua shared with the rest of the region was compounded by forty-six years of a one-family dictatorship.

In sum, even though the process of capitalist development begun by the introduction of coffee production was incomplete, Nicaragua took a critical step forward through this new interchange with the world economy. Coffee production initiated the formation of a social division of labor previously unknown to Nicaragua, proletarianizing and semiproletarianizing the population.[25] It accelerated the concentration of land. It briefly brought a modernist bourgeoisie to the forefront of government decision making. The short liberal experiment, although retaining many elements of Nicaragua's precapitalist past, laid the foundation for the next wave of capitalist development that began in the second half of the twentieth century.

Cotton Production

The introduction of cotton to Nicaragua's agroexport repertoire in 1950 had profound consequences for the entire society. Cotton gave a new impetus to the process of integrating the country into the capitalist world economy. Cotton signaled the consolidation of agrarian capitalism and an agroexport-based economy in Nicaragua.

Cotton had been produced on a small scale during the colonial era, when it was used to make sailcloth for the León-based shipbuilding industry. But it was not until the 1950s and the worldwide boom for export crops caused by the Korean War that large-scale cotton production became an integral part of Nicaragua's agroexport economy. As Robert G. Williams (1986) argues, this period of increased demand for cotton was differentiated from earlier such periods by the introduction of chemical pest control in agricultural production. Nicaragua (and Central America more generally) had responded to previous booms in the international cotton market by increasing production, but it had not been able to sustain its exports in less than peak market conditions because of elevated production costs arising from significant pest-related crop losses. The "insecticide revolution" eliminated this last obstacle.

Like coffee before it, the expansion of cotton production began with a boom. Cotton acreage tripled between 1950/51 and 1951/52 (calculated from CONAL, 1973). By 1954/55 the area planted with cotton had multiplied fivefold since the beginning of the decade.[26] Cotton's importance in generating foreign exchange also increased dramatically during this period. The crop had brought in only 5 percent of Nicaragua's foreign exchange earnings in 1950 (calculated from República de Nicaragua, 1959:28). But by

1955 cotton had surpassed coffee as a foreign exchange earner, accounting for 39 percent of the country's export earnings, as opposed to 35 percent for coffee. Nicaragua soon replaced some of the world's traditional cotton producers.[27] By 1967 Nicaragua had become the eleventh largest cotton producer in the world (Belli, 1968:64).

The state played a central role in this process of expansion. It supported the growing cotton industry through the development of related infrastructure and generous credit policies. Government spending for infrastructure alone increased from 27.2 million córdobas in 1950 to 88.4 million córdobas in 1955 and reached 154.7 million córdobas in 1963 (Belli, 1975: 23).[28] These expenditures consisted of improvements of roads, bridges, agriculture, energy, transport, storage facilities, communications, and other services. International lending agencies provided extensive assistance to the various Central American governments during this period to stimulate investments geared toward cotton production (Williams, 1986). Infrastructural modernization was crucial for making the cotton region more accessible to interchange with the world market.

Perhaps of equal importance for the expansion of the cotton industry was the financial assistance offered by the state to cotton producers. Bank credits for cotton production increased from 22.6 million córdobas in 1952/53 to 108.2 million córdobas in 1955/56 (CONAL, 1973:Table X-65). Private banks, which in 1952/53 had not provided any credit for cotton production, were authorizing an additional 25.9 million córdobas by 1955/56. Between 1952/53 and 1961/62, bank credits covered an average of 80 percent of the acreage planted with cotton (calculated from CONAL, 1973:Table X-70). At one point in the mid-1960s the banking system supplied credit for 89 percent of the area cultivated with cotton, although this figure was generally in the range of 70 to 75 percent during the 1960s and 1970s (calculated from BCN, 1979:31, 74). The extensive coverage of cotton acreage by bank credit was unparalleled by that for any other crop. This credit also provided for more and more of the expenses associated with cotton cultivation. For each *manzana* planted, the government provided credit for between 70 and 80 percent of the production costs (Ordóñez, 1976:54 and Appendix 3). Abundant bank credit was crucial in promoting the large-scale adoption of cotton production because of prohibitive input costs. As Williams (1986:24) succinctly stated, "Cotton is a cash hog." Tremendous outlays of cash were required before payment for the crop began to come in, eight months after the production cycle began.

A significant part of this outlay went to the input that made the cotton boom possible—insecticides. Insecticides and their application together represented approximately 27.4 percent of production costs in 1962/63 (calculated from CONAL, 1973:Table IV-29). Although this figure remained relatively stable in the ensuing years, heavy insecticide use led to the need for yet another chemical input.[29] Cotton cultivation in general and insecticide use in particular greatly depleted the soil, requiring the increased application of fertilizers. Fertilizers averaged around 10 percent of production costs in the 1960s and 1970s. Thus these two inputs alone made up more than one-third of cotton's production costs.

Multinational corporations were the primary source for these two key inputs. Initially, chemical inputs for cotton were imported in processed, packaged form and applied directly to the cotton fields. Eventually, Nicaragua assumed the role of mixer and packager of chemical inputs for cotton that were sold on the Central American market, limiting its imports to the raw materials required for this new industry.

A second important category of cotton inputs also had to be imported: machinery, tractors, trucks, and airplanes. Although these products represented less of the total import bill than chemical inputs, they created a further dependence on the international market (Biderman, 1982). Consequently, though cotton was responsible for the generation of a significant percentage of Nicaragua's foreign exchange earnings, its production was also highly dependent on imports, thus requiring the expenditure of foreign exchange. The net result was that cotton production multiplied Nicaragua's links to the world market.

The Nicaraguan state's active role in promoting the expansion of cotton production contrasted markedly with its relatively passive posture regarding economic development in the years between Zelaya's ouster and the rise of cotton production. Changes in the Somoza family were an important influence in this increased involvement in agroexport production. Initially, the Somozas were primarily interested in appropriating the country's already existing wealth instead of stimulating new growth, but the family's economic behavior was modified in the 1950s. Though the Somoza family never did become directly involved in cotton cultivation (as it had with coffee), "the Somoza regime which controlled the Nicaraguan state [began to] act . . . as though it believed that the best way to consolidate its power was to further the accumulation process" (Biderman, 1982:85). Cotton production did further the accumulation process. It gave rise to a series of related industries, modernized the financial sector, and changed the face of Nicaraguan society.

Table 2.1

Land Distribution according to Size of *Finca*, 1963

Size Groups[a]	Farm Size (*Manzanas*)	Percent of Farms	Percent of Area
Microfincas	Less than 1	2.2	—
Subfamily	1–5	33.2	1.5
	5–10	15.4	1.9
Family	10–20	13.0	3.2
	20–50	14.4	8.1
Medium	50–100	10.7	12.4
	100–500	9.6	31.7
Multifamily	500–1,000	1.0	10.7
	1,000–2,500	0.4	10.3
	More than 2,500	0.1	20.2
		100.0	100.0

Source: Calculated from Ministerio de Economía, 1966:Tables C and D.

[a]The various size groups are defined as follows:

Family: A farm that has enough land to maintain a family using the predominant level of technology.

Subfamily: A farm that does not have sufficient acreage to satisfy the basic necessities of a family or employ all of the family members throughout the year.

Medium: A farm with enough acreage to employ others in addition to family members but that does not involve a complex division of labor.

Multifamily: A farm that is large enough to employ a permanent work force in addition to family members and that has a hierarchical division of labor.

(Note: These definitions come from the Comité Interamericano de Desarrollo Agrícola, as cited in CEPAL et al., 1980:46). For more extensive data on land tenure in the Central American region as a whole see CEPAL et al. (1980:48).

The adoption of large-scale cotton production accelerated the stratification process within the rural social structure. The key regions where cotton cultivation expanded (the Pacific coastal plain and the department of Masaya; see map 2.1) had previously been occupied by cattle raising and subsistence production. As cotton consumed more land, it displaced peasants who had heretofore worked this land. The region's land tenure patterns were greatly affected, with the concentration of land increasing dramatically (see table 2.1). The ideology of "economies of scale" was one argument given for increased land concentration. More important, however, most of the cotton producers were members of the newly developing capitalist class. They had the means and the will (when the world market price for cotton was high) to dominate the fertile Pacific coastal plain with the cultivation of this export crop.[30] According to the agricultural census of 1963, medium and large producers controlled 89 percent of that year's cotton acreage.[31] Data from the 1971 agricultural census point to the stability of this pattern: medium and large producers controlled 91 percent of the cotton acreage that year (calculated from Warnken, 1975:Table 20). Table 2.1 illustrates the extent of concentration in landownership throughout Nicaragua by 1963, which became more accentuated during the next decade.

The replacement of cattle raising and subsistence production by cotton required the removal of large numbers of peasants. As had been the case fifty years earlier during the coffee boom, the displaced had several options open to them when they left their land on the Pacific coast.[32] Some of these peasants chose to move to the agricultural frontier, which by this time had been pushed even farther east (Real, 1974). Nueva Guinea, in particular, received many of the displaced. This area had been targeted for resettlement by one of Somoza's "agrarian reform" programs. The land to which these *campesinos* were relegated was distant from markets and roads, often not on level terrain, and generally less fertile than that they had left. The sale of their labor on the agroexport estates during several months of the year was usually necessary to ensure their survival.

The second option for the displaced was entry into the wage labor force. According to a study of Nicaragua by the Fondo Internacional de Desarrollo (FIDA) (1980:12), "the cotton boom during the 1950s let loose a dramatic process of proletarianization of the *campesino* population." It pushed more and more of this previously self-sustained sector of the population into the wage labor force.[33] A significant increase in Nicaragua's level of urbanization occurred at this time. The proportion of Nicaragua's population residing in urban areas grew from 35.2 percent to 47.7 percent in the two decades following the initiation of the cotton boom (calculated from Ministerio de Economía, 1974:v). The Pacific region was the area most affected by the expansion of the urbanized population, coinciding with the growth in export production in that part of the country. Many of the new urban dwellers continued to migrate back to the cotton region to work in the harvest. Lack of steady employment left them no other alternative.

Yet cotton cultivation differed from coffee in its effects on the precapitalist relations of production previously characterizing the region. As Carmen

Diana Deere and Peter Marchetti, S.J. (1981:44) observed, "Whereas the development of coffee production had been compatible with noncapitalist relations of production interior to the haciendas and the coexistence of subsistence production and export production, the development of cotton production required the 'clearing' of the haciendas as modern infrastructure was to be laid."

This difference was evidenced in a number of ways. For example, an examination of land tenure patterns shows a significantly higher level of land concentration in the two key cotton-growing departments (León and Chinandega) in comparison with that of the two key coffee-growing departments (Matagalpa and Jinotega). Although the percentage of farms falling into the *microfinca* and subfamily categories was higher in León (48 percent) and Chinandega (54 percent) than in Matagalpa (44 percent) and Jinotega (36 percent), these farms constituted approximately the same percent of the area cultivated in both regions (calculated from Ministerio de Economía, 1966:Table 26). At the other extreme, multifamily farms occupied significantly more of the area cultivated in León (48 percent) and Chinandega (58 percent) than in Jinotega (22 percent) and Matagalpa (32 percent). Thus the trend toward smaller peasant farms in the Pacific cotton-growing region was accompanied by a tendency for the largest farms to occupy more land there.

It is even more revealing that legal ownership of the land was significantly more prevalent in the key cotton-growing departments than in the coffee-growing departments. In León and Chinandega, 86 percent of the agricultural land had legal titles, compared to 54 percent and 58 percent in Matagalpa and Jinotega, respectively (calculated from Ministerio de Economía, 1966:Table 26).[34] Legalization of landownership has been integral to the expansion of agroexport capitalism throughout Central America (see Williams, 1986). The new capitalist class's growing need for land was in large part resolved through the sudden delegitimization of landownership that was not validated by legal titles. Most of those who formed the *minifundio* sector had never had legal title to the land they worked (which, in many cases, went back several generations). These farmers were, therefore, easily evicted from the land as the expanding cotton capitalists (like the coffee bourgeoisie before them) found mechanisms to "legalize" their own right to the land.

Finally, in the cotton-growing region precapitalist forms of rental arrangements disappeared overnight as rent paid in cash became the modus operandi. Payment in money characterized 85 percent and 77 percent of the rental transactions in Chinandega and León, respectively, in 1963 (calculated from Ministerio de Economía, 1966:Table 26). In contrast, only 12 percent of rental property was paid for in cash in Jinotega, and the figure for Matagalpa was 23 percent. Cash rental payments required participation in the money economy. Most subsistence producers had previously had only limited interaction with the money economy. This shift away from rent in kind or labor services signaled a restricting of the rental market and the gradual elimination of precapitalist production relations.

In sum, cotton production brought about a profound transformation of the rural social structure in the regions it touched. The consequences of its introduction were much more far-reaching than those of any other crop in the history of Nicaragua's economic development.

The Consolidation of Nicaragua's Agroexport Economy

Cotton production revolutionized western Nicaragua's social structure in the twenty-five years following its introduction. It also firmly integrated the nation's economy into the international market and consolidated Nicaragua's agroexport production, making it the base of the country's economy.

Although no longer Nicaragua's most important crop, coffee production also began a new period of expansion at this time. The number of acres planted to coffee more than doubled between 1950 and 1963 (CEPAL, 1966:28). Most of this expansion took place in Nicaragua's north-central region, particularly in the department of Jinotega. This growth accentuated the differences in the social structure between the Pacific highlands and the central mountain region that had emerged with coffee cultivation. The central mountain region had more room for expanding acreage under cultivation. Consequently, although the concentration of land increased there during this period, the process was not as extreme as that in the Pacific highland region: whereas 65 percent of the farms in Carazo (on the Pacific coast) in 1963 were under ten *manzanas* in size, and the largest farms occupied 32 percent of the land, in Jinotega only 36 percent of the farms were smaller than ten *manzanas*, with the largest farms occupying 22 percent of the agricultural land (calculated from Ministerio de Economía, 1966:Table 26).

Several other export products were developed at this time and further consolidated Nicaragua's agroexport economy. The production of sugar, seafood, tobacco, bananas, and, most important, beef expanded. The expansion of beef production for export constituted the third and final phase in the evolution of Nicaragua's agroexport economy. There had been cattle *haciendas* in Nicaragua since colonial times. The export of tallow, hides, and beef had been important in the economy of that era. But the introduction of coffee had eclipsed beef as a key agricultural product, and the expansion of cotton had displaced the cattle *hacienda* from the Pacific coastal plain during the 1950s. Yet cattle raising made a strong comeback in the late 1960s, becoming one of Nicaragua's four most important agroexport products.

Following the increase in coffee production, cattle were raised primarily to satisfy the domestic demand for beef. Cattle raising and meat processing remained traditional in nature. In response to a growing demand for beef in the world economy, however, a modern U.S. Department of Agriculture (USDA)–approved beef packing plant was built in Nicaragua in 1957. Most of the demand came from the burgeoning fast-food industry in the United States. These new developments coincided with a temporary downturn in the cotton economy. The result was an expansion in beef exports throughout Central America, from 30 million pounds in 1963 to 180 million pounds in 1973 (Williams, 1986).

To meet this demand, Nicaragua's cattle herd grew by 46 percent between 1963 and 1971 and beef exports doubled during the same period.[35] As it had previously done with cotton, the state played a key role in facilitating the expansion of this latest export product. Further infrastructural development was geared toward modernizing cattle raising (Williams, 1986), and aid was also administered in more direct forms such as the importation of breeding cattle from the United States and the establishment of an artificial insemination center. International financing was readily available to support the state in these endeavors because beef was seen by the international development agencies as the key to export-led growth in the region.

Although intensive cattle raising was adopted at this time, extensive cattle raising remained the predominant form of production, which necessitated a significant expansion in the area dedicated to cattle raising. Between 1963 and 1971 the area occupied by pastures grew by 31 percent at the national level. Much of that expansion took place in central Nicaragua and on the agricultural frontier. Acreage in pastures in the department of Zelaya alone (where most of the agricultural frontier is located) increased by more than 500 percent between 1963 and 1971 (calculated from 1971 agricultural census data in Warnken, 1975:124, and 1963 census data in Ministerio de Economía, 1966:14, 18). By 1971, 72 percent of Nicaragua's pastures were

situated in the central and southern interior and East Coast regions (calculated from Warnken, 1975:124).

Cattle raising was commonly combined with precapitalist production relations. A dynamic evolved whereby the *minifundistas* who had been pushed
to the agricultural frontier during the cotton boom were once again displaced, having been bought out by large cattle ranchers after several years of
working the land and deforesting it. The *campesinos'* need for cash forced
them into this relationship, which repeated itself every few years.[36] Some
subsistence production was also carried out on the cattle *haciendas*. Small
plots were occasionally made available to *campesinos* for rent in kind, labor
services, or cash. This rental relationship offered the landowner more
cleared land at no extra expense.

Concentrated landownership was the norm in cattle production. Almost
50 percent of the pasture land was concentrated on farms larger than five
hundred *manzanas* in 1971, that is, on multifamily farms or *latifundios*, a
pattern that had been established during the previous decade (calculated
from Ministerio de Economía, 1966:Table 28, and Warnken, 1975:124).
This suggests the extent of *campesino* displacement resulting from the expansion of cattle raising. The resurgence of cattle production for export transformed the country's interior.[37] It also reinforced the capitalist/precapitalist
relationship that cotton production had begun to eliminate. Yet cattle raising
ultimately had the same effect as cotton, further marginalizing the *campesino*
sector.

The expansion of cattle production in Nicaragua's interior coincided with
the state-supported development of sugar, tobacco, and bananas as new
export crops. Government assistance came in the form of subsidized irrigation, agricultural credits, and technical assistance. These three crops were
among the most irrigated-intensive crops in Nicaragua. Their production
was geared almost entirely to the U.S. market. Sugar, tobacco, and bananas
joined coffee, cotton, and beef production in consolidating Nicaragua's
agroexport economy. Although Nicaragua was no longer dependent on the
production of one export crop, agroexport production remained the critical
generator of capital.

The Nicaraguan economy experienced an unprecedented expansion following the introduction of cotton and the other products adopted shortly
thereafter. The first fifteen years of this period, in particular, were characterized by dramatic growth: the average growth rate of the Gross National
Product was more than 6 percent annually for the period between 1950 and

1964.[38] The average annual rate of growth in agriculture alone between 1950 and 1977 was 4.7 percent, one of the highest rates in the world (CEPAL, 1979b:17)

Although agriculture was the key to economic expansion at this time, other sectors were also affected by the modernization of the economy. Capital generated by agroexport production formed the basis for a number of financial institutions that were established in the 1950s (Wheelock, 1980: 141–89). These financial institutions in turn promoted growth in other areas of the economy. A shift in loan patterns of the country's banks provides evidence of the efforts to foster development in new areas: "In 1960, agriculture received over 40 percent of all credit issued by the domestic financial system; in 1978 and 1979, only a little more than 20 percent went to this sector" (BCN, as cited in Enríquez and Spalding, 1987:107). Housing construction and manufacturing absorbed more and more of the credit offered by the banking system.

A limited process of industrialization was also begun during this period. This industrial growth took several forms: the development of agroindustry and agricultural input and consumer goods industries. Growth in all of these areas was associated with the Central American Common Market.

Central American industrialization was largely a product of the U.S. Alliance for Progress, which was created following the overthrow of Batista and the initiation of Cuba's revolutionary transformation in the hope of preventing "another Cuba" from emerging elsewhere in the region. One of the Alliance's key programs in Central America was the CACM, which was heralded as the solution to the region's developmental difficulties. Yet the benefits derived from the industries it stimulated in each country were counterbalanced by serious limitations.

The first form of industrial development promoted by the CACM, agroindustry, accompanied the expansion in agroexport production. Agroindustrial development included the construction of sugar refineries and cattle slaughterhouses. Thus the products toward which this industrialization was oriented were now exported in semiprocessed form. Growth in this area also included the processing of some of Nicaragua's agricultural products for the domestic market. For example, the cottonseed oil industry experienced a great expansion at this time. Most of the manufacturing that was introduced following the cotton boom was concentrated in foods and beverages: food, beverages, and tobacco accounted for over 60 percent of gross manufactured output in 1960 (Weeks, 1985a:136). Textile and clothing production, based on a combination of local cotton and imported synthetic fibers, made up another 15 to 20 percent of gross manufacturing output.

Industrial growth also took the form of manufacturing of agricultural inputs, primarily mixing chemical inputs, such as fertilizers and pesticides, for agricultural production. Whereas in 1952 only 25 percent of the insecticides sold in Nicaragua were mixed inside the country, that figure had risen to 40 percent by 1955 and to 98 percent by 1959 (Belli, 1968:40). Growth in this sector continued with the formation of the CACM in the 1960s, which also stimulated the domestic manufacturing of other assorted consumer goods. Nondurable consumer goods predominated, with durables contributing only 0.6 percent to gross manufacturing output (Weeks, 1985a:139). This pattern conformed to the traditional import-substitution model of industrialization, in which manufacturing of consumer durables and machinery follows that of consumer nondurables.

The overall model of industrialization was characterized by several serious limitations, however.[39] Foremost among these was the extremely heavy reliance on imported inputs. On the average, 30 percent of all imports in the 1960s were destined for manufacturing (calculated from SIECA, 1975b: 294). This figure rose to 39 percent in the 1970s, reaching a high of 48 percent in 1979 (calculated from SIECA, 1981:304–5). The expanding chemical industry, for example, imported over 50 percent of its inputs.[40] What is at issue here is the problem that faces all import-substitution schemes: ultimately, one type of imports is being replaced by another. Overall dependency is not lessened but may be increased.

A related issue is that much of Nicaragua's CACM-associated industrial development was of a "last touch" nature. "Last touch" or "final touch" industries are those in which industrial production is restricted to the final stages of a consumer goods production process. Most of the processing has already occurred elsewhere. This type of industry produces only limited benefits for the country where the last touch industry is located because the value-added content of the product, hence the surplus to be gained, is usually less than the cost of the imported product (see Torres Rivas 1980a). In the case of the CACM, the earlier stages of processing were carried out in the United States. Furthermore, this industrial development was capital-, not labor-intensive. Consequently, export-oriented agriculture was pushing people out of its regions of expansion, and industrial development was unable to absorb this population.

In addition, the CACM model was based on the premise that unifying the markets of the region would facilitate the development of industry by increasing demand, which was too limited in any one of the individual countries. The implicit assumption was that the market would be expanded not only by a broadening of the region's traditional consumers of nonbasic goods, the bourgeoisie, but that it would grow to include groups heretofore excluded from purchasing these goods, the popular classes. That is, it was recognized that there was a limit to growth inherent in the extreme concentration of wealth. But CACM industrialization did not create any redistributive mechanisms that would overcome this obstacle to development. On the contrary, according to Edelberto Torres Rivas (1980a:36), an increase in the concentration of wealth in the region coincided with the growth of the CACM.

Equally important, CACM-stimulated industrial development did not bring about the consolidation of any of the national economies of the region. Instead, the end product of this process was the development of a bifurcated export orientation in each of these economies. Some regional trade of manufactured goods was stimulated by the CACM, but in the case of Nicaragua the percentage of manufactured goods exported to countries outside of the region was significantly greater than that exported to CACM countries in 1970.[41] And Nicaragua continued to be dependent on an unrelated agroexport market. The development of industries that would be integrated into the rest of each country's economy was not on the CACM agenda.

In sum, by the end of the 1960s Nicaragua's economy was heavily dependent on export agriculture. The growth associated with agroexport production had led to the development of a limited industrial base. Although it stimulated the modernization of the country's financial sector and several other key sectors of the economy, agriculture remained at the center of the economy, and export production was predominant within agriculture.

Nicaragua's dependence on agroexport production had a number of consequences. This sector "monopolized the greatest number of cultivated *manzanas*, the greatest number of salaried workers, and the greatest percentage of the state's resources" (Núñez, 1981:13).[42] Agroexport dependency made Nicaragua's economy vulnerable to the vacillations of the international market. Furthermore, "since Nicaragua had little in the way of modern techniques or infrastructure, it was forced to compete in the world market on the basis of its cheap labor, a feature which had to be constantly reinforced for the traditional agroexporting system to function" (Kaimowitz and Thome, 1982:224–25). These consequences would continue to condition

Nicaragua's development, even as efforts were made to transform it following the overthrow of Somoza.

Insufficient Food Production and Rural Poverty

As agroexport production consumed more and more of Nicaragua's prime agricultural land, basic grains farmers were increasingly displaced to less productive land. Basic grains production had traditionally been carried out by small- and medium-sized farmers.[43] These were the same producers forced off the land by the expansion of agroexport production. They were displaced to small plots on the agroexport estates or to the agricultural frontier. Regardless of which of these options they chose, the land these producers moved to was marginal compared with what they had previously farmed. The results were twofold: food production stagnated and the standard of living of these *campesinos* deteriorated.

The Pacific coastal plain was the area most affected by the cotton boom. Before the expansion of cotton, this area had been central to the nation's basic grain production. The region that had once been known as Nicaragua's granary was rapidly turned over to agroexport production. The cattle-raising boom that followed reinforced this pattern, pushing basic grains production farther and farther east.[44]

The consequences of producing food crops on marginal land were compounded by the lack of attention paid to the basic grains sector by the state. In credit distribution and technical assistance the state clearly favored export agriculture (see Enríquez and Spalding, 1987). The *campesino* sector was forced to rely on private lenders for loans made at usurious rates. Low prices for basic grains added to the plight of their producers. These disadvantages combined to produce a stagnation in the country's food crop production.

Before the expansion of export agriculture in the 1950s and 1960s, Nicaragua had been self-sufficient in basic food crops. The cotton boom and the expansion in beef, sugarcane, and tobacco production changed that. Production increases in basic grains did occur in some regions in the country's interior, but they were not sufficient to keep pace with the growth rate of the population. In contrast to the dramatic yield increases in export crops, yields of food crops showed no improvement because of their marginalization. The net results were that by the mid-1950s Nicaragua had to start importing food and per capita consumption of these products began to decline.[45]

The other side of declining food production was a deterioration in the living standard of the *campesino* population. All the factors that negatively affected the nation's food production simultaneously affected the small- and medium-sized *campesino* farmers who carried out that production. The size of their plots was reduced with each successive expansion in agroexport production. Between 1952 and 1963 the proportion of farms smaller than ten *manzanas* increased from 35 to 50 percent.[46]

At the same time, the proportion of family farms (those between ten and fifty *manzanas*) diminished from 37.4 to 28 percent of all farms as these *campesinos* were pushed into the *minifundio* sector. The changing pattern in land tenure was reflected in the drop in income experienced by this sector. Estimates of rural family incomes from the early 1970s indicate that a majority of the rural population did not earn enough to meet minimum nutritional requirements.[47] Many *campesinos* were forced to look for other ways to supplement their income. The wage labor market was their primary alternative.

Some salaried work was available to them in the agroexport sector, but this work was primarily seasonal. Only 19.8 percent of the agricultural labor force was able to obtain permanent wage employment (Deere et al., 1985:78). It was very common for *campesinos* to work most of the year on their tiny plots of land and a few months of the year as wage laborers on the agroexport estates.

The social services available to the rural poor also put them at a disadvantage. Health conditions were poor for most Nicaraguans during the Somoza years. Life expectancy was only fifty-three years, the lowest for Central America (Bossert, 1981:261). The infant mortality rate was 120 per 1,000 live births (AID, 1976a:22). Malnutrition affected an estimated 55 percent of children below the age of five.[48] All these health conditions were worse in the countryside. The poverty that characterized the lives of most of the rural population predisposed this sector to health problems. For example, the scarcity of potable water in the countryside exacerbated all of the above-mentioned health conditions.[49] Access to health care services was also extremely limited in rural areas: "In 1973, over half of the the hospital beds in the country were in the three major cities and [there were] only five health facilities with beds . . . in rural areas" (Bossert, 1981:262).

Educational services similarly favored urban areas. Even though 45 to 47 percent of the population lived in rural areas in the mid-1970s, only 27 percent of the primary school teachers were located outside of urban areas.[50] Only 5.3 percent of children finished primary school in the coun-

tryside, as opposed to 44 percent in urban areas. Many areas were so isolated that they had no access to educational facilities. Predictably, illiteracy
rates were significantly higher in rural areas than in the cities. The national
illiteracy rate was estimated to be 50 percent, yet in some rural areas this
figure exceeded 80 percent (MED, 1980:30–42).

The Somoza Regime

The general outline of agroexport dependence and rural poverty described
above was duplicated in other countries in the region, but Nicaragua's development was unique in that one family dominated the process of political
and economic change (see Millett, 1977). All of the countries in the region
were characterized by highly concentrated landownership. The politi-
cal/military structure typically enforced this unequal distribution of resources. Nevertheless, in Nicaragua, the Somoza family used its control over
the National Guard and the political structure to appropriate a disproportionate part of the nation's wealth, excluding even much of the bourgeoisie from this process.

The dominance of the Somozas over Nicaragua's economy delayed the
formation of an independent capitalist class until the development of large-
scale cotton production in the 1950s. The Somoza family did not become
directly involved in cotton production as it had with coffee, thereby creating
an opening that had not existed since Zelaya's time for a capitalist class to
emerge. Tension developed between this nascent class and the Somoza regime when the latter attempted to control certain aspects of cotton production (see Navas et al., n.d.; Spalding, 1987). This tension, however, did not
reach critical proportions until most other sectors of Nicaraguan society
were already organized in opposition to Somoza.

Although the Somozas were not directly involved in cotton production,
they did take advantage of the impact the cotton boom had on the rest of the
economy. When beef production expanded in the 1960s, the Somoza family
moved in to dominate the most profitable part of the production process, the
processing stage. The family "controlled the only two meat-processing
plants licensed to export" (Kaimowitz and Thome, 1982:225). Its position
in the dairy industry was comparable (Wheelock, 1980:170). The family
also controlled 50 percent of the country's sugar mills, 65 percent of com-

mercial fishing, and 40 percent of commercial rice production, to mention only a few of its assets (Kaimowitz and Thome, 1982:225).

The Somozas' financial interests extended beyond agriculture, however. The family also played a central role in the incipient industrial sector. In addition to the agroindustrial concerns mentioned above, they owned textile plants, cement works, construction material companies, and the country's key transportation companies. The establishment of the Central American Common Market strengthened the family's position in each of these areas.

The 1972 earthquake facilitated the Somozas' expansion into yet another sector, services and banking. Anastasio Somoza Debayle (the third Somoza to rule Nicaragua) was chairperson of the National Emergency Committee, a temporary governing body set up to respond to this national disaster, which enabled the family to take full advantage of the (U.S.) $600 million in relief funds that poured into the country following the earthquake. This venture proved so profitable that he moved next to "create his own bank, the Banco de Centro América, alongside the [Somoza] group's two modest finance houses, NIAPSA (a housing loan company) and Interfinanciera" (Weber, 1981:17). Suffice to say, "there was no branch of economic activity in which the [Somoza] group did not control major assets" (Wheelock, 1980:174).

The family's expanded economic holdings following the 1972 earthquake were not well received by the rest of the Nicaraguan upper class. The Somozas were perceived to have overstepped their bounds in monopolizing the profit-making possibilities of the earthquake reconstruction. This was a turning point in the relationship between the regime and the Nicaraguan bourgeoisie. Certain elements of the bourgeoisie would eventually join the opposition movement that overthrew the Somoza dynasty in 1979.

Before the bourgeoisie's final defection from the Somoza camp, a popular opposition movement had been formed. The FSLN had succeeded in bringing together a number of diverse opposition groups and was recognized as their vanguard. The rural poor composed an important part of this movement. Each expansionary wave of agroexport production caused a worsening in the conditions to which the *campesino* population was subjected and, in turn, generated a reaction by this sector. The political tension produced by these conditions was expressed in violent landlord-tenant confrontations, organized land takeovers, and evictions. Between 1964 and 1973, 240 land invasions took place in the cotton region alone (Núñez, 1981:79). The expansion of cattle raising in the country's interior produced even more dramatic results. Early guerrilla warfare, organized by the FSLN, found support among the *campesino* population that had been the most hard hit by spreading pastures.[51]

A generalized discontent emerged in the *campo*. The countryside, where the injustices of the Nicaraguan social structure were clearest, became a critical area of operations for the FSLN in the years preceding Somoza's overthrow.

Agrarian Reform, Somoza-Style

Somoza was aware of the time bomb ticking away in the countryside. He responded to the growing opposition with a two-pronged approach: reform and repression. When reform did not produce the desired *campesino* passivity, it was replaced by repression.

During the 1960s and 1970s Somoza directed a number of reform projects aimed at eliminating unrest in the countryside without affecting the status quo. Two agrarian reform projects were central to this effort. The projects were carried out through the Instituto Agrario de Nicaragua (IAN) and, later, the Instituto de Bienestar Campesino, or Campesino Welfare Institute (INVIERNO).[52] The underlying assumption of these programs was that the provision of land titles to a sector of the *campesino* population would increase the food supply and combat the "wave of international communism [that was] invading the Nicaraguan countryside" (Tijerino, 1962).

IAN was founded in 1963. Several programs were implemented under its auspices, the two most important of which were a land titling program and a land colonization program. The land titling program was designed to instill in its *campesino* beneficiaries an interest in maintaining the status quo. It was also aimed at legitimating the landownership of those who had migrated to the agricultural frontier. All of the titles authorized by this program applied to farms located in the central region and the agricultural frontier.[53]

The land titling program's impact was extremely limited. By the late 1970s it had affected only 16,500 families (IAN, 1974a:2). IAN's beneficiaries were not provided with credits, inputs, or technical assistance, any of which might have helped them at least marginally to improve their production levels. These contradictory policies suggest the goal of instilling an identification with their property in the beneficiaries, without necessarily raising their standard of living.

The colonization program was similarly limited in effect. It established a total of sixty-three colonies, incorporating 41,052 *manzanas* (IAN, 1974a:3), but only 2,651 families participated in the program. Most of the colonies were established on the agricultural frontier and Nicaragua's Atlantic coast.[54] The titling and colonization programs were clearly designed to ease the relocation of *campesinos* from the Pacific coastal plain to the agricultural frontier. Yet these reform measures, which hypothetically might have helped the *campesino* sector, were legislated primarily to promote the expansion of the agroexport sector.

In 1975 the Campesino Welfare Institute was established. The U.S. Agency for International Development (AID) provided a significant part of the funding for INVIERNO. INVIERNO's development projects were concentrated in the principal coffee-growing regions of the country: the Pacific highlands of Carazo and the central highlands of Matagalpa and Jinotega. These areas were characterized by extreme land fragmentation and poverty. The interior region had also been noted for intermittent FSLN guerrilla operations.

INVIERNO's stated purpose was to increase production levels through a myriad of projects, with agricultural loans as the centerpiece of the program. The limited size of the loan program was indicative of INVIERNO's reach: only 2,882 clients received credit through it (BNN, 1976:2).[55] The total quantity of credit allocated through the program was 8.2 million córdobas (U.S. $1.2 million). The interest rate on INVIERNO's loans was exorbitant (18 percent), surpassing even that charged on loans to large producers. Requirements for receiving loans restricted the number of *campesino* families who could apply to the program. High interest rates and stringent loan requirements indicate that the program targeted better-off *campesinos*.

None of the projects incorporated into INVIERNO's program seriously affected the existing agrarian structure. Ultimately, INVIERNO differed little from IAN in its aim of securing the allegiance of a small sector of the *campesino* population under threat of being influenced by the guerrillas.

It has been argued that INVIERNO also sought to ensure the availability of sufficient quantities of workers for the agroexport harvests (Núñez, 1981; Biderman, 1982; CIERA, 1982b). By charging high interest rates on its agricultural loans, INVIERNO increased the indebtedness of loan recipients. The poor quality of the land worked by this sector made it difficult to produce enough to repay the loans and interest. Consequently, these farmers were usually forced to supplement their income by working in the agroexport harvest, particularly the coffee harvest. INVIERNO was ostensibly established to promote basic grains production, yet its most important accomplishment was to strengthen the already existing agrarian structure.

All of the agrarian reform programs developed by the Somoza government in the 1960s and 1970s shared the common goal of reducing the social tension generated by the extreme inequalities inherent in Nicaragua's agrarian social structure. They were clearly not oriented to changing that social structure. Indeed, "the State's half-hearted and poorly funded efforts to respond to the plight of small food producers, in particular, and to the agrarian crisis, in general, contrasted sharply with its subsidized accumulation-oriented activities on behalf of large capitalist producers of irrigated rice and agroexport products" (Biderman, 1982:152). The discrepancy in the Somoza government's treatment of these two sectors was apparent to at least some of those whose lives it affected. As might have been anticipated, Somoza's agrarian reform programs were not always successful in achieving their primary goal of eliminating the growing unrest in the countryside. When agrarian reform failed, repression was Somoza's next line of attack.

By the mid-1960s the FSLN's base of operations was the countryside. When the last wave of Somoza's repression began, it was focused there. When his regime began to feel the effects of the armed opposition, Somoza imposed a state of siege in 1975, providing the news blackout needed to send the National Guard on "search and destroy" missions. Indiscriminate bombing was carried out, and napalm and defoliants were used. A generalized state of terror reigned in the countryside: "Peasant huts were burned out and their crops destroyed, women raped . . . the number of those who died in the 33 months of the state of siege can never be calculated, but 3,000 is a frequent estimate" (Black, 1981:89). Somoza's repression caused a momentary lull in guerrilla activities in the *campo*, but Somoza was ultimately unable to stop the growing tide of opposition.

Even when the Somoza government began to comprehend the threat implied by the opposition movement, it was unwilling to address the social conditions that had given birth to this movement. Somoza's refusal to deal with the social inequities generated in part by Nicaragua's agroexport economy would eventually lead to the downfall of his regime.

Civil War and Revolution

On July 19, 1979, the Somoza dynasty was finally brought down. Anastasio Somoza Debayle, the son of Anastasio Somoza García (the first Somoza to assume power, in 1932), was the opposition's immediate target in Nicaragua's civil war, but the struggle went far beyond Somoza for the vast majority of those who fought against him. For many people, Somoza's overthrow signified the possibility of a social order characterized by a more equitable distribution of the country's resources. This vision of the future included the objective of correcting the imbalances between agroexport and food crop production. The implementation of an agrarian reform program was a prerequisite for achieving these goals.

Recognition of the need for an agrarian reform went beyond a theoretical understanding of Nicaragua's agroexport dependency. The FSLN had spent many years organizing the poor and fighting the National Guard in Nicaragua's countryside. The *campesino* population had been a critical base for the FSLN: "It was the peasantry who provided knowledge of the land, served as the information network, and were key in provisioning the guerrilla forces . . . the peasantry and land-less rural workers also provided the 'raw material' of the guerrillas" (Deere and Marchetti, 1981:47). The first *campesino* struggles were primarily focused on economic issues—wages, working conditions, and living conditions on the export estates—but they became more political in nature as Somoza's repression increased in ferocity. The need for a political and economic transformation, which would include the restructuring of agriculture, became more apparent with each new organizing effort in the countryside.

By 1977–78 a coalition of opposition forces was in the process of formation. In addition to much of the *campesino* population, the coalition included the "radicalized and mobilized urban masses . . . millionaire industrialists . . . much of the private sector, traditional opposition parties, most of the organized church hierarchy, and tens of thousands of other Nicaraguans" (Fagen, 1981:5). At the head of this coalition was the FSLN.

From the outset, the development and transformation of the economy was a principal goal of the Nicaraguan revolution. This was to be operationalized as development of a mixed economy, diversification of Nicaragua's trading partners, expansion of economic infrastructure, and, more generally, implementation of policies designed to redistribute the nation's resources, such as agrarian reform and food development programs (Government of National Reconstruction, 1982:6). The Government of National Reconstruction (GNR) was formed by the opposition just before Somoza's ouster. It sought to represent the interests of the majority of the population in implementing the policies outlined above, and this "logic of the majority" meant a "logic of the poor," that is, Nicaragua's working class and its *campesino* population. Under this guiding logic, the agrarian reform program became critical to the new government's revolutionary platform. An agrarian transformation was essential if the needs of Nicaragua's rural poor were to be met.

3

The Nature of
Agroexport Production

The euphoria of victory quickly gave way to the hard realities facing the new Nicaraguan government. Somoza and his associates had sacked the country's treasury during their last months in power, leaving the victors with an external debt of $1.5 billion and an economy that the war had brought to a halt.[1] Reactivation of the economy was the new government's first priority. But even beyond resolving this immediate crisis, certain parameters delimited revolutionary policy making, not the least of which was the agroexport economy inherited by the Sandinistas. The generation of foreign exchange earnings required to meet the foreign debt and to enable Nicaragua to continue importing food, consumer durables, and inputs for basic industry remained a serious challenge.

Early on in the revolutionary process it was realized that agroexport production would have to continue to be the motor of accumulation, generating foreign exchange for the foreseeable future.[2] The industrialization process that had taken place in Nicaragua was of a restricted nature and had not brought about a consolidation of the economy. Moreover, the crisis in the Central American Common Market set limits on the industrial sector's potential for generating foreign exchange earnings. Beginning in the 1970s, this crisis become more severe with the worsening of the regional economic situation. Intraregional trade was especially hard hit. The Nicaraguan industrial sector was not equipped either to meet domestic demand or to generate substantial foreign exchange earnings (see Weeks, 1985b; Brundenius, 1987).

In addition to these macroeconomic factors, several other factors more specifically related to the revolutionary process negatively affected Nicaragua's existing industrial sector. During the insurrection, Somoza had responded to increasing opposition among sectors of the bourgeoisie by ordering extensive bombing of their factories. Overall damage to the industrial sector resulting from the civil war was estimated by the United Nations to be approximately (U.S.) $150 million (CEPAL, 1979b:37). Later, just as the process of economic recovery was gaining momentum, Nicaraguan industry was struck by U.S. economic retaliation.

In 1981 the Reagan administration imposed an economic blockade against Nicaragua aimed at destabilizing the Sandinista regime (Maxfield and Stahler-Sholk, 1985:258) by using its veto power in multilateral lending agencies to block numerous loans to Nicaragua. It also attempted to pressure other countries not to make bilateral loans to Nicaragua. The blockade deepened the foreign exchange crisis the new government had encountered upon its assumption of power. Traditional industry was hardest hit by the foreign exchange shortage, "particularly those firms which relied heavily on imported inputs or spare parts" (Sholk, 1983:19; see also Weeks, 1985a:193–94). The foreign exchange crisis resulted in the closing of many factories and further shrinkage of the industrial sector.

Bringing the industrial sector more in line with Nicaragua's domestic needs and existing economic structure was one of the new government's early goals. It was believed that to push forward Nicaragua's economic development, the country must not simply be a producer and exporter of primary products but also a processor of those primary products and an exporter of the products it processed. Agroindustry came to be seen as the centerpiece of this new strategy of development (Wheelock, 1984b). Major investments were made in developing the agroindustrial sector.[3] This sector was seen as Nicaragua's hope for the future (see Wheelock, 1984a). Until the agroindustrial sector was fully operative, which would not be for some time, the export of primary products remained the key source of foreign exchange earnings. Even after this new sector was functional, it would continue to be dependent on many traditional agroexport crops as critical inputs.

Cotton, coffee, sugarcane, and beef production would therefore remain at the center of the Nicaraguan economy, at least in the initial stages of the revolutionary process.[4] Yet the continuing dependence on agroexport production conditioned revolutionary policy making insofar as any policy that might have a negative impact on this sector had to be evaluated in terms of its overall effect on the economy. At the same time, for the new government to maintain its legitimacy, it would have to fulfill its promises to implement social reforms leading to greater equity.

The agrarian reform, which was perhaps the most important social program carried out by the Sandinista government, was particularly affected by Nicaragua's dependence on agroexport production. The goals of the agrarian reform included redistribution of the nation's agricultural resources and production increases aimed at raising the standard of living of the rural poor, both of which required a major transformation of the agrarian structure. In the process of implementing this structural transformation, the agrarian reform had a significant impact on the agricultural relations of production that had been the basis of export agriculture in prerevolutionary Nicaragua.

The need to maintain agroexport production while carrying out an agrarian reform created serious tensions for revolutionary policy making. George Black (1981:266) succinctly summarized this dilemma: "Not only is there acute imbalance between the two sectors of agriculture [basic grains and agroexport production], but plantation labour has been profoundly stigmatized by the years of Somocismo. And that very plantation labour is the key to emergency economic reactivation." Thus the effect revolutionary policies that pushed forward the social transformation would have on the national economy had to be taken into account in the new government's planning process because economic reactivation was a precondition for that same transformation.

The issue of the labor supply in export agriculture was a striking example of the tensions confronting agrarian reform policy makers. Many of the policies aimed at improving the lives of the rural poor disturbed the delicate balance that had developed to meet seasonal labor demands in the agrarian sector. This effect was particularly felt during the critical months of the harvest. FIDA (1980:146) characterized this dilemma in a discussion of the limited options open to revolutionary policy makers in their efforts to achieve economic reactivation and transformation: "The policy of strengthening and reorganizing the *campesino* sector tends to break one of the fundamental givens on which the functioning of the agroexport sector is based: the existence of a reserve labor supply whose low level of income and absence of alternative sources of employment has left them at the disposition of this sector for use during the agroexport harvests, without causing this sector additional cost during the rest of the year." Thus surfaced the contradiction between harvest labor requirements, which were essential to maintaining agroexport production, and the need for basic structural changes in the agrarian sector to bring about a more equitable distribution of the nation's resources. This relationship between agrarian reform and labor supply problems exemplifies the dilemmas that confronted the Nic-araguan revolution more generally.

The historical development of agroexport production gave rise to a labor system that was dependent on large numbers of seasonal workers during the harvest months. This process was accentuated with the adoption of each new export crop. A characterization of the production process of Nicaragua's major export crops (coffee and cotton) follows that highlights the role of seasonal labor in agroexport production.[5] This description portrays coffee and cotton production as they appeared in the mid-1970s. Any references to post-1979 coffee and cotton production will be designated as such. The following chapter describes the dilemma that arose in coffee and cotton production as a result of the process of revolutionary change that was set in motion in 1979. In order to understand this dilemma, however, it is essen-tial to first become acquainted with prerevolutionary coffee and cotton production.

Coffee Production

Seasonal variation in demand for labor emerged with the introduction of indigo production in the early seventeenth century, but this labor pattern did not have a major impact on agricultural relations of production until the adoption of coffee cultivation at the end of the nineteenth century. Jaime Biderman (1982:55) notes that in addition to integrating Nicaragua into the world market, coffee production generated "significant changes . . . in the internal division of labor, and both land and labor began to be transformed into commodities via the privitization of land and the dispossession of small producers who, having lost their means of production, were forced to sell their labor power." Coffee, however, did not monopolize all of the arable land in the regions where it was cultivated. Coffee farms varied enormously in size. There were many producers with only a few *manzanas* and a small number of producers with very large plantations. The following discussion will focus on the medium- and large-sized capitalist growers because they have been the most important in terms of quantity of coffee produced.[6] Even more significant for the purposes of this study, these producers also employed the greatest number of seasonal laborers.

Extensive cattle grazing often was, and still is, combined with coffee production. An INCAE (1982a:Table 12) study showed that on those coffee *fincas* that produced a second agricultural good (more than 76 percent of the sample), cattle raising was the most frequently chosen alternative. This pattern was particularly common in the central mountain region, where 21 percent of the national cattle herd was located (calculated from Warnken, 1975:124). In contrast, only 7 percent of Nicaragua's cattle were raised in the Pacific central region, which included Carazo (the second most important coffee-growing region). The absorption of land for coffee and cattle left only tiny plots for growing basic grains. The *campesinos* who worked these *minifundios* traditionally sold their labor during the agroexport harvests on the large plantations to supplement the meager income they earned from basic grains.

The Nonharvest Months

In the late 1970s Nicaraguan coffee production practices were still relatively rudimentary. Because cultivation continued to be carried out predominantly in mountainous areas, mechanization of soil preparation was impossible. Technological advances were limited to the application of chemical fertilizers and pesticides and the cultivation of higher-yielding varieties of coffee trees, yet even these advances remained extremely restricted. By 1960, only 1.5 percent of the farms surveyed in a government study of coffee production used fertilizer (Dirección General de Estadísticas y Censos, 1961).[7] Furthermore, cultivation of traditional, lower-yielding varieties of coffee plants remained the norm (Gariazzo, 1984:16–17). Consequently, Nicaragua's yields were significantly lower than those of other coffee-producing countries in the region (see Wheelock:1980).

Limited advances in the level of technology employed on coffee farms were both evidenced in and influenced by the relatively small number of coffee producers who obtained loans to finance their production. In the late 1950s only 37 percent of Nicaragua's coffee farms received agricultural credit, of which 45 percent was provided by the banking system and 55 percent by private lenders and export firms (Dirección General de Estadísticas y Censos, 1961). Although the annual capital outlays required in coffee production once a farm was established and producing were smaller than those of some other crops, these figures suggest the lack of interest among coffee producers in modernizing their production practices. When the demand for coffee rose, producers expanded acreage rather than intensifying production.

In 1980 the new government initiated a program under the auspices of the Comisión Nacional de Renovación de Cafetales (CONARCA) to modernize Nicaraguan coffee production. CONARCA's primary goal was to stop the spread of a coffee fungus, *la Roya*, that had affected the country's coffee production since 1976. Although it soon proved impossible to eradicate *la Roya*, a new strategy of controlling its spread through the application of a fungicide was adopted.[8] CONARCA's other key goal was to raise production levels by replacing traditional varieties (primarily Borbón and Arábigo) with higher-yielding varieties of coffee trees (particularly Caturra). By the end of CONARCA's renovation program in 1983, ninety-six hundred *manzanas* of coffee had been renovated in Carazo.[9] Nonetheless, most of Nicaragua's coffee production was not affected by this modernization process.

During most of the year, work on the coffee *finca* consisted of the maintenance and replanting of coffee trees. Maintenance activities entailed pruning, weeding, and fertilizer application (where it was carried out). The trees were pruned once, shortly after the harvest. Weeding was done, on the average, three times during the year. In addition, on most well-established *fincas* some planting was done during the nonharvest months each year. Coffee trees take about three years to become fully productive. After approximately five years of production, each tree's yield begins to diminish. The productive life of coffee trees averages about twenty years. Consequently, some planting was done each year to maintain the productivity of the *finca*. But unless a *finca* was expanding, planting did not occupy a significant amount of labor time.

Between harvests permanent workers had other tasks such as caring for the owner's other crops and farm animals. One coffee plantation I visited had, in addition to 150 *manzanas* of coffee, 20 *manzanas* of cacao, a citrus orchard, several small banana groves, sugarcane, corn, and farm animals. All the crops and animals except the coffee, cacao, and bananas would eventually be used or consumed on the *finca*. It was common to have a small area cultivated with crops grown for consumption on the *finca*. Some of the permanent workers were also given access to tiny parcels of land to grow staple crops for their own use. This arrangement proved mutually beneficial for workers and plantation owners: "The ceding of land on the *finca*, free of charge, to the workers was part of a strategy employed by producers (especially large- and medium-sized producers) designed to retain this labor force without having to completely provide for their and their family's subsistence. This strategy also enabled producers to utilize their labor in a

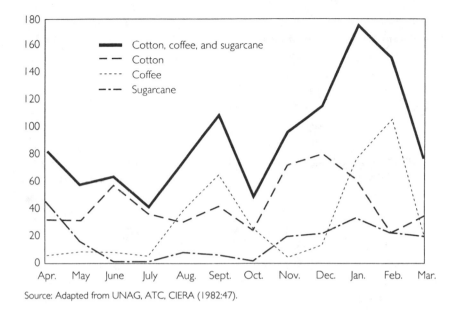

Source: Adapted from UNAG, ATC, CIERA (1982:47).

Figure 3.1
Monthly Agroexport Labor Requirements

flexible manner" (INCAE, 1982a:40). Thus lending out small plots of land provided a means of lowering the reproduction costs of the permanent work force.

Wheelock (1980:84) called this maintenance period the "preparatory period." He concluded, from a survey of forty-nine *latifundios*, that the number of workers employed during this preparatory period was significantly less than during the harvest period: "The number of workers [was] reduced to a minimum—to 10 percent of the number of harvest laborers." (The agroexport work force is made up primarily of temporary [70 percent] as opposed to permanent [30 percent] workers, and figure 3.1 shows how labor requirements vary from month to month.)

The preparatory period lasted approximately from February to November. This time frame varied according to the *finca*'s location, with the harvest starting and ending earlier in warmer areas within a region. The harvest also took place earlier in the Pacific region departments of Managua and Carazo than in the central departments of Matagalpa and Jinotega. But aside from these minor variations, the crop cycle was the same: nine months of "dead time" and three months of harvest.

The Harvest

As harvest time approached, a noticeable gearing up occurred throughout the coffee growing regions. The harvest began when the rainy season ended.[10] It was then that the beans began their final stages of maturation.

According to Wheelock (1980:84), the harvest occurred in three stages that were distinguished by variations in labor demands corresponding to the coffee beans' cycle of maturation. Coffee beans reach an optimal picking point, after which they either fall to the ground or dry on the tree.[11] Beans harvested after this optimal point are typically of lower quality than those harvested earlier, and their value is correspondingly diminished.

Coffee beans mature on a given *finca* at a varied rate. Significant variation on the same tree is even common. Consequently, a tree will be picked several times during the harvest. Nevertheless, there are peak moments in any given area when the majority of beans are ready to be picked.

After being picked, the beans were taken to a coffee *beneficio* (processing plant), either on the same *finca* or in the area of the *finca*.[12] Coffee processing consists of removal of the husk, washing the beans to eliminate the honeylike substance that coats them, and drying the beans. Before 1979 larger *beneficios* often also carried out international marketing of the coffee. According to David Kaimowitz (1980:9), "there were fifteen coffee exporting firms in the country but the largest five controlled two-thirds of all the coffee exported." Immediately following Somoza's ouster in 1979, the revolutionary government nationalized all international marketing of export goods. The marketing of coffee was then assumed by a state agency, the Empresa Nicaragüense de Café (ENCAFE).[13]

Harvesting the beans was by far the most labor-intensive task in the entire cycle of coffee production. Table 3.1 demonstrates the significant difference in labor-intensity per *manzana* between harvesting and all other activities in the coffee production process. Almost 33 percent of the estimated labor time required to cultivate a *manzana* of coffee was concentrated during the three months of the harvest (INCAE, 1982a:70). Coffee is one of the two most labor-intensive crops Nicaragua produces, the other being tobacco.[14]

Harvest labor was recruited from the surrounding *fincas* and hamlets, nearby towns and cities, and sometimes even outside the department in

Table 3.1

Average Labor Supply Requirements per *Manzana* of Advanced-
Technology Coffee

Activity	Person/Days per *Manzana*	Percent	Months
Pruning	11	9.2	March/April
Monitoring of shade trees	6	5.0	March/April
Weeding	9	7.5	March/June–August/September
Replanting	1	0.8	June
Clearing the undergrowth	6	5.0	June
Suckering	5	4.2	July
Fertilizer application	12	10.0	June/September
Insecticide application	4	3.3	June
Fungicide application	8	6.7	April/July
Herbicide application	9	7.5	June/September
Harvest[a]	45	37.5	October/February
Other (drainage, etc.)	4	3.3	May/September
TOTAL	120	100.0	

Source: INCAE (1982a:Table 18).

[a]Calculating an average of 200 pounds per *Manzana*, including transporting to the *beneficio*.

Note: The figures used in this table for the various activities involved in coffee production are coefficients that indicate, in their most simple form, the average time required (person/days) to realize the tasks inherent in the productive cycle of a specific crop and/or animal, according to their biological cycle. These coefficients are then multiplied by the overall number of productive units—acreage cultivated with coffee and other crops and animals on the *finca*—permitting an estimation of the total labor demand (INCAE, 1982a:64–65).

which the *finca* was located. Smaller *fincas* relied on family labor to meet their harvest labor needs. INCAE (1982a:Table 24) found that during the 1979/80 harvest up to 40 percent of harvest labor requirements on smaller *fincas* were met through the employment of relatives and neighbors. In contrast, less than 6 percent of medium-sized producers and none of the larger producers used family labor. Reliance on workers from off the farm but within the department was the most common form of meeting the latter two sectors' harvest labor requirements (more than 50 percent). Nevertheless, there were a significant number of larger producers whose principal source of harvest labor was from outside the department (37 percent).

When a *finca* had been in operation for several years, harvest laborers began to return each year. Several Miskito harvest workers whom I interviewed were en route to a very large *finca* (employing six to seven hundred harvest workers), where they had worked the previous year (interview 117, two coffee harvest workers, December 3, 1983). These two laborers traveled each year from Nicaragua's Atlantic coast to the Matagalpa region to work in the coffee harvest. They would continue to return to the same farm each harvest until a more attractive alternative arose.

The first stage of the coffee harvest took place during November and the first half of December. Only approximately 20 percent of the beans were mature at this point (Wheelock, 1980:85). Serious recruiting was carried out during this period to ensure an adequate labor supply for the next, most important, stage of the harvest.

During the second stage of the harvest, between mid-December and mid-January, approximately 50 percent of the coffee beans were picked. It was during this stage that demand for coffee pickers was the highest. Labor requirements were determined by the number of *manzanas* under cultivation, the type of coffee tree being harvested, and the level of technological development characterizing the *finca*. Coffee tree varieties differ depending on the density at which the trees may be planted and the yield each type produces. Consequently, higher-yielding varieties and those that are planted at greater density will require larger numbers of workers than those with lower yields and densities.

The three main varieties of coffee grown in Nicaragua are (in descending order of productivity) Caturra, Borbón, and Arábigo. Not surprisingly, the larger farms used more advanced levels of technology and grew the most productive varieties of coffee: more than 60 percent of the most technologically advanced farms were larger than fifty *manzanas*, and more than 80 percent of the large producers grew primarily the Caturra variety of coffee tree (INCAE, 1982a:Table 10). At the other extreme, 57 percent of the farms employing the lowest levels of technology were smaller than twenty *manzanas* and grew Arábigo, Borbón, and two other varieties of coffee trees in greater quantities than Caturra. All of these factors coincided to produce the greatest demand for harvest labor on the largest coffee farms.

In addition, demand for coffee pickers varied by region. In absolute numbers, the demand for harvest labor was greater in the north-central region of the country than in the Pacific highlands because coffee acreage was significantly more extensive there.[15] Yet in relative terms, the demand for coffee pickers was greater in Carazo than in Matagalpa and Jinotega because the level of technology characterizing coffee production in the former department was more advanced, thus yields were correspondingly higher (Gariazzo, 1984:151).

There are no data on the absolute number of workers employed in the coffee harvest, though an estimate can be obtained using the coefficient for per *manzana* harvest labor requirements shown in table 3.1. For example, using the area under coffee cultivation in the 1977/78 agricultural cycle, 120,000 *manzanas*, the number of person/days required for that harvest would have been 5.4 million or approximately 90,000 people during the peak period from mid-December to mid-January.[16] This figure is a rough estimate, but it does provide an indication of the magnitude of harvest labor requirements.

This large work force included men, women, and children. In a survey of 454 harvest workers carried out by the Instituto Centroamericano de Administración de Empresas (INCAE) (1982b:Table 7) in 1980, 34.1 percent were women. Wheelock (1980:85) calculated the percentage of women in the harvest work force to be even higher, 40 percent. The same INCAE study found the participation of children between the ages of ten and fourteen to be 21.7 to 22.7 percent, according to gender. Wheelock stated that children's participation in the harvest "was not just of a supplementary or marginal nature, rather it was daily, such that of a crew of 35–40 pickers, there would be 4–6 children between the ages of 7–11." Furthermore, it was common for several members of the family to work in the harvest together.[17] Clearly, the coffee harvest was heavily reliant on female and child labor.

Living conditions for permanent workers on the coffee *latifundio* were generally worse than those described in Chapter 2 for the rural population as a whole. Harvest workers' living conditions were even less desirable: "Permanent workers [had] individual lodgings which [were] quite rudimentary, with no running water or electricity, but seasonal harvest workers live[d] in even more deplorable conditions. They [were] crowded into 'galerones' (dormitories) with no distinctions as to sex or age, no sanitary services or ventilation, and a high incidence of disease" (Biderman, 1982: 65). On the coffee *fincas* I visited, temporary workers lived in closet-sized rooms with dirt floors, no lights, and no windows. Six wooden bunks for sleeping were built on two levels into three walls of each small living quarter.

These living conditions were so dismal that, following the establishment of the revolutionary government, the Ministry of Labor (MITRAB) began issuing *normativas laborales* (work standards) that specifically addressed the issue of the living quarters of coffee harvest workers. (*Normativas laborales* were also issued for cotton harvest workers.) These "norms" described in detail what constituted acceptable living conditions, including the need for ventilation, cleanliness, and so on, but enforcement of these *normativas* did not appear to be very successful. Life on the coffee *finca* was so unpleasant that temporary workers would not seek it out. Seasonal labor continues to be looked upon as a last resort for the rural population.

The final stage of the coffee harvest took place between the middle of January and the beginning of February. The remaining 30 percent of the coffee beans were picked during this stage (Wheelock, 1980:85). Demobilization of the harvest labor force was begun at this time, although approximately 40 percent of the pickers stayed on to finish the harvest.

As the harvest on one *finca* ended, workers often moved to other *fincas* where the harvest was still under way. INCAE (1982b:Table 29) found that approximately 31.2 percent of the coffee pickers it surveyed worked in more than one harvest in 1979/80. These laborers were more likely to move to another coffee *finca* than to a cotton *finca* (only 5 percent also worked in the cotton harvest). Even though not all of the work force employed at the peak of the harvest was able to work all three stages of the harvest on the same *finca*, its members generally managed to find work during most of the harvest. In the above-mentioned survey approximately 87.2 percent of the coffee pickers worked throughout the 1979/80 harvest, as opposed to 73 percent of the cotton pickers (INCAE, 1982b).

The harvest was usually finished by the end of February, with some regional variation. Temporary workers returned to their *minifundios* or the urban informal sector until the harvest mobilization began once again nine months later. After a brief pause, the permanent work force began the cycle anew with the first activities of the preparatory period.

Cotton Production

The introduction of large-scale cotton production to Nicaraguan agriculture in 1950 had profound consequences for the entire society. The expansion of capitalism into the agrarian economy, which had begun at the end of the nineteenth century when coffee was introduced, was accelerated with the massive increase in cotton cultivation in the 1950s and 1960s. The transformation of land and labor into commodities caused by coffee production was both more extensive and more thorough with the development of cotton production.

The expansion of cotton production took place on the Pacific coastal plain from Masaya, north through León and Chinandega, to the Honduran border. This plain had traditionally been used by *campesinos* for basic grain production. The development of cotton production displaced these basic grains producers by pushing them onto marginal land within these departments, onto the rapidly expanding agricultural frontier in central-eastern Nicaragua, or into the growing population of the landless. The result was a striking transformation of the coastal plain region: "The cotton 'boom' completely changed the productive profile and social structure of the departments of León and Chinandega and part of Masaya" (FIDA, 1980:12). Although the cotton boom greatly increased the concentration of land in the areas where its cultivation expanded, the extent to which this process occurred varied between cotton departments. The concentration of land was most extreme in Masaya, where by 1963, 82 percent of the farms were smaller than ten *manzanas* (calculated from Ministerio de Economía, 1966:Table 26). The small farmer's access to land was becoming more and more restricted. While concrete changes resulting from the expansion of cotton were generally confined to these three departments, the implications of these changes for agricultural relations of production went far beyond departmental boundaries. The seasonal labor patterns characteristic of coffee production were even more pronounced in cotton. As cotton production consumed ever-increasing numbers of *manzanas*, thereby displacing more and more *campesinos*, demands for harvest labor grew commensurately. Seasonal labor became fully institutionalized as a fundamental characteristic of export agriculture in Nicaragua.

The Preharvest Months

The cotton production cycle roughly corresponded to that of coffee, except for a delay of several weeks. The first stage of the cotton cycle began between mid-February and mid-March, depending on when the previous harvest ended, and lasted approximately 105 days (see figure 3.2). During this stage the soil was prepared for planting. Whatever remained of the previous harvest was plowed under, thereby recycling nutrients back into the soil.

Harvest and sale	105 days soil prepara-tion and planting	105 days cultivation								Harvest and sale
January	February	March	April	May	June	July	August	September	October	November	December

Source: Perdomo (1979:Appendix I).

The cycle begins between February 15 and March 15. The harvest begins between November 1 and 25. The selling phase often begins simultaneously with the harvest. When a producer sells the cotton in its ginned form, the sale of one harvest may overlap with the soil preparation of the next cycle.

Figure 3.2

The Cotton Production Cycle

This tilling of the land also ventilated the soil and brought to the surface any parasite larvae that it contained. Early exposure to the elements killed the larvae. Since pests were a perennial problem in cotton production, attacking them before the cotton was planted reduced the need for controlling them later.[18]

Planting usually began in mid- to late June, after the rainy season had begun.[19] Rainfall was crucial for the germination of the newly planted cottonseeds. Fertilization was often done at the same time as planting. This first stage of cotton production ended when the seeds had been planted.

Labor requirements during this first stage depended on the level of mechanization characterizing each *finca*. The development of cotton production introduced a level of mechanization previously unknown to Nicaraguan agriculture. Facilitated by Somoza's generous credit policies, the larger producers mechanized many preharvest operations. Because medium- and large-sized producers controlled most of Nicaragua's production, a significant amount of cotton production probably was mechanized.[20]

Tractors were increasingly used for plowing, planting, and pesticide application. According to Biderman (1982:92), "the 'tractorization' of these preharvest operations contributed decisively to the expansion of cotton area and production by increasing labor productivity and reducing unit costs . . . it also initiated a profound transformation in the use of labor, which became increasingly proletarian yet seasonal in character." Thus the increased pro-

Table 3.2

Employment in Cotton Production, Permanent and Temporary,
1960/61–1978/79

Crop Year	Permanent	Temporary	Total	Percent Temporary
1960/61	4,075	44,820	48,985	92
1961/62	5,366	64,389	69,755	92
1962/63	6,710	80,515	87,225	92
1963/64	8,240	98,879	107,119	92
1964/65	9,566	114,797	124,363	92
1965/66	10,140	121,685	131,825	92
1966/67	10,767	129,208	139,975	92
1967/68	12,546	135,914	148,460	92
1968/69	11,264	122,037	133,301	92
1969/70	9,303	100,783	110,086	92
1970/71	8,177	88,586	96,763	92
1971/72	9,365	101,451	110,816	92
1972/73	21,091	158,185	179,276	88
1973/74	25,935	202,295	228,230	89
1974/75	20,350	180,602	200,952	90
1975/76	14,322	157,543	171,865	92
1976/77	16,980	198,104	215,084	92
1977/78	18,651	192,725	211,376	91
1978/79	14,890	158,832	173,722	91

Source: Adapted from Biderman, 1982:180.

ductivity of the permanent work force resulting from mechanization exacerbated the natural differential in labor requirements characteristic of cotton production.

There is some disagreement in the literature on Nicaragua's coffee and cotton production concerning the extent of this differential in each crop. Wheelock (1980:84) estimated that 90 percent of the total labor force in coffee production was employed in the harvest months and only 10 percent was employed on a year-round basis. Figure 3.1 appears to substantiate that claim and confirm that the differential was greater in coffee than in cotton production. Biderman (1982:65), however, suggested that 80 percent of the work force was employed for harvest and 20 percent year-round in coffee production and argued that mechanization of preharvest operations in cotton production resulted in 90 percent employment for harvest and 10 percent year-round.[21] The data cited in table 3.2 substantiate this claim with respect to cotton production, demonstrating that in certain years the differential was as extreme as 92/8 (see also Núñez, 1981:53; and Centro de Investigación de la Realidad Nacional, 1978). It is not essential to determine here which of these estimates is most accurate; all of these descriptions provide evidence of the dramatic seasonal labor requirement differentials that have evolved with the development of cotton and coffee production.

The effects of tractorization on labor requirements in the first stage were similar for the second stage. This next stage primarily entailed the protection of the seed once it had germinated: "After the seed germinates sundry types of insects attack the tree and farmers usually spend great efforts in combating the noxious pests, chiefly with pesticides" (Belli, 1968:82). Weeding and some pruning were done during this stage. Thus the technology implicit in the phrase *tractorization* included the application of pesticides, chemical fertilizers, and sometimes chemical defoliants. The same tractors used to till the soil and plant the cotton were used to apply these labor-saving chemicals. Later, spraying by airplane became the norm on any *finca* larger than five *manzanas*.

All of these labor-saving technologies had a dramatic effect on the size of the permanent work force: "Since labor was therefore no longer needed on a year-round basis, cotton growers retained only an indispensable minimum number of permanent workers required for preharvest operations, and made the rest of their labor requirements a variable cost" (Biderman, 1982:94). Table 3.3 shows the number of person/days required for each activity in the cotton production process in 1980. Preharvest tasks made up 43.7 percent of these person/days and were spread over nine months. In contrast, harvest labor requirements, which made up 56.3 percent of total labor requirements, were restricted to three months of the year.

On coffee *latifundios* permanent workers found employment during the preharvest period in caring for other crops produced on the *finca*. It was not uncommon for other crops to be grown for consumption on the *finca* or even for sale to local markets. The combination of coffee cultivation and cattle raising was also common. Cotton was very different in this sense. The incidence of cattle raising combined with cotton production was significantly less than with coffee. Of all the farms surveyed by INCAE (1982a:Table 5), among those that had a second crop (46 percent), only approximately 5.4 percent raised cattle. Furthermore, 54 percent of all the cotton *fincas* had no second crop of great importance, as opposed to coffee, in which only 24 percent of those sampled did not have a second key crop.

Table 3.3

Average Labor Supply Requirements per *Manzana* of Cotton

Activity	Person/Days per *Manzana*	Percent	Months
Pruning, plowing, harrowing, planting, fertilizing, furrowing, insecticide and herbicide application	3	5.5	May–November
Weeding	18	32.7	August–November
Thinning	3	5.5	August–September
Harvest[a]	31	56.3	December–March
Total	55	100	

Source: INCAE (1982a:Table 11).

[a]An average of 400 pounds per *manzana* and 130 pounds per person/day.

Note: The figures in this table are coefficients. See the note to table 3.1 for an explanation.

This pattern of specialization was another expression of the increasingly capitalist nature that Nicaraguan agriculture was assuming with the growth of cotton production. Cotton farms were typically large, mechanized operations, leaving little space for the continued existence of earlier modes of production. This development had significant consequences for the labor force employed in cotton production. It meant that fewer workers were employed during preharvest months in the cultivation of other crops and livestock on the cotton *finca* than on coffee farms. The opportunity for other types of employment besides preharvest cultivation operations on the cotton *finca* was limited. When lack of other employment opportunities on the *finca* was combined with a high level of mechanization of preharvest cotton operations, labor requirements during this "dead time" became minimal.

The Harvest

The preharvest period ended in November. The second stage of preharvest operations lasted approximately 150 days (see figure 3.2). The ideal time to pick cotton is roughly 150 days after it is planted. The cotton harvest is similar to the coffee harvest in that not all of the bolls mature at the same time. Therefore, the plants are usually picked twice, the second picking 10 to 15 days after the first. Timing is of the essence in cotton production. In the harvest, timing plays a central role in the quality of cotton produced and, therefore, its value. The earlier cotton is picked after it reaches the maturation point, the higher the quality and the more valuable it will be. Conversely, "late harvests affect the yields of ginned cotton, the length, uniformity and resistance of the cotton fiber" (Wong, 1978:15).

Perhaps the most important way that tardiness in the harvest affects the quality of cotton is that the bolls fall to the ground after they reach the height of their maturation process. Cotton picked from the ground is marketable, but it is usually of lower quality because it is dirtier. It also requires special handling during the ginning process. Generally, the longer mature cotton is left in the field and the more it is exposed to the elements, the greater damage the cotton fibers will sustain.[22] Consequently, picking ideally begins when 60 percent of the bolls are open (Wong, 1978:17).

Once the cotton was picked, it was sold either to export houses and intermediaries *en rama* (in its unginned form) or to the cotton ginner to become *oro blanco* (white gold). The proportion of cotton sold *en rama* in the mid-1970s varied between 24 and 41 percent (calculated from CONAL, 1975:71; and Oficina Ejecutiva de Encuestas y Censos, 1978b:45–47). Small producers often sold their cotton unginned to receive a cash return sooner, which enabled them to meet early loan repayment deadlines. Most of the cotton, however, was sold first to ginning companies and entered the open market for export after it was processed. As with coffee, control over cotton exporting was concentrated. By the mid- to late 1970s, four export firms controlled approximately 56 percent of the cotton export market (calculated from INIES, 1983b:Table 30). Likewise, following Somoza's overthrow, the international marketing of cotton was nationalized. The Empresa Nicaragüense de Algodón (ENAL) was established with the mandate of purchasing cotton from growers and selling it on the world market.

Cotton ginning entailed separating the cotton fiber from the seed. All extraneous materials that had gotten mixed in with the cotton as it was picked were also removed in this process.[23] Ginning facilities were usually located in the areas where cultivation took place and traditionally were dominated by large producers and exporters. This pattern developed because "groups of cotton producers wanted to increase their vertical integration, or in the case of exporters, they wanted to be assured they would have cotton to sell" (Arias, 1977:5). With the nationalization of Somoza's and his close associates' property and of international cotton marketing, approxi-

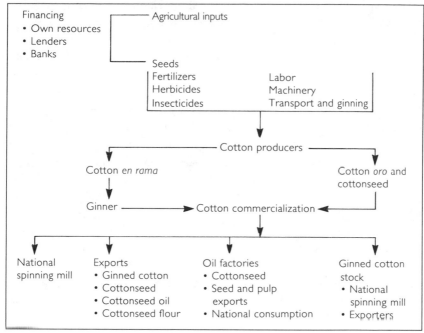

Source: Perdomo (1979:Appendix 5).

Figure 3.3

The Cotton Cultivation and Commercialization Process

mately 32 percent of the country's ginning facilities became government-owned.[24]

From the gin, the cotton was taken to storage facilities or directly to the port of Corinto for export. In the early 1980s, less than 10 percent of Nicaragua's cotton crop remained in the country (interviews 130 and 132, representative of multinational agricultural inputs firm and manager of state-owned cotton ginning facility, March 6, 1984). Cotton that was not exported was usually of inferior quality and was used in the production of mattresses. Most of the cottonseed was sent to local factories, where it was processed into cottonseed oil. In the past, however, very small quantities of cottonseed have been exported. Figure 3.3 illustrates the various stages of cotton production and commercialization.

The cotton industry developed into a streamlined enterprise, symbolizing the degree to which cotton production had become organized along classically capitalist lines. The following discussion examines the extent of proletarianization of the work force that this capitalistic organization brought about.

Maturation of the cotton plant triggered the mobilization of harvest workers. Although mechanization of the harvest somewhat reduced harvest labor requirements, pickers were still in high demand. Harvest laborers represented more than 90 percent of the total number of workers employed in cotton production. Furthermore, harvest wages made up 60 to 70 percent of total annual wages (Biderman, 1982:94). Table 3.2 illustrates the growth in employment of both temporary and permanent laborers in cotton production between the 1960/61 and 1978/79 crop cycles. Employment in cotton grew by more than 250 percent in the first half of the 1960s alone (from 48,895 workers in 1960/61 to 131,825 in the 1965/66 crop cycle). A peak was reached in 1973/74 of 228,230 workers, 89 percent of whom were temporary. The average number of workers in the 1970s was close to 190,000, of whom approximately 90 percent were harvest workers. Cotton employed far more workers than any other crop. Cotton harvest workers alone "constituted over half of the estimated economically active population in agriculture" (Biderman, 1982:94).

Agricultural employment in cotton dropped after 1979 because Nicaragua's civil war drastically reduced the acreage planted in cotton (see table 3.4). Although cotton acreage increased after 1979, it was still significantly less than it had been for most of the 1970s. Coffee acreage, to the contrary, was relatively unaffected by the civil war (see table 3.4). Consequently, some evening out of the agricultural labor force occurred after 1979, at least among Nicaragua's two major export crops.

Demand for harvest labor varied according to the cotton acreage planted. But beyond this truism, "smaller production units not only [did] not employ as much labor, they, themselves [the producers and their families] join[ed] the rest of the workers in the harvest" (Centro de Investigación de la Realidad Nacional, 1978:215). INCAE (1982a:Table 14) found that approximately 25 percent of small producers relied primarily on family members and neighbors to meet their harvest labor requirements. The number of cotton producers who relied on family labor was, however, significantly less than the approximately 40 percent for coffee producers. This difference is an indication of the accelerated process of proletarianization that accompanied the expansion of cotton production. Cotton producers were more reliant than coffee producers on wage labor to meet harvest labor needs.

Table 3.4

Harvested Area for Major Crops, 1960/61–1987/88

(in thousands of *manzanas*)

| | Agroexport Crops | | | | | | Basic Grains | | | | | |
| | Cotton | | Coffee | | Sugarcane | | Rice | | Beans | | Corn | |
Crop Year[a]	Mz.	%	Mz.	%	Mz.	%	Mz.	%	Mz.	%	Mz.	%
1960/61	82	16	118	24	23	5	31	6	54	11	187	38
1961/62	107	19	123	22	29	5	34	6	66	12	207	36
1962/63	134	23	128	22	30	5	32	6	61	10	201	34
1963/64	165	26	119	19	34	5	31	5	61	9	229	36
1964/65	191	27	126	18	35	5	32	5	67	10	249	35
1965/66	203	27	129	17	27	4	33	5	75	10	279	37
1966/67	215	28	129	17	32	4	33	4	80	10	282	37
1967/68	209	25	130	15	34	4	34	4	83	10	352	42
1968/69	188	23	126	16	41	5	34	4	85	10	345	42
1969/70	155	23	124	18	43	6	37	5	58	9	261	39
1970/71	136	19	120	17	46	6	48	7	67	9	299	42
1971/72	156	21	118	16	44	6	48	7	70	10	294	40
1972/73	211	29	119	17	43	6	43	6	57	8	244	34
1973/74	259	32	119	15	45	5	36	4	67	8	293	36
1974/75	254	27	119	13	52	5	47	5	93	10	374	40
1975/76	205	26	120	15	59	7	42	5	80	10	298	37
1976/77	283	31	120	13	60	7	30	3	97	11	324	35
1977/78	303	34	120	13	57	6	35	4	88	10	303	33
1978/79	248	27	135	15	59	7	39	4	95	11	325	36
1979/80	64	10	140	22	53	9	51	8	76	12	240	39
1980/81	135	20	134	20	56	8	47	7	78	11	231	34
1981/82	133	17	126	16	63	8	59	7	108	14	294	38
1982/83	129	18	126	17	65	9	63	9	98	14	235	33
1983/84	168	21	128	16	62	7	63	8	126	15	266	33
1984/85	164	20	126	16	61	8	55	7	118	15	270	34
1985/86	124	19	121	19	61	9	51	8	103	16	188	29
1986/87	85	13	104	16	61	9	56	8	142	21	225	33
1987/88	85	13	103	16	60	9	55	8	96	15	261	39

Sources: 1960/61–1978/79: BCN (1979:74–84).

1979/80–1987/88: MIDINRA, unpublished data (March, 1989).

[a]Crop year is from April through March.

Harvest labor was also recruited from surrounding *fincas*, hamlets, towns, and cities and in some cases even outside the department where the *finca* was located. More than 50 percent of the medium- and large-sized producers included in INCAE's (1982a:Table 14) survey stated that their harvest labor needs were met by hiring workers from within the department. Nicaragua's cotton harvest also traditionally attracted migrant labor from Honduras and El Salvador. Migrant laborers from El Salvador typically worked on cotton plantations in Puntañata (at the point of the peninsula in Chinandega), traveling there by ferry. Honduran laborers usually were concentrated in northeastern Chinandega, close to the Honduran-Nicaraguan border. Very little of this migrant labor force traveled as far as the department of León looking for work. Employing foreign laborers was more common among large producers (35.8 percent), although a few (16 percent) medium-sized producers also relied on imported labor.[25] For some large producers in Chinandega, as much as 50 percent of their harvest labor force was composed of foreign laborers (interviews 205 and 206, large private producers, July 20, 1987).

As was the case in coffee production, women and children often participated in the cotton harvest. Orlando Núñez (1981:74) argued that "in spite of [all the other recruiting mechanisms relied upon, including foreign laborers] the shortage of labor [was] so delicate that cotton producers resorted to all sorts of means so that they would not lose their precious product, including the employment of women and children from the labor camps at the moment of the harvest." Although women's participation in the cotton harvest was slightly less than in the coffee harvest, they still represented a significant part of the work force: 28 percent (INCAE, 1982b:Table 8), compared with 34.1 percent among coffee pickers. The presence of children in the cotton harvest was also less than that in the coffee harvest but remained at a level that made them important in meeting harvest labor requirements: 17.3 to 17.8 percent, varying by sex (INCAE, 1982b:Table 6), as opposed to 21.7 to 22.7 percent among coffee pickers.

Living conditions for cotton harvest workers were as deplorable as those for coffee harvest workers, yet the living quarters of the cotton workers were even worse because of the environmental conditions characterizing their physical location. According to Douglas L. Murray (1984:10), the pesticide use that was central to cotton production often contaminated cotton workers' living areas. Workers were exposed to aerial spraying, and their food and water were frequently contaminated.[26]

Adverse living circumstances were combined with the unfavorable climatological conditions that coincided with the cotton harvest. The harvest takes place during Nicaragua's dry season, which is characterized by very high temperatures and veritable dust storms. Furthermore, 85 percent of the cotton acreage was concentrated in the departments of León and Chinandega (Velásquez, 1977:1), where temperatures reach their highest levels, making working conditions extremely difficult.

Cotton harvest workers traditionally endured these conditions an average of sixty-nine days a year before they were "deproletarianized."[27] One study found that approximately 29.5 percent of those who worked in the 1980 harvest were employed on at least one other *finca* when they were let go, including 9.9 percent who also participated in the coffee harvest (INCAE, 1982b:Table 29). But when the harvest came to an end, these workers were left to find their own means of survival until they were needed for the next harvest.

El Tiempo Muerto

The development of agroexport production created a work force that could swell to enormous proportions to meet harvest labor requirements and be largely dispensed with when the harvest terminated. This process was heightened by the mechanization of many preharvest operations in cotton production. But aside from a small difference in proportion, the principle was the same for both cotton and coffee harvest workers: the vast majority of harvest workers had to fend for themselves the other nine months of the year. These workers learned to eke out an existence during the "dead time" (*el tiempo muerto*) working small plots of land on which they produced basic grains, participating in the urban informal sector, or joining the ranks of the unemployed. Foreign laborers faced the same options when they returned to their native countries during the nonharvest months. Although there were some differences in the ways coffee and cotton pickers supported themselves and their families during these months, a general picture can be drawn of the marginal existence that led them once again to offer their labor power in the next harvest.

The Minifundio

As the cultivation of coffee expanded in the last decade of the nineteenth and the early part of the twentieth centuries, it gradually reduced the ability of the *campesino* population to be self-sustaining agricultural producers. The adoption of several other export crops in the 1950s and 1960s only reinforced this pattern, pushing them onto small, infertile plots of land.[28] The *campesino* population was largely excluded from receiving technical assistance and agricultural credits.[29] And Somoza's protection of the intermediaries who offered short-term credit to subsistence producers at usurious interest rates further guaranteed the latter's poverty. The same intermediaries were also the *campesinos'* key link to the market. Thus these tiny producers were forced to accept the low prices offered by this sector of middlemen. All of these factors combined to force many *campesinos* to search for means to supplement their income. The option they most frequently relied on was working in the harvests.

In the most comprehensive survey of harvest workers carried out to date, it was found that a full 54.5 percent of the coffee and 46.8 percent of the cotton harvest workers were semiproletarian (CIERA, 1981:Table 15).[30] That is, they participated in the wage labor force only part of the year and worked on their own farms the rest of the year. This pattern varied somewhat by region and crop. Nevertheless, these figures underline the strong interdependence between *minifundio* and export crop production.

The link between *campesino* and agroexport production was stronger in the coffee sector than in the cotton sector, as seen in the figures shown above. This tendency was clearer in Nicaragua's two key coffee-growing departments than in the country as a whole: in Matagalpa, 53.5 percent of the coffee harvest workers were semiproletarian (and 23.5 percent proletarian), and in Jinotega, 55.4 percent were semiproletarian (and 17.1 percent proletarian) (see CIERA, 1981:Table 15). By contrast, in the country's other important coffee-growing region, Carazo, 46.8 percent of the harvest workers were semiproletarian (and 26.1 percent proletarian). Carazo is located in the more developed Pacific region. There, population pressure, combined with the concentration of land brought on by the spread of coffee production, pushed *campesinos* off the land and into the rural and urban work force and the informal sector at a much faster rate than in the central mountain region.[31]

The effects of the expansion of agroexport production on the composition of the labor force were especially evident in Nicaragua's cotton-growing regions. In the country's most important cotton-producing department, Chinandega, 37.1 percent of the harvest workers were proletarian in origin and 37.7 percent were semiproletarian (CIERA, 1981:Table 15). In León, the country's second most important cotton department, 32.4 percent of the harvest workers were proletarian in origin, and 42.8 percent were semi-proletarian. Semiproletarian workers composed even more of the cotton harvest labor force in Masaya and Managua, 45.8 percent and 59.1 percent, respectively. Thus, where cotton production had advanced the furthest, in Chinandega, it had gradually proletarianized the labor force. Yet more than one-third of the cotton harvest labor force in Chinandega continued to come from the *minifundio* sector.

The harvest labor needs of the agroexport growers were thus largely met by *minifundistas*. This labor force did more, however, than offer its labor during this annual period of need. Its seasonal nature also responded to another requirement of the agroexport producers: it collected wages only during several months of the year. The agroexport producers had to pay harvest workers an absolute minimum if they were to earn a profit because of the differential profit scale between international capital (which bought their products on the world market) and the producer.[32] The need for cheap labor was easily accommodated by the fact that harvest wages were "only" supplemental income: "What was important about the semiproletariat, was that the wages they were offered for their seasonal labor could be very low because the reproduction of this labor force did not have to be guaranteed by this wage alone" (CIERA, 1982a:2). These wages were not expected to sustain workers and their families because they had a small parcel of land that supported them through the rest of the year.

The Urban Informal Sector

Another important source of harvest labor was the urban informal sector. The expansion of cotton production displaced large numbers of *campesinos*, who either moved to the agricultural hinterland, where they worked tiny plots of land, every year being pushed further into the frontier as agroexport production expanded, or moved into urban areas. Managua was a major "pole of attraction"; its share of the total population increased from 9.8 to 20 percent between 1950 and 1970 (calculated from Oficina Ejecutiva de Encuestas y Censos, 1978a:5, 27). Those who migrated to urban areas were increasingly incorporated into the informal sector because the demand for formal industrial labor was much smaller than the population migrating from rural areas (Jarquín, 1974). Although its wages were low and irregular, the informal sector allowed these workers to maintain a marginal existence. This work was insecure, however, and many recent émigrés chose to supplement the meager incomes they earned in the informal sector with harvest wages. INCAE (1982b:Table 17) found that 30.4 percent of the cotton harvest labor force and 21.8 percent of the coffee harvest labor force came from urban areas in 1980.

Harvest laborers were also found among the ranks of the unemployed. Not surprisingly, the cotton harvest attracted more of the unemployed (who composed approximately 15 percent of the harvest labor force) than the coffee harvest (approximately 10 percent of the harvest labor force).[33] When other employment was unattainable, the agroexport harvests at least provided wages for several months.

In some years the heavy labor demands of the harvest period were not met. As the acreage planted with export crops expanded, a corresponding increase in the demand for harvest workers occurred. Harvest labor supply problems were first encountered when coffee production was just beginning (Cumberland, 1980). Deere and Marchetti (1981:43) noted that vagrancy laws passed in the late 1800s "fined workers who did not participate in the coffee harvest and who could not prove some other form of employment." The *minifundio*–export production relationship was found to be the best solution to these early labor supply problems.

In more recent years the shortages were felt most acutely in cotton production when cultivation increased dramatically and labor requirements increased correspondingly. The first remedy cotton producers turned to was mechanization: only 13 harvesters were registered in the country in 1963/64, but this figure had grown to 161 by 1966/67, and 17 percent of cotton output that year was harvested mechanically (CONAL, 1967:Table VI-2; and 1976:37). One study reviewing the pros and cons of mechanizing the harvest during this time of crisis (Ministerio de Economía, 1965) cited the increased profits to be gained by mechanizing because it reduced labor costs: as harvest labor became scarce, wages had risen. This study also noted that early harvesting, which was facilitated by mechanization, reduced problems in the quality of the cotton when the harvest was extended over too much time.

The benefits of mechanization, however, were accompanied by a long list of problems. Not the least of these was that machine-picked cotton is of lower quality than cotton picked by hand. The disadvantages inherent in mechanization of the harvest were sufficient to lead Nicaraguan cotton producers to continue relying primarily on temporary laborers to pick the crop. Thus, though the use of mechanical cotton harvesters posed a temporary solution to labor supply problems, it was not seen as a panacea. By the late 1960s, their use was already in decline, so that only 4.9 percent of the 1970/71 harvest was carried out by machines (IRCT, 1982:Table 2).

The decline of mechanical harvesters was also related to the boom-and-bust cycles characteristic of agroexport production. By 1970, cotton production had reached the low point of one of these cycles and acreage was down so that fewer workers were required for the harvest. Moreover, this low point coincided with the adoption of another remedy for harvest labor supply problems: the introduction of imported labor.[34]

Honduras and El Salvador were Nicaragua's main sources of imported labor. Following the 1969 war between El Salvador and Honduras, the exodus of laborers to Nicaragua provided a needed safety valve for population pressures within both countries. In the case of El Salvador, this pressure had been one of the causes of the war (Dorner and Quiros, 1973). For Nicaragua, this bracero-type program provided harvest laborers, thereby reducing the need for mechanical harvesters.[35] In addition, imported labor helped to keep wages low. By increasing the size of the labor pool, Salvadoran and Honduran immigrants undermined the bargaining position of Nicaraguan harvest workers.

By the early 1970s, cotton producers had resolved the temporary labor supply problem by using a combination of mechanization and imported labor. Cotton acreage expanded once again, reaching the all-time high of 310,846 *manzanas* in 1977 (see table 3.4). Determined agroexport producers (often with the help of the state) had found means of resolving labor supply difficulties, which enabled them to continue expanding their production. Yet implementation of the agrarian reform program, which began immediately following the establishment of the revolutionary government in 1979, was to make the nature of this seasonal labor system problematic.

In sum, prerevolutionary Nicaragua was characterized by the seasonal variation in labor demands typical of agroexport production. These demands were met by employing large numbers of workers during the peak harvest period. Once the harvest was finished, the workers went back to their *minifundios*, the urban informal sector, or their native countries. This pattern of varying labor demands contributed, on one hand, to the growth produced by the expansion of cotton production, which was growth solely in terms of capital accumulation. On the other hand, the increase in underemployment and unemployment that accompanied this growth contributed greatly to both urban and rural poverty, especially the latter. One of the by-products of this process was the development of rural unrest. The extent to which this unrest had grown by the late 1970s was evidenced in the large number of rural-based people who fought or participated in other ways in the war that led to the overthrow of Anastasio Somoza Debayle. The FSLN was able to gain the support of the *campesino* population not only because of that group's opposition to Somoza's tyranny but because of the FSLN's program for a profound agrarian reform. Even before the victory celebrations were over, agrarian policies were being enacted by the new government, formalizing and extending the reform process that had begun during the war.

4

The Dilemmas of
Revolutionary Policy

Agrarian Reform and the

Problem of Labor Supply

An Introduction to the Problem

When the revolutionary process was initiated in Nicaragua in July 1979, a new emphasis on addressing the needs of the majority of the population was adopted, which focused on Nicaragua's poor, especially the rural poor. The Government of National Reconstruction initiated the process of restructuring Nicaraguan society to promote two objectives: economic development and income redistribution. Because agriculture plays such an important role in the country's economy, and because the political support of the agrarian population was critical for the government's revolutionary program, the most profound changes were carried out in the agrarian sector.

Agrarian reform policy makers quickly found, however, that efforts to pursue their twin objectives created certain tensions for the revolutionary process. Nicaragua's economic development remained largely dependent on the production of several key export crops. Export earnings generated by these crops were crucial, even for further growth in the agricultural sector. Yet a delicate balance had developed between the agroexport and *campesino* sectors as the former expanded. Agroexport production depended on a large seasonal labor supply, a significant portion of which came from the *campesino* sector. The agrarian reform, however, threatened to offset the balance between these two sectors of agriculture. The possibility of reducing the economic necessity that drove *campesinos* to participate in the agroexport harvest each year was inherent in the objective of improving income distribution in the *campo*. This chapter addresses the growing tension between agroexport production and agrarian reform as the reform gradually undermined the previously existing productive structure that had come to be the basis of export agriculture.

The Nicaraguan agrarian reform was designed to meet three basic objectives: to raise the standard of living of the rural population, to guarantee the nation's food self-sufficiency, and to increase the generation of foreign exchange earnings by strengthening the country's agroindustrial base. Meeting these objectives meant "promoting development of the productive forces, changes in the relations of production, and democratization of political power. Through rational organization of the APP [Area Propiedad del Pueblo, i.e., the state sector] and development of the cooperative system, these changes [would] become the foundation of a new type of accumulation based on agricultural production" (MIDINRA, 1983:21). In late 1981, the vice-minister of agrarian reform, Salvador Mayorga (1982:102), summarized the results of a series of reform measures that had been implemented with the goal of creating an agrarian sector more oriented to the needs of the rural poor: "a) Greater access to land for poor rural workers; b) Reduced rents on agricultural land; c) A weakening in the control of intermediaries and access to better prices for small farmers; d) An increase in the amount of credit extended to small farmers who produce basic grains; [and] e) An increase in the salaries of agricultural workers." Underlying the implementation of the reform measures that had brought about these changes was the assumption that achieving a better balance between production of basic grains for domestic consumption and production for export would facilitate an improved standard of living for the rural poor and ensure Nicaragua's food self-sufficiency.

Transforming the relationship between *campesino* and export agriculture, however, required that "a new functional equilibrium be established in the assignment of resources between basic grain and agroexport production. This equilibrium refer[red] not only to the spatial integration of these two types of production, but especially to the crucial problem of seasonal labor demands" (FIDA, 1980:154). Explicitly, by providing more resources for production in the *campesino* sector and thereby increasing the income earned by those who depended on this production, the traditional necessity of this population to sell their labor on the agroexport plantations should have been reduced, if not eliminated. This brings us back to the central problem under study: How can agroexport production be expanded at the same time that an attempt is made to reorient the priorities of agricultural production toward meeting the needs of the rural poor? More concretely, What was the nature of the relationship between agrarian reform and the harvest labor supply problems that were encountered in the agroexport sector beginning in 1979? To understand the tension between agroexport production and agrarian reform, one must analyze the first several harvests that occurred after the Government of National Reconstruction came to power in July 1979. Although expression of this tension took time to develop, the initial indications that it would emerge as a problem can be found in the harvest that was carried out later that year.

The First Post-Somoza Harvest

The civil war seriously affected Nicaragua's agricultural production. The final insurrection, which occurred during the months traditionally dedicated to planting the year's crops, particularly hurt production. Overall losses incurred by the agricultural sector during the war were estimated by CEPAL (1979b:37) to be approximately (U.S.) $27.7 million.

The 1979/80 cotton crop was especially hard hit by the war. Planting season coincided with the last two months of the war, when the final insurrection was at its height. Limited planting did take place in the few weeks following July 19. But cotton acreage was dramatically reduced from the few years preceding 1979: 64,000 *manzanas* were planted in 1979/80, compared with the 248,000 *manzanas* planted in 1978/79 (see table 3.4). This significant reduction in cotton acreage restricted problems meeting harvest labor requirements to the largest farms. Only approximately 21 percent of the large producers and 16 percent of the medium-sized producers interviewed by INCAE (1982a:Table 16) had problems finding workers for the cotton harvest.

Coffee production, although less directly affected by the war, did also experience labor supply problems. More than 55 percent of the medium and large producers in INCAE's survey (1982a:Table 27) encountered difficulties meeting their harvest labor requirements. In addition, more than 62 percent of this sample had labor supply problems during both the harvest and preharvest months. Coffee acreage was not affected by the fighting, but yields were lower in 1979/80 than in either the preceding or following years.[1] Many producers had been unable to conduct required maintenance activities during the final months of the war. Efforts to control the spread of Nicaragua's principal coffee disease (*la Roya*) through timely application of fungicides during this period were particularly affected. Some coffee-processing facilities were also destroyed.

More important for the present discussion, however, massive dislocation characterized the months immediately following the war. A breakdown in transportation, difficulties with food supplies, and the disappearance of the previous labor recruitment system all contributed to the shortage of harvest laborers during this first post-Somoza coffee harvest (see Deere and Marchetti, 1981; and Kaimowitz, 1980). Although none of these factors could be attributed to the agrarian reform per se, coffee producers cited several factors that did stem from revolutionary policies: "a) a political orientation being developed in the workers; b) the new policy of intensive basic grain cultivation, which took workers away from the coffee *fincas* to work in these crops; and c) the application by state enterprises of an intensive labor policy designed to attend to these new enterprises and reduce the unemployment generated by the war" (INCAE, 1982a:95). It could be argued that implementation of the measures mentioned by these coffee producers was still not sufficiently advanced by the time of the 1979/80 harvest to have contributed to the labor shortage. The intensive grain cultivation policy in particular was probably not sufficiently developed to have taken away a significant number of former harvest workers. But the state farms, formed on confiscated Somocista property immediately following Somoza's ouster, were certainly employing more workers than these *fincas* had previously employed.[2] Thus what these producers already saw as a fact was rather the beginning of a tendency that was to become more pronounced in each of the following harvests.

Although the 1979/80 coffee harvest cannot be considered representative of post-Somoza harvests, for the first time concern arose "regarding the extent to which meeting rural workers' and peasants' demands ha[d] dried up the labor market" (Deere and Marchetti, 1981:63). The agrarian reform–agroexport dilemma would become even more apparent in the 1980/81 harvest, where it found its clearest expression in the cotton sector.[3]

The 1980/81 Cotton Harvest

The 1980/81 crop cycle was the first "normal" year for cotton production following the civil war. The drop in production during the 1979/80 cycle was followed by a gradual increase in acreage during the next few years, although production still fell short of prerevolutionary years (see table 3.4).

The doubling of cotton acreage between the 1979/80 and 1980/81 crop cycles created a corresponding increase in demand for labor, particularly in the harvest period. The expansion in acreage and labor demand coincided with the implementation of agrarian reform measures, which combined with several other factors to produce a labor shortage in the 1980/81 harvest that had a significant negative impact on the agroexport sector. The data cited below illustrate the severity of the problem during the 1980/81 crop cycle.

The cotton harvest usually takes place between December and March, and the most intense work is done in January and February. Yet because of the labor shortage, the 1980/81 harvest lasted until the beginning of May.[4] This delay resulted in the deterioration in the quality of the cotton. In addition, in many areas the plants were only picked once so that later-blooming bolls were not harvested.

In quantitative terms, whereas the expected ratio of workers per *manzana* was 0.7, the actual ratio was approximately 0.33 during the 1980/81 harvest.[5] In other words, there was a deficit in the number of harvest workers of approximately 50 percent. This deficit occurred at a time when the demand for labor was half what it had been traditionally because of the production decline during the insurrection. If cotton acreage had approximated that of previous years, this shortage would have been of disastrous proportions, but even with reduced acreage, it was still serious.

Various factors combined to produce this critical shortage. Together they represented the dissolution of the pre-1979 labor system, which was brought on by the process of revolutionary transformation. An examination of the factors that caused the labor shortage will shed light on the dilemma that faced agrarian planners. Agrarian policies would have to address this dilemma before serious limitations in agroexport production resulted.

Campesinización and the Harvest Labor Supply

The effects of a number of agrarian reform policies combined to play a key role in fostering the labor shortage experienced in the 1980/81 cotton harvest. These policies worked together to produce what is commonly known in Latin America as *campesinización*. *Campesinización* refers to the creation of conditions that permit the reproduction of peasant households as petty agricultural producers, thereby eliminating their need to participate in the wage labor force. It resulted from a variety of agrarian reform policies, including land redistribution, the reallocation of agricultural credits, rent ceilings, and guaranteed producer prices for the crops traditionally grown by *campesinos*. Large numbers of peasants who previously had no choice but to supplement their income by working in the harvest could now choose to stay at home and work on their own farms.

The Redistribution of Land

Somoza's overthrow was followed by an immediate confiscation of the family's property, as well as that of its cronies. Government decrees 3 and 38 authorizing this confiscation laid the basis for the establishment of a state sector that came to include 1.4 million *manzanas* of land (MIDINRA, 1982:42).[6] This new sector, the Area Propiedad del Pueblo, incorporated approximately 20 percent of Nicaragua's agricultural land. The scattered cases of land takeovers organized by the FSLN, which had occurred in the last months of the war (primarily in the north Pacific region), were legalized by these decrees. Agricultural communes had been set up on this land, foreshadowing one of the organizational forms that would be adopted following the announcement of the confiscation measures on July 20, 1979. The nationalization process begun by these two decrees constituted the first phase of the agrarian reform. The second phase was not begun until mid-1981.

The agrarian reform ministry decided it would be most productive to maintain intact the large, modernized agroexport estates, which constituted the better part of the area nationalized in the first phase. Efficient production on these estates was crucial for the continued generation of foreign exchange earnings (Wheelock, 1984a).[7] Nevertheless, small farmers were granted greater access to land; three hundred thousand *manzanas* were distributed informally to *campesinos* who organized cooperatives (*La Prensa*, 1982b).

Small farmers were organized into cooperatives so they could obtain the greatest benefit from the redistributed land. These cooperatives took a number of forms, the most common of which were Credit and Service Cooperatives (CCS) and Sandinista Agricultural Cooperatives (CAS). In the CAS, land was pooled and production was carried out collectively. In contrast, CCS members joined together to receive credit and technical assistance but otherwise worked individually.

The cooperative movement developed rapidly. By mid-1980, 2,512 cooperatives had been formed, 53 percent of which were CAS and 47 percent of which were CCS.[8] One-third of the newly formed CAS were located on state land and the remainder on private land. Former *minifundistas* made up approximately 75 percent of the cooperatives' membership (Marchetti, 1981:58). Whereas in early 1979 only a handful of cooperatives existed, two years later a significant part of the rural poor was opting to try this new form of organization.

Mounting pressure on the new government in the form of land invasions by the *campesinos* and decapitalization by the propertied classes finally forced the promulgation of the Agrarian Reform Law on August 21, 1981 (*La Gaceta*, 1981).[9] This law initiated the second phase of agrarian reform by authorizing the confiscation of idle or underused land on large estates. Land that had not been farmed for two years was defined as idle, and underused farms were defined as those on which less than 75 percent of the acreage was cultivated. The law specified that on the west coast and in the coffee-growing regions of Matagalpa and Jinotega only those who owned more than five hundred *manzanas* could be affected. This area included the key agroexport regions. The size specification for the rest of the country was one thousand *manzanas*. The law also affected land rented for cash, labor, or in kind by large landowners (with the above-mentioned size specifications). Those who owned more than fifty *manzanas* on the Pacific coast or one hundred *manzanas* elsewhere and rented this land for labor or in kind could be affected as well. This last specification reflected the new government's desire to eliminate "archaic" forms of land tenure. Finally, the Agrarian Reform Law authorized the confiscation of land belonging to those who had left the country. Landowners were to be compensated according to the situation characterizing each farm.

Ratification of the Agrarian Reform Law signaled a change in emphasis in terms of the social organization of the reformed sector. If large estates were deemed to be more efficient and productive in their existing form, they would be maintained in this form even after the Agrarian Reform Law facilitated their confiscation. The political climate in which the law was enacted, however, was such that its goal was to respond to the *campesinos'* demand for land. Indeed, small producers proved to be the chief beneficiaries of this second phase.

Implementation of the law began at a relatively cautious pace. In the first nine months of its existence only 231,295 *manzanas* were confiscated.[10] Redistribution proceeded even more slowly than land confiscation. In this same period only 20 percent of the confiscated land, or 47,709 *manzanas*, was turned over to the *campesino* sector (CIERA, 1982b:130). Titles to this land were given to 146 cooperatives and 41 individuals.[11] Because the goal was to ensure that the land would be used productively, the process of assigning it took time. Another factor determining the pace of land distribution to the peasantry was the concern among certain agrarian reform officials that this would lead to *campesinización*, thus reducing the size of the labor force available for the agroexport harvests (see Kaimowitz, 1986). Nonetheless, confiscation and redistribution were accelerated after the first year. By the end of 1983, 426,508 *manzanas* had been redistributed (see table 4.1). Titles for an additional 198,634 *manzanas* were granted for land that had previously been occupied and worked without legal title (MIDINRA, 1986b:53). To that point, 25,395 families had benefited from the reform. Table 4.2 illustrates the transformation that had taken place in the agrarian sector by December 1983.

After that, land redistribution and titling moved even faster in response to the escalating Contra war. The government hoped to fortify its political base by increasing the population of agrarian reform beneficiaries. The granting of land titles to squatters, most of whom had farmed their parcel of land for many years without legal title, received priority. By December 1984, the total number of *manzanas* that had been redistributed or for which a legal title had been granted reached 1,955,682, of which approximately 34 percent was redistributed land and 66 percent represented the legalization of titles (see table 4.1 and MIDINRA, 1986b:53).

The formation of cooperatives had also accelerated after 1980: by October 1982, a total of 2,849 cooperatives existed, with 68,434 members.[12] The majority of those associated with cooperatives belonged to CCS (63.2 percent), rather than CAS (11.5 percent) or practiced precooperative forms of production. In the three years since Somoza's overthrow, tremendous advances had been made in the cooperative movement. Cooperative formation and the land distributed by both phases of the agrarian reform had resulted in a significant increase in the amount of land available to the rural poor.

Some land had already been made available to former landless and land-poor rural workers by the time of the 1980/81 cotton harvest. The beneficiaries included cotton and coffee pickers, although there appeared to be differences between the two groups. INCAE (1982b:131) found that, at least in the initial stages of the agrarian reform, land redistribution benefited cotton pickers more than coffee pickers: among the former who cultivated small parcels of land in 1980, 31 percent had begun this cultivation after

Table 4.1

Land Redistributed and Families Benefited, October 1981–December 1988

Form	1981/82		1983		1984		1985	
	Area (%)	Families (%)	Area (%)	Families (%)	Area (%)	Families (%)	Area (%)	Families (%)
Sandinista Agricultural Cooperatives (CAS)	106,398 (80)	6,739 (85)	240,119 (82)	10,734 (79)	195,558 (81)	8,604 (76)	61,235 (57)	5,119 (44)
Credit and Service Cooperatives (CCS)	3,342 (3)	771 (10)	36,179 (12)	2,533 (19)	28,146 (12)	2,347 (21)	15,388 (14)	4,344 (37)
Work Collectives (CT)	–	–	245 (0)	32 (0)	2,993 (1)	139 (1)	3,033 (3)	313 (3)
Individuals	22,827 (17)	383 (5)	17,398 (6)	298 (2)	14,141 (6)	264 (2)	20,790 (19)	264 (2)
Dead Furrow Cooperatives (CSM)	–	–	–	–	–	–	7,443 (7)	1,574 (14)
Totals	132,567 (100)	7,893 (100)	293,941 (100)	13,597 (100)	240,838 (100)	11,354 (100)	107,889 (100)	11,614 (100)

(continued)

Table 4.1 (*continued*)

Form	1986		1987		1988		TOTALS	
	Area (%)	Families (%)	Area (%)	Families (%)	Area (%)	Families (%)	Area (%)	Families (%)
Sandinista Agricultural Cooperatives (CAS)	149,759 (48)	6,310 (41)	129,569 (73)	4,457 (50)	38,853 (68)	5,102 (57)	921,491 (69)	47,065 (61)
Credit and Service Cooperatives (CCS)	26,147 (8)	2,146 (14)	18,788 (10)	1,446 (16)	5,630 (10)	1,656 (19)	133,620 (10)	15,243 (20)
Work Collectives (CT)	12,107 (4)	707 (5)	3,949 (2)	177 (2)	1,182 (2)	202 (2)	23,509 (2)	1,570 (2)
Individuals	110,652 (35)	4,531 (30)	15,512 (9)	1,880 (21)	8,654 (15)	866 (10)	209,974 (16)	8,486 (11)
Dead Furrow Cooperatives (CSM)	16,367 (5)	1,523 (10)	10,191 (6)	918 (11)	3,059 (5)	1,051 (12)	37,060 (3)	5,066 (6)
Totals	315,032 (100)	15,217 (100)	178,009 (100)	8,878 (100)	57,378 (100)	8,877 (100)	1,325,654 (100)	77,430 (100)

Source: CIERA (1989: vol. 9, p. 56).

Table 4.2

Changes in Land Tenure by Property Sector

(in thousands of *manzanas*)

Property Sector	1978		1983		1987a	
	Area	%	Area	%	Area	%
Individuals	8,073.0	100	5,232.0	65	4,874.5	60
More than 500 Mz.	2,920.0	37	1,132.5	14	769.0	9
200–500 Mz.	1,311.0	16	1,021.0	13	968.8	12
50–200 Mz.	2,431.0	30	2,391.0	29	2,426.6	30
10–50 Mz.	1,241.0	15	560.5	7	581.3	7
Less than 10 Mz.	170.0	2	127.0	2	128.8	2
Cooperatives	–	–	1,183.6	14	1,730.0	22
APP	–	–	1,657.0	21	1,076.8	13
Abandoned	–	–	–	–	391.7	5
Total	8,073.0	100	8,073.0	100	8,073.0	100

Source: Data for 1978 and 1983 are from Wheelock (1984a:Table 5); for 1987 from Dirección General de Reforma Agraria, MIDINRA (unpublished data, 1988). Percentages may not agree exactly because of differences in rounding.

aIn 1988 MIDINRA began to use a new system to describe the structure of land tenure (see CIERA, *La reforma agraria en Nicaragua: 1979–1989* (Vol. IX). Consequently, in order to be able to assess the changes that have occurred in the land tenure structure using identical categories only the data through 1987 have been included in this table.

July 1979. The corresponding figure for coffee pickers was 23.6 percent.[13] Access to a better standard of subsistence, which was made possible through land redistribution, reduced the need of these workers to offer their labor in the agroexport harvests (see Barraclough, 1982). Thus land redistribution contributed to *campesinización*.

The Redistribution of Agricultural Credits

Perhaps the most important policy change contributing to the 1980/81 cotton harvest labor shortage was that affecting the distribution of credits for agricultural production. Comandante Jaime Wheelock, former minister of agricultural development and agrarian reform, acknowledged the role of credit policies in fueling the labor shortages: "We already know that in many areas, particularly in the western region [where most cotton production was concentrated] we've had productivity problems . . . now that the revolution has opened up credit possibilities for small farmers, we've noticed that they want to stay on their own land and this has had sharp repercussions on the export-economy" (quoted in Marchetti, 1981:61). The reorientation of credit policies was a central feature of Nicaragua's agrarian reform.[14] The new credit programs were aimed at facilitating structural changes in the agrarian sector and increasing basic grain production.

Nicaraguan credit programs had traditionally reinforced the status quo of unequal distribution and given priority to agroexport production. Credits played a critical role in agricultural production because they facilitated the necessary investments in inputs, wages, and so on and ensured financial solvency until the harvest was completed and the returns began to come in. Somoza's credit policies emphasized providing this important assistance to large agroexport producers. Cotton production alone consistently received more than 50 percent of the agricultural credit disbursed (BCN, 1979).

Marginal smallholders typically received less than 10 percent of the agricultural credit. Because small- and medium-sized *campesino* producers traditionally had been Nicaragua's primary growers of basic grains, these discriminatory credit policies also served to maintain basic grain production at very low levels. Nicaragua's basic grain yields were below those of many Third World countries (see FAO, 1972; and USDA, 1974).

The agrarian reform's goals of ensuring Nicaragua's self-sufficiency in food and of raising the rural poor's standard of living required a restructuring of credit policies. The Sistema Financiero Nacional, which was set up after the country's banking system was nationalized in 1979, was responsible for carrying out this reorganization. One of the most important results of the new credit policies was a significant increase in the amount of credit made available to marginal smallholders. Between 1979 and 1980, the amount of credit offered through the Rural Credit Program for smallholders increased almost fivefold, from 178 million córdobas to 831 million córdobas (CIERA et al., 1984). Furthermore, the proportion of small- and medium-sized *campesino* producers receiving benefits within the program jumped from 11 percent in 1978 to 40 percent in 1980 (Enríquez and Spalding, 1987:111–14). Small producers, in particular, were targeted to receive credit: "Although only a third of the more prosperous, medium-sized producers and 'rich peasants' who received credit in 1980 were receiving credit for the first time that year, over 65 percent of the poorest peasants receiving credit in 1980 were newly enrolled."

The organization of cooperatives played a part in this dramatic increase in financing for the *campesino* sector. Credit and Service Cooperatives facilitated the application for and better use of these newly allotted credits.[15]

Cooperative formation also fostered more efficient use of technical assistance, which usually accompanied agricultural credits.

The few years following this first enormous increase in credit allocated to the *campesino* sector were characterized by a more cautious approach to the distribution of credits. The amount of credit provided for this sector was reduced in 1981 because the massive distribution of credit in 1980 did not produce all of the desired results. Production increases were less than expected, and loan repayments were significantly below what they should have been.[16]

Repayment and production difficulties were indicative of the legacy of Somocismo and underdevelopment inherited by the revolution. Unforeseen problems arose because the government's new policies targeted a sector of the population that was not accustomed to receiving credit. For example, credits were not always used in ways that would result in more basic grains being available for urban consumers. In some cases, this was a simple product of many years of deprivation. Thus, instead of investing the credit in production, people bought goods they had previously been unable to buy. In other cases, an increase in production was accompanied by an increase in the consumption level of those same producers.

In addition, a festive ambience prevailed in the year following Somoza's overthrow. It was reflected in the expression used to characterize that first year's credit policies, "la piñata" (the party). This radical break with the past led to a decline in productivity among salaried workers on many farms. Small farmers who received credit for the first time probably considered it their due after so many years of exploitation.

Administrative difficulties resulting from inexperience and poor planning also contributed to the credit-related problems that arose that first year. In some cases, credits were distributed too late in the season to effect a change in the year's crop. In other cases, they were distributed in areas so remote that the crops they helped produce could not be delivered to urban areas. An estimated 10 percent of the corn and bean crops may have been lost in this manner (Collins, 1982:53). Furthermore, the increased availability of credit could result in expanded production only if it was accompanied by additional agricultural inputs. Because such inputs were not consistently available, the credit functioned as a consumption subsidy and contributed to raising inflation in the countryside. Finally, the growing gap between price ceilings for basic grains set by the government and the cost of consumer goods in the countryside also contributed to less-than-hoped-for increases in staples reaching urban consumers through official channels.

Improved access to credit may have raised the consumption levels of the rural poor in the short run, but the long-term difficulties resulting from a growing *campesino* debt and mounting shortages of staple goods caused the government to modify its new credit policies. Credit distribution was more restricted in 1981 and thereafter, and the amount of acreage financed was reduced by more than 40 percent (calculated from Banco Nacional de Desarrollo, 1984), but this did not indicate a reversion to pre-1979 credit policies. The emphasis on providing credit to basic grain as well as to agroexport producers continued. The amount of credit allocated to the *campesino* sector continued to increase, albeit at a slower pace, after the first dramatic expansion of credits in 1980.[17]

Increases in credit allocations to the rural poor contributed to restructuring the agrarian sector. Even in the first year of their implementation, the new credit policies helped to increase the food security of a significant part of the *campesino* sector (Barraclough, 1982:42). Cotton and coffee harvest workers were among the beneficiaries of the new credit program, although, as was the case with land redistribution, more cotton pickers than coffee pickers benefited. The proportion of coffee pickers receiving credit jumped from 9.3 percent in 1978 to 17.5 percent in 1980 (INCAE, 1982b:131). Credit beneficiaries among cotton harvest workers similarly increased from 22.4 percent to 41.5 percent in 1980.

This unprecedented subsidization of small farmers was bound to have an effect on the harvest labor pool. The increase in food security that resulted from the redistribution of credits undermined the fundamental motivation that had led these workers to the harvest in the past—hunger.[18] Thus greater access to credit reduced the number of *campesinos* who were willing to leave their plots to work on the agroexport estates during the harvest.

The New Rent Ceilings on Agricultural Land

Land redistribution and increased access to credit were complemented by ceilings placed on rents for agricultural land. The ceilings were intended to improve the standard of living of the rural poor through restructuring the agrarian sector and to increase basic grain production, thereby working toward national self-sufficiency in food.

Rental prices for agricultural land in the Somoza years had reflected the dominance of agroexport production within this sector of the economy. Rents on the fertile Pacific coastal plain had been extremely high, reinforcing the growing concentration of land among the small group of capitalist cotton producers. This situation characterized all of the country's rich agricultural land. The only variation was in which dominant crop came to replace *campesino*-produced basic grains. In prerevolutionary Nicaragua, rental prices contributed to the increasingly marginal existence and indebtedness of the *campesino*.

Setting rental ceilings was thus seen as crucial to opening up more land to the *campesino* sector. The strategy of establishing rental ceilings also reflected the political context in which the agrarian reform was taking place. Because the right to private property had been guaranteed when the Sandinistas took power in 1979, there was a limit to the amount of land that could be confiscated. Rental ceilings enabled the GNR to respect private property and, at the same time, make more land available to the *campesino* sector.

Rental ceilings varied according to the type of crop grown and the region. The ceilings were designed to bring rents down to approximately 10 to 15 percent of what they had been before 1979: cotton land was now supposed to rent for the equivalent of (U.S.) $30 per *manzana* and land where corn and beans were to be grown for the equivalent of (U.S.) $10 per *manzana*.[19] The law also required large landowners to rent out, at official rates, any land they left uncultivated.

There was, however, some opposition to the rental ceilings. The government was not always able to prevent evictions or to enforce the ceilings, and opening up uncultivated land on the large estates was even more problematic. Nevertheless, this law had significant implications for structural change in the rural sector. FIDA (1980:110) attributed the following changes to the rental law's implementation: "1) A reduction in the number of *campesinos* who paid their rent in kind, and their transformation into renters; 2) An expansion in area controlled by the *campesino* sector; 3) The relocation of renters to land in more fertile areas; and 4) The *campesinización* of a sector of the agricultural proletariat." The regulation of rents had the potential of bringing to an end years of control by the rural upper class over the subsistence of tenant farmers. Although no concrete figures are available of the number of *campesino* families who benefited from the new regulations, it is reasonable to assume that more land was made available to the *campesino* sector through their implementation. Thus both land redistribution and rent ceilings increased *campesino* access to land. Simultaneously, the economic coercion that had traditionally forced the rural poor to seek supplemental income in the agroexport harvest was reduced.

The Empresa Nicaragüense de Alimentos Básicos

Increased availability of agricultural credit, land redistribution, and rent ceilings were all designed to provide the *campesino* sector with access to the inputs necessary for basic grain production. The new government also implemented policies intended to improve the terms of trade between the countryside and the city, thereby encouraging production and facilitating improved consumption by the urban poor. Toward this end, the government set guaranteed prices for basic grains. These prices were to be enforced through government purchasing and distribution of goods produced by the *campesino* sector.

A few months after Somoza's overthrow, the Empresa Nicaragüense de Alimentos Básicos (ENABAS) was established. ENABAS was to be responsible for purchasing and distributing a variety of basic food products. Government involvement in the marketing of basic grains was not new to Nicaragua. What was new was the motivation behind it. ENABAS was supposed to encourage basic grain production by offering better prices to the *campesinos* than they had received in the past, thereby also raising their standard of living. In the prerevolutionary period, the Instituto Nacional de Comercio Exterior e Interior (INCEI) had been responsible for marketing basic grains.[20] INCEI purchased grain from producers and operated a direct distribution system. Its prices reflected one of the institution's primary purposes—to keep grain prices artificially low. Even in years when there were relative grain shortages in the world market, INCEI kept prices down. One consequence was that basic grain producers were forced to supplement their artificially reduced incomes with wages earned in the agroexport harvests. In other words, these small farmers were forced to subsidize the rest of the economy.

ENABAS was established with the mandate of transforming the domestic distribution system so that it would work in favor of both small producers and consumers, instead of against them. ENABAS's initial goal was to purchase approximately 40 percent of the basic grain crop (MIPLAN, 1980:95). It was assumed that if the price for this much of the crop was guaranteed, intermediaries would have to match that price. On the consumer's end, it was hoped that ENABAS would stabilize the market against speculators' attacks on sales of basic goods by putting more goods on the market when prices started to rise. When it did not have enough goods on hand, ENABAS would be able to import the goods required to meet consumer demand. It was also supposed to implement a new subsidization program aimed at benefiting the urban poor. (ENABAS usually sold basic grains at lower prices than it paid producers.)

ENABAS did not succeed in meeting these ambitious goals during its first year of operation (1980). For various reasons ENABAS purchased significantly less than its target of 40 percent of the basic grains crop—12 percent for corn and 24 percent for beans (CIERA, 1983b:23).[21] The most important of these reasons was that the government's purchasing prices were set too low. Prices paid to producers for corn and beans rose 33 percent and 22 percent respectively between 1979 and 1980, but inflation during the same period was 35 percent.[22] Moreover, manufactured goods became increasingly scarce in rural areas, driving prices even further upward. But pricing problems were not the only reason that ENABAS did not purchase more corn and beans. ENABAS's infrastructure, particularly its transport and storage facilities, was inadequate for the demands placed on it. And its bureaucratic mechanisms for making grain purchases (including payment in checks and quality controls) could not compete with the arrangements that had traditionally characterized the relationship between intermediaries and *campesinos*. ENABAS learned many important lessons during this first year. Among other changes implemented after 1980, producers' prices were adjusted upward to compete with those offered by private purchasers. ENABAS did succeed in increasing its purchasing in each of the subsequent years, although corn purchases still fell short of its 40 percent goal (CIERA, 1983b:23).

The problems encountered by ENABAS in replacing traditional intermediaries were symptomatic of the more general problems that confronted the new government in its efforts to transform the agrarian sector. A complex set of relations had been developed over many years, and replacing them would take time. It was not uncommon for an intermediary to arrive at a farm offering agricultural credit and inputs and return to the farm at harvest time to purchase what was produced, thus canceling the *campesino's* debt. In contrast, although the credit offered by the government was now available at much lower interest rates, several trips to the nearest branch office of the bank were usually required to complete the transaction. For those living in isolated areas, this could mean more than a day's walk into town. Once the *campesino* had obtained this necessary resource, the local government-run agricultural inputs outlet (PROAGRO) was the next stop. Inputs at PROAGRO were frequently in short supply so items that could not be obtained there had to be purchased on the open market, usually at very elevated prices, or done without. After the harvest, the *campesinos* had to bring their crop to the nearest ENABAS purchasing center, frequently incurring a significant expense in the process. Finally, ENABAS provided them with a certificate to be cashed at the local bank in payment for the crop. The bank branch office would not necessarily have enough cash on hand to pay all the producers for their crops at the same time. Thus several trips to the bank might be required to complete the last stage of this process.

In sum, although the traditional intermediaries usually exploited the dependency of the *campesino* population on the functions they performed, the system worked. In contrast, the course leading through the new state system, composed of multiple bureaucracies, was laden with potential for bottlenecks. Several efforts were made during the early 1980s to streamline this process so that, for example, one rural outlet would perform all of these functions. Yet the problems remained to be resolved.

ENABAS's efforts to control the distribution of basic grains were more successful than its purchasing efforts. It was able to guarantee a subsistence quota of basic grains to urban consumers at fixed prices. Although the market price for beans went up 37 percent between 1981 and 1982, ENABAS's price for consumers remained stable (Utting, 1987:146). Stabilizing consumer prices while producer prices continued to rise meant that ENABAS had to subsidize urban consumption: "In the first six months of 1982, for example, speaking only in terms of the price differential [between the government's purchasing price and selling price], the state's subsidy for the four basic grains was 55 million córdobas [or (U.S.) $5.5 million]."[23] By 1984 the government was forced to begin cutting subsidies on basic items. The growing government deficit, in part caused by subsidies, led to this decision.

Nonetheless, exerting some control over product marketing and pricing for internal consumption allowed the government to eliminate some of the middlemen who had reaped enormous profits over the years at the expense of the small farmer. Rose J. Spalding (1983) argues that state control over as little as 10 to 20 percent of the market can exert a significant influence over prices. Even this initial attempt by ENABAS to control prices probably strengthened the bargaining position of the small farmers vis-à-vis private purchasers. This strengthened position, when added to the other agrarian reform measures, lessened the *campesino* sector's need to look beyond the *minifundio* for supplemental income.

The Harvest Wage Scale

The regulations governing wages for harvest workers were another factor contributing to the harvest labor shortage of 1980/81. Whereas the various agrarian reform policies worked to improve the standard of living of the *campesinos* on their *minifundios*, thereby facilitating a process of *campesinización*, the new wage regulations inadvertently served to discourage workers from coming to the harvests.

Anastasio Somoza García (the first of the three Somozas to rule Nicaragua) had promulgated a series of labor regulations in the 1940s, primarily to provide international legitimacy to the regime. This legislation, including minimum wage laws, was rarely enforced, and many workers did not know it existed.

When the Sandinistas came to power, a series of reforms aimed at protecting the rights of workers were undertaken. As part of this effort, the Ministry of Labor (MITRAB) established a minimum wage for agricultural workers, which immediately raised wages by 30 percent.[24] But because minimum wages had rarely been enforced under Somoza, implementation of the new regulations meant that the wage increase was, in many cases, actually greater than 30 percent. This initial wage increase contributed to fueling the inflationary trend begun during the insurrection, as well as provoking temporary shortages of some consumer goods in rural areas. Nevertheless, it indicated the new government's intention to govern in the interests of the workers and *campesinos*.

Part of the new wage program specifically addressed workers hired for the harvest. Minimum wages were established for the myriad of positions offered during both the preharvest and harvest periods. During the first year, perhaps because of lack of experience as well as inadequate planning, the wage scale for harvest workers was set too low in real terms, thus reducing the incentive to work during this period. Because living and working conditions characterizing harvest labor are extremely arduous, wages had to provide a significant incentive to attract temporary workers, particularly when traditional forms of economic and political coercion were weakened or eliminated. The more secure position obtained by the *campesinos* through the agrarian reform measures increased their bargaining power in the sale of their own labor and enabled them to reject a wage scale that was not commensurate with their rising expectations and standards.

According to agrarian reform officials, harvest wage scales were traditionally characterized by two basic elements: first, harvest wages were approximately equal to preharvest wages, and second, Nicaraguan harvest wages were higher than those offered in neighboring countries.[25] In the 1980/81 harvest, however, the relationship between preharvest and harvest wages was broken, with the latter being approximately 60 to 70 percent of the former. The harvest wage was also inferior in purchasing power to that paid in prerevolutionary Nicaragua.[26] Inflation had played a key role in undermining the significance of minimum wage laws.

In addition to the comparatively high salary traditionally offered for working in the harvest, laborers had been attracted by the availability of manufactured goods at relatively low prices (CIERA, 1984a:9). Wages earned in the harvest gave them access to goods that otherwise would have been beyond their means. Many of the manufactured goods were brought into Nicaragua by Salvadoran and Honduran workers, who used the income earned through sale of the goods to supplement wages earned in the harvest. Manufactured goods became extremely scarce after 1979, particularly in rural areas. Instead of being offered at attractive prices at the harvest, these goods often were sold for double what they cost on the open market in Managua and quadruple the government-established price (calculated from CIERA, 1984a:16). These factors, combined with the effect of the harvest wage scale on foreign laborers, led several agrarian reform officials to cite low wages as the primary cause of labor shortages in the 1980/81 cotton harvest.

Opinions differ, however, on the potential of increased wages to bring out more pickers. Following the logic of the agrarian reform officials, increasing wages should result in an absolute increase in the number of laborers who seek work in the harvest. Therefore, if a labor shortage develops, raising wages should attract the quantity of workers required to eliminate the shortage. This issue was faced by the Regional Commission on the Labor Force for the region of Matagalpa and Jinotega (Nicaragua's most important coffee-growing region) during the 1983/84 harvest.[27] As the harvest was moving into its last stage, the commission was forced to decide whether raising the minimum wage from 10 to 15 córdobas per *lata* (the unit used to measure the amount of coffee beans picked by a given worker) would provide the necessary incentive to reduce the serious shortage of harvest labor. A wage increase of 3 córdobas per *lata* was finally decreed. Several commission members, however, expressed to me their disagreement with the logic that higher wages would necessarily attract more laborers or increase the productivity of laborers already working in the harvest (interview 129, Comisión Regional de la Fuerza de Trabajo, Matagalpa/Jinotega, February 3, 1984). They reasoned that harvest workers' priorities were such that once they earned a certain amount of money, they stopped working. A recent study, which concurred with this supposition, argued that the rationale that higher wages would increase participation in the harvest followed a "proletarian logic," rather than a "*campesino* logic" (Aznar, 1986:125–27). According to this study, *campesinos* prioritize their own agricultural production, thus leaving the harvest earlier (or not participating at all) when possible.[28] Consequently, raising the wage would only result in their leaving the fields earlier in the day.

Several cotton producers, representing both the state and the private sector, echoed this argument when speaking of labor shortages during the 1983/84 harvest (interview 130, MIDINRA and private producer, March 6, 1984). They referred to the "*campesino* mentality," which led these workers to fix a certain daily goal that would cover their immediate expenses. The *campesinos* had no inclination to earn more than that amount if it required additional work and an extension of the time spent away from their own *fincas*.

Judging the accuracy of these depictions of the *campesino* mentality is not essential to the present discussion, but it is important to realize that a debate about the relationship between wages and labor availability was occurring.[29] The unresolved nature of this debate makes it difficult to estimate the weight reduced wages played in the 1980/81 harvest. Nevertheless, because consumer goods were in short supply in rural areas, increased wages would have had little material significance for workers and would have added to the inflationary spiral already under way. Suffice to say that the errors made in setting the wage scale contributed to the labor shortage.

Salvadoran and Honduran migrant workers, who had traditionally participated in the cotton harvest, were also influenced by the wage scale. In the past, Nicaragua had offered better wages for harvest labor than its neighbors. Consequently, Salvadoran and Honduran workers had been attracted to Nicaraguan cotton harvests since the early 1970s. Their participation in the harvest helped keep wages low because their numbers were plentiful and the opportunities in their own countries were limited.[30] The harvest wages set by MITRAB for 1980/81 were, however, in real terms lower than those offered in El Salvador and Honduras.[31] As a result, fewer workers

than usual migrated to Nicaragua to participate in the harvest. It is unknown how much weight these migrant workers carried in the harvest labor
force, though estimates range from 2 percent to 8 to 12 percent.[32] Given this
uncertainty, it is impossible to know exactly how much the closing off of this
labor source affected the 1980/81 cotton harvest labor shortage. It must
simply be concluded that the effect of reduced wage scales on imported
labor constituted another factor contributing to the harvest labor shortage in
1980/81.

In sum, government-set wages did not offer sufficient incentive for traditional cotton pickers to participate in the harvest. The agrarian reform had
provided them with other options so that they were, for the first time, able
to reject a harvest wage scale that was too low; they could stay at home on
their own land rather than working in the agroexport harvests. Then vice-
minister of agrarian reform, Salvador Mayorga (1982:102) acknowledged
the relationship between agrarian reform and labor shortages in the agroexport harvests in a description of the reform program: "These [greater access
to land, credit, and better prices] and other measures, and more fundamentally, the rupture in the bases that sustained the somocista model of development, have provoked a sudden consequence in the agricultural sector: a
shortage of seasonal labor in the coffee and cotton harvests, as a result of the
tendency toward campesinización of the semiproletariat." Thus agrarian
reform policies leading to campesinización set the stage for harvest labor
shortages, while reduced wage scales made the shortages more serious by
removing previously existing incentives for participation in the harvest labor
force.

Additional Factors Not Originating in Government Policies

Several other factors that were not directly related to the government's
agrarian reform policies also contributed to reducing the labor supply. These
were geopolitical, conjunctural, or both in nature. Although they must be
taken into account to understand what happened in the 1980/81 harvest,
they were less important than the fundamental tension that the agrarian
reform policies caused in the agroexport sector.

Regional turmoil reinforced low wages in reducing the number of foreign
workers available for the 1980/81 cotton harvest. This turmoil escalated
following the ouster of Somoza in July 1979. A coup d'etat on October 15,
1979, in El Salvador set in motion a popular struggle that had been gestating

throughout the 1970s in that country. By mid-1980 a full-scale war had broken out with a guerrilla movement growing in strength by the month.

Nicaragua's first "normal" post-Somoza cotton harvest came at a time when the disruption caused by El Salvador's civil war prevented many laborers from migrating to work in Nicaragua's harvests. In addition, many Salvadorans had already gone into exile by this time. Finally, the political and ideological differences between the two regimes made migration back and forth between the two countries increasingly difficult.

The revolution also altered Nicaragua's relationship with the conservative regime in power in Honduras. The overthrow of the Somoza dictatorship triggered a frantic search by the United States for a new guardian for its interests in the region. The Reagan administration chose Honduras to fill this void. The Honduran regime's predisposition to accept this role was apparent even during the Carter-Reagan transition months, which coincided with the 1980/81 harvest. Honduras's conservative, military-dominated government was not sympathetic to the revolution in Nicaragua. The growing tension between the two countries diminished the ease with which workers moved back and forth across the border.

Somoza had developed a compatible, labor-sharing relationship with the right-wing regimes in both El Salvador and Honduras, which served as a safety valve for the latter two governments in reducing mounting population and employment pressures. And Salvadoran and Honduran laborers helped to keep Nicaraguan harvest wages low and to fulfill the labor requirements created by the expansion of seasonally labor-intensive agroexport production in underpopulated Nicaragua. The change in regime in Nicaragua in 1979 brought an end to that relationship, thereby reducing the availability of foreign workers for its agrocxport harvests.

Two final factors contributed to the 1980/81 labor shortage, although they carried less weight than those previously discussed. First, immediately following Somoza's ouster in 1979 the Sandinista guerrilla army was restructured to form the Sandinista Popular Army (EPS) (see Gorman, 1982). In the last months of civil war against Somoza the National Guard disintegrated, and many of its former members fled into Honduras. It was then necessary to establish a new army, based among those who had been guerrillas.

This new army was to be different from its predecessor. The National Guard had served primarily to repress opposition to the Somoza regime (see Millett, 1977). In contrast, the EPS was established, first and foremost, to protect the revolution. The EPS was also supposed to have an ongoing relationship with the civilian population, as opposed to maintaining itself as a caste above civil society, as the National Guard had done. With these goals in mind, the Ministry of Defense began to develop a new army.

In its formation this new army drew upon several sectors of the population that had previously helped constitute the agroexport harvest labor force. The EPS incorporated many former *campesinos* or the teenaged sons and daughters of *campesinos*. The urban informal sector was perhaps an even more important contributor of personnel to the EPS. The instability that characterized the dead time for this sector made the reasonable, stable wages offered by the EPS attractive. Furthermore, the year-round employment offered by the EPS proved a powerful incentive for both sectors. In addition, an immense political appeal was attached to being a member of the EPS immediately following Somoza's ouster.

As regional tension increased, it became necessary for the Nicaraguan government to expand its defensive resources. This necessity would increase in importance in the next few years, but even the initial formation of the EPS absorbed some workers from the traditional harvest labor force. Thus the restructuring of the army contributed to the 1980/81 labor shortage.

A final factor was the dislocation that followed the civil war. Two years of war and several months of generalized insurrection (the final insurrection) had forced many people to flee their homes, some escaping to refugee camps outside the country and some moving to safer places within Nicaragua. Transportation, food distribution, labor-recruiting systems, and other norms were disrupted. The glue that had held Nicaraguan society together for so long momentarily came apart. Many of the societal relations disrupted by the war had not yet been reestablished by the time of the 1980/81 harvest. One consequence of this dislocation was that many traditional harvest workers did not arrive for the harvest.

In conclusion, agrarian reform policies, an inappropriate harvest wage scale, the cutoff of Salvadoran and Honduran migrant labor, the formation of a new army, and the dislocation following Nicaragua's civil war combined to produce a labor shortage in the 1980/81 cotton harvest. All of these factors taken together ruptured the labor system that had made agroexport production possible in the past. At the heart of this rupture was the agrarian reform.

The process of *campesinización*, resulting from land redistribution, rent ceilings, increased availability of credit, and guaranteed prices, provided alternatives to harvest labor for the *campesino* sector. Therefore, its effect on the harvest shortages was serious and long term. It had the potential to undermine the seasonal labor supply system that was central to agroexport production. An examination of the several harvests that followed this first key year will help us to understand the seriousness of the threat the agrarian reform posed to the relations of production underlying agroexport production.

The Labor Supply Debate
and Post-1980/81 Harvests

The Debate

The serious labor shortage in the 1980/81 harvest was widely acknowledged, although its severity was disputed. Some disagreement exists, however, about the extent to which subsequent harvests have been affected by labor shortages. The issue of labor shortages in the agroexport harvests proved to be sensitive because acknowledgment of their persistence called into question the feasibility of carrying out the agrarian reform program while agroexport production was still central to the economy. This issue raised the dilemma of the extent to which the new government could meet political demands for reform while the country's financial solvency remained dependent on the same political and economic structure that gave rise to the revolution in the first place.

Labor shortages in the agroexport harvests brought to a head an internal debate in the agrarian reform ministry over the speed and manner in which the reform should proceed. This debate had existed since the agrarian reform began. The key issue of contention was whether state farms or cooperatives should be the organizational form promoted by the agrarian reform (interview 97, MIDINRA, August 8, 1983; see also Deere et al., 1985). Kaimowitz (1986) has argued that disagreement within the ministry over this issue stemmed from conflicting analyses of the nature of Nicaragua's agricultural sector. Among other things, the two opposing sides disagreed on the composition of the agroexport harvest labor force. According to what Kaimowitz (1986) terms the "capitalist agroexport model," whose chief proponent was the agrarian reform minister, Jaime Wheelock, semiproletarian workers formed the basis of this labor force. Thus land redistribution would undermine this sector's participation in the labor force, whereas state farms would redress some of the social and economic problems of the agrarian sector without reducing the size of the harvest labor force. This logic was one motivation behind the government's slowness in redistributing land to the *campesino* population in the early 1980s.

On the other hand, "propeasant model" proponents (to use Kaimowitz's terminology) argued that the harvest labor force was not composed primarily of semiproletarians, but of proletarians (see Havens and Baumeister, 1982, whose work forms the basis for Kaimowitz's conclusions). Thus land redistribution would not affect labor availability for the agroexport harvests. Furthermore, this model's proponents considered cooperatives to be the correct path to socialism.

The harvest labor force came from several sectors, with perhaps the most important being the poor peasants who formed the semiproletariat (representing between 37.7 and 55.4 percent of the workers, depending on crop and region). (See the Appendix for a discussion of the strengths and weaknesses of the various data sets that characterize this work force.) Clearly, greater precision in the data describing the agroexport harvest labor force would be useful in analyzing this problem. Nonetheless, the larger question of the direct correlation drawn by propeasant model proponents between the proletarian nature of this work force and its consequent lack of interest in the agrarian reform needs further examination.

For example, the same survey on which the "proletarian thesis" (which underlies the propeasant model) was based included several questions concerning the proletarian harvest workers' perceptions of the agrarian reform. It was found that "almost half of the workers interviewed, who were wage laborers year-round, connected the idea of an improvement in their standard of living with a 'campesino option' [i.e., having increased access to land and/or agricultural credit]" (quoted in Vilas, 1984:120). Thus the semiproletariat population was not the only sector to whom the options opened up by the agrarian reform appealed. A significant part of the fully proletarianized population was also drawn to the *campesino* option.

The announcement of the Agrarian Reform Law in July 1981 signaled a shift in emphasis from state farms to cooperatives. After mid-1981, land redistribution accelerated and formation of cooperatives was strongly encouraged. The issue of labor shortages in the agroexport harvests called into question the wisdom of this shift in emphasis. Therefore, those who favored the new emphasis on cooperative formation were somewhat reluctant to acknowledge that labor shortages continued to be a major problem and to question their relationship with the agrarian reform.

Government officials from several agencies related to the agrarian reform claimed that labor shortages had ceased to be an issue. They argued that the problem had been solved and that neither the 1981/82 nor the 1982/83 harvests had experienced labor shortages. These officials argued that the principal cause of the shortage in 1980/81 was the wage scale and that this was rectified in the following years.[33] In other words, readjusting the minimum wage upward provided the incentive that had been lacking in the previous year.

According to these officials, a significant increase in the level of mechanization of the cotton harvest was also under way and would further reduce any risk of labor shortages. Forty percent of the cotton harvest was to be picked by machine in 1981/82. Finally, they argued that the 1981/82 cotton harvest was normal and even ended earlier than usual. Better organization and increased mechanization had resolved the labor supply problem.

Officials who saw harvest labor problems as no longer being an issue could be characterized as primarily agrarian reform planners, who addressed this issue from a planning, as opposed to an implementation, perspective. They had the unenviable responsibility of designing solutions to agrarian reform problems. Evidence suggests, however, that the scope and persistence of the problem may have led them into some wishful thinking when they claimed that improved wage policies and increased mechanization had resolved this complex problem.

On the other side of the debate were those who argued that the problem of harvest labor shortages remained to be resolved. This perspective could generally be characterized as representative of those who were involved in the implementation of agrarian policies. These implementers included agroexport producers, workers, union officials, and government technicians. High-level policy makers commonly shared this perspective because they were required to analyze agrarian reform measures within the context of the rest of the economy, and they bore responsibility for the overall effectiveness of the agrarian reform.

The Three Subsequent Years

Evidence from the three succeeding years left little doubt that each of the subsequent harvests was affected by labor shortages. This evidence included substantial media coverage of labor shortages, the mobilization of large numbers of volunteer coffee and cotton pickers, and numerous statements by producers, workers' organizations, and government officials concerning the shortages. In addition, increases in the level of mechanization of the harvest, which were proposed following the 1980/81 harvest labor shortage, did not occur to the extent initially hoped for. The number of harvesting machines imported did increase following Somoza's ouster, but only 15 percent of the cotton crop was harvested by machine in 1981/82 (as opposed to the predicted 40 percent). The remainder of that harvest was completed by hand. In sum, neither decreases in labor requirements nor substantial expansion of the labor supply occurred in the several years following the 1980/81 harvest.

The Nicaraguan media devoted extensive coverage to labor shortages during the 1982/83 and 1983/84 harvests, reflecting concern that the shortages would provoke losses in the harvests.[34] *Barricada*, the official organ of the FSLN, portrayed the problem in a typical front-page headline: "To Cut Coffee in Matagalpa: Pickers Needed." The article stated that Matagalpa "could be declared an emergency zone because of the shortage of 5,000 workers in the coffee harvest" (*Barricada*, 1982:1).

During both the 1982/83 and 1983/84 harvests the media also devoted extensive coverage to the mobilization of volunteer harvest labor forces.[35] The relative success of both the cotton and coffee harvests was commonly attributed to the participation of volunteer pickers. In a ceremony celebrating the demobilization of the volunteer battalions in the coffee harvest, Wheelock heralded the volunteers as "hombrecitos del futuro" (*Barricada*, 1983e). The heavy reliance on volunteer harvest workers points to the continued shortage of labor.

In addition to the media, high-level agrarian reform, labor, and planning ministry officials expressed concern about the continuing problem posed by insufficient numbers of harvest workers (interviews 131, MIDINRA, March 15, 1984; 119, MIPLAN, March 26, 1984; 118, MITRAB, March 30, 1984). Labor shortages were characterized as the most serious problem confronted during the 1983/84 cotton and coffee harvests. According to these officials, the problem had not been resolved following the 1980/81 harvest. Indeed, the shortages had become more severe. Representatives of the Rural Workers' Association (ATC) and numerous private producers concurred that the harvest labor shortages were not limited to the first post-Somoza cotton harvest.

The reasons cited for these continuing shortages did not change radically in the following few years. In the 1982/83 and 1983/84 harvests, *campesinización* and military mobilizations were the most commonly mentioned causes for the labor shortages. Regardless of their political perspective or economic position, informants connected the advancement of the agrarian reform and mobilizations resulting from the counterrevolutionary war with the labor shortages in the agroexport harvests (interviews 131, MIDINRA, March 15, 1984; 124, medium-sized private producer, February 23, 1984; 115, UNAG, November 10, 1983).

The various factors that facilitated the process of *campesinización* were mentioned as contributing to the reduced size of the cotton and coffee harvest work forces. The growing accessibility of land, credit, and guaranteed prices generated new options for traditional harvest laborers, leading many of them to decide against working in the agroexport harvests. A medium-sized capitalist coffee producer anticipated a 30 percent loss in his 1983/84 harvest because only 50 percent of his harvest labor requirements had been met (interview 124, private coffee producer, February 23, 1984). He cited guaranteed prices for basic grain producers as the most important reason for labor supply difficulties. (An excellent harvest of basic grains occurred during the 1983/84 crop cycle.[36]) According to this producer, the prices ENABAS had offered basic grain producers provided the necessary incentive for them to stay on their own farms and focus their attention on basic grain production.

A medium-sized capitalist cotton producer attributed the 1983/84 labor shortages to land titling and the various training programs offered to *campesinos* through the agrarian reform (interview 130, March 6, 1984). These measures, which were integral to the agrarian reform, presented new options to traditional harvest workers. This informant concluded that once traditional pickers had other options, they stopped working in the harvests.

Finally, a Ministry of Planning seminar entitled "Employment and Agrarian Reform" cited all the measures that together constituted the agrarian reform as leading to *campesinización*: "The distribution of land by the agrarian reform, availability of credit, the virtual elimination of exploitative rents, progressive improvements in *campesinos'* living conditions, the cooperative movement, etc., appear to have acted as disincentives for the incorporation of poor *campesinos*, semiproletariat, and a good part of the subproletariat, in the export harvests" (MIPLAN, 1984:5). The agrarian reform had made it more profitable for the rural poor to become *campesinos* rather than to continue being agricultural wage laborers. Land and credit were readily available and were, slowly but surely, raising the standard of living of the *campesino* sector.

Guaranteed producer prices also made basic grain production attractive (as the coffee producer cited above had mentioned). Carlos M. Vilas (1984:121) found that producer prices alone made direct production more profitable than harvest wage labor. He compared producer prices for corn and beans during the 1979/80 through 1982/83 period and calculated that producer prices for corn had increased 35 percent more than cotton harvest wages and 56 percent more than coffee harvest wages; likewise, producer prices for beans had increased 31 percent more than cotton harvest wages and 50 percent more than coffee harvest wages. Furthermore, agricultural wages had not kept pace with inflation. Working one's own land, instead of participating in the agroexport harvests, had not only become possible but economically advantageous.

Relative vs. Absolute Labor Shortages

Implementation of the various revolutionary programs led to a reduction in the number of people who were willing to work in the harvest. But in addition to causing an absolute shortage of harvest workers, the changes brought about by the revolutionary process also led to relative labor shortages. That is, those workers who did arrive to work in the harvest picked less while at the harvest and participated during a shorter period of time than they had in the pre-1979 period.[37] This phenomenon was a result of the changing nature of the harvest labor force and the transformation of labor relations.

The composition of the harvest labor force changed after 1979. It appears that the participation of women and children increased over what it had been in the Somoza period.[38] According to CIERA (1984a:22), children between the ages of eight and fourteen represented only 4 percent of the cotton harvest labor force in 1977/78, but by 1981/82 they represented 16.9 percent and in 1983/84, 26.8 percent.[39] Although comparable figures for children's participation in the 1977/78 coffee harvest are unavailable, Aznar (1986:67) found that on the farms included in his sample, 27.8 percent of the labor force harvesting coffee in 1985/86 were children under fourteen years of age.[40] Likewise, a study of women's participation in the agroexport labor force (CIERA et al., 1987:19) found that the percentage of women working in the harvest had increased dramatically: whereas they composed 32 percent of the cotton harvest labor force in 1980/81, by the 1984/85 harvest this figure was 56 percent, and their participation in the coffee harvest increased from 28 to 41 percent.[41]

Assuming this changing pattern of labor force participation by sex and age to be real, the reasons for its occurrence appear to stem from the war. That is, many young men were drafted into regular army units, reserve units, or local militias. Thus women filled the void left by the removal of those men from the labor force. In his study of employment in coffee production, Aznar (1986:67) found women's participation to be significantly stronger on state farms (55.1 percent) than in either the private (38.2 percent) or cooperative sectors (41.5 percent) during the 1985/86 harvest.[42] One possible explanation of this phenomenon was that young men working on state farms were more likely to be mobilized for the defense. Therefore, young men of draft age often avoided being where they were likely to be picked up. A MIDINRA study, however, found this sex/age pattern to be the opposite in terms of which sector incorporated more women and children (interview 194, MIDINRA, June 16, 1987). Clearly, further research must be carried out before more definitive statements can be made.

This change in the composition of the labor force is significant because women and children typically harvest less per day and participate a shorter amount of time than their male counterparts. INCAE (1982b:Tables 32 and 33) found that men harvested an average of 34 percent more coffee and 29 percent more cotton than women.[43] Likewise, Thos Gieskes and Peter Valkenet (1986:44) estimated that men harvested 67 percent more coffee than children.[44] Furthermore, women's greater household responsibilities typically meant that once they had completed the minimum amount of work necessary to provide them with a certain designated income (which is self-established), they tended to leave the harvest rather than working extra hours or days (see CIERA et al., 1987). Consequently, the increased participation of women and children in the harvest labor force after 1979 resulted in less coffee and cotton being picked per worker than in previous years, when men made up a larger part of the labor force. Thus the expanded role of women and children in the harvest contributed to the relative labor shortage, though it perhaps mediated the absolute shortage.

The relative shortage of harvest labor also resulted from the transformation that occurred in labor relations following the ouster of Somoza. Labor productivity in both industry and agriculture dropped with the change in regimes.[45] Labor productivity in the harvest was no exception to this pattern (see CIERA, 1984a; interview 194, MIDINRA, June 16, 1987). In a speech intended to encourage increased labor productivity in the 1986/87 coffee harvest, Jaime Wheelock stated that the absolute labor shortage could be partially resolved by increasing the productivity of those workers who did participate in the harvest, thus suggesting the extent to which productivity had fallen: "How are we going to combat the economic crisis? We are going to combat it with work, with an extra effort; we can't overcome this economic situation if it is not through our own efforts, that is, as opposed to working three or four hours [a day], working seven, eight, nine, ten, or twelve hours; becoming two Nicaraguans instead of one" (Wheelock, 1986:7). The length of the workday for agricultural workers was traditionally six to seven hours.

The state sector was harder hit by dropping labor productivity than either the cooperative or private sectors. One agrarian reform analyst hypothesized that this pattern had developed because the state sector had been more affected by changing labor relations than either of the other sectors (interview 194, MIDINRA, June 16, 1987). That is, on state farms *el patrón* and *el capataz* (the plantation owner and foreman) no longer controlled the production process. State administrators had taken over this role. Thus both workers and administrators were state employees. The new state administrators did not have the same relationship with the workers that their predecessors had. The repressive, paternalistic functions previously fulfilled by plantation owners and foremen had disappeared. The vacuum in authority that resulted was evidenced in drops in labor productivity.[46]

In contrast, *el patrón* and *los capataces* still existed in the private sector. Therefore, though labor relations had likely improved somewhat on private farms, the previously existing authority structure had remained intact. Union organizing on these farms had undoubtedly raised wages, but "the boss" continued to maintain control over the production process and productivity.

Labor productivity in the cooperative sector was affected by two factors. First, the workers themselves were the owners of their farms. It was clearly in their own interest to maintain productivity. Second, the harvest labor force in the cooperative sector was largely composed of cooperative members, their immediate families, and other relatives.[47] Thus this labor force had a common interest in maintaining a reasonably high level of productivity.

In all three sectors of production productivity was reduced when workers had to participate in the defense of the farms on which they worked. Productivity was lost both because of the actual work time spent guarding the farm and because of the exhaustion typically caused by being awake most of the night (after working all day) when the guard shift occurred at night. Another reason for reduced productivity was the upsurge in labor organizing that occurred after 1979. A certain percentage of formerly productive labor time was occupied by union meetings or meetings of the cooperative membership, depending on the sector.

Low levels of labor productivity in both industry and agriculture became a focus of growing concern for government policy makers, particularly after 1985. By 1986 the goal of increasing labor productivity had become central in government planning and policy implementation.[48] The contribution made by reduced labor productivity to the relative labor shortage experienced in the agroexport harvests became a factor in the new focus on understanding and responding to the reasons behind its occurrence. Thus the government recognized that the labor shortage had two aspects, one absolute and one relative, and both had to be addressed if this dilemma was to be resolved.

The Growing Informal Sector

Traditionally, part of the harvest labor force had come from the part of the urban population that had been unable to obtain employment in Nicaragua's small formal industrial sector and was unqualified for more skilled work. This informal sector was largely composed of recent émigrés from rural areas, who had been pushed off the land as agroexport production expanded. Although its impact was not felt immediately, the changes that the informal sector has undergone since 1979 have also affected the availability of harvest labor.

Up to 1979, participation in the informal sector was the last resort when all other alternatives had failed. Wages were typically low, and employment was unstable. The agroexport harvests provided a means of supplementing wages earned in the informal sector. The revolutionary government, however, implemented policies that fostered increased, year-round participation in the informal sector.

Growth of the informal sector was a result of expanded participation by those who were previously employed in the formal sector and by increased rural-urban migration, which placed this new pool of labor in the informal sector. The shift from formal to informal sector employment, which occurred in a part of the already urbanized population, resulted from several determinants, including the closing down of many formal sector activities, particularly in industry, and the weakening of formal sector wages by inflation to such an extent that informal sector wages became significantly more remunerative.[49] Whereas wage increases in the formal sector were controlled by the government in an unsuccessful effort to slow down inflation, informal sector wages were not controlled and therefore became substantially higher than those of the formal sector. Informal sector wages also became higher than wages offered in the agroexport harvests. Thus the stable and reasonable wages for three months of the year, which previously attracted those from marginalized urban areas to participate in the cotton and coffee harvest, could no longer compete with conditions in the informal sector. It became more profitable to remain in the informal sector during the entire year than to participate in it nine months of the year and join the harvest labor force for the remaining three months.[50]

In addition, rural-urban migration accelerated after 1979, and many new urban dwellers joined the ranks of those employed in the informal sector. The reasons for this increase in rural-urban migration were numerous; some stemmed from revolutionary policy making but others did not. These reasons included war-related relocations (150,000 people, or 10 percent of the rural population, had been relocated by October 1984, many of whom migrated to urban areas [UNRISD, 1986:197]); difficulties related to the design of policies oriented to the peasant sector such as the problems in the government's effort to replace the functions of intermediaries in the countryside and the terms of trade crisis that developed between the countryside and the city; the disproportionate allocation of social resources to urban areas, evidenced in the subsidization of consumer goods, primarily in Nicaragua's cities (Utting, 1987); and "increasing income differentials between rural and urban low income groups" because of the large profit margins that could be obtained in the urban informal sector (UNRISD, 1986:197–201).

The Contra War

Although various agrarian reform measures stimulated the process of *campesinización* that underlay the harvest labor shortages, this process was compounded by the mobilization of thousands of people into various branches of the military to fight the Contra forces. By early 1982 it had become common knowledge that the Reagan administration had organized and was providing the Nicaraguan Contras with material and technical assistance in their efforts to overthrow the revolutionary government.[51] The strongest of the Contra groups had its base among the former National Guardsmen who had fled to Honduras with the downfall of Somoza. Later, several other Contra groups formed within the exile community, operating out of both Honduras and Costa Rica. A series of scattered skirmishes between the Contras and the Nicaraguan army in 1981 had, by early 1983, developed into a genuine war. In early 1982 the Contras were thought to be too weak and divisive to pose a serious threat to the Sandinistas.[52] This characterization continued to hold true in the succeeding years. Yet the death and destruction they caused had escalated to the point that by 1983, tens of thousands of Nicaraguans were mobilized to fight them.

These mobilizations affected all sectors of Nicaraguan society. Reserve battalions and militias composed of government functionaries, factory and agricultural workers, Sandinista Youth, and others were sent to the front. The precise numbers of soldiers forming the various branches of the military were not made public for security reasons, but Stephen Gorman and Thomas W. Walker (1985:112–13) estimated that "the army expanded from 13,000–18,000 in 1980 to around 24,000 in the period from 1981 to 1983, to probably over 40,000 in 1984." In addition, they suggested that the number of militia members numbered between 60,000 and 100,000 in 1984. Although it was impossible to know what percentage of the agricultural labor force was affected by these mobilizations, military mobilization was repeatedly mentioned as a cause of the 1983/84 harvest labor shortage. Coffee production appeared to be harder hit than cotton production because the central coffee-growing region extended into areas that were under constant attack by the Contras.[53] People in these regions were also incorporated into civil defense units, charged with the defense of their communities. An ATC official estimated that up to 40 percent of the organization's membership from the Matagalpa-Jinotega region was mobilized into defense units in 1983 (interview 100, ATC, August 18, 1983). Cotton harvest workers were also mobilized, although to a lesser degree than coffee pickers.

Counterrevolutionary operations followed several strategies during this period. From the beginning they were designed to harass army and militia units, as is typical of guerrilla warfare, but they also aimed at terrorizing the civilian population into opposing the Sandinistas.[54] Fear of being attacked by the Contras sometimes led people to decide not to work in the harvests. This was particularly the case for the coffee harvest in the country's north-central region. Coffee cultivation extended all the way to the Cordillera de Dipilto, which marks the border between Nicaragua and Honduras. Contra incursions from Honduras constantly passed through this area. The eastern border of the coffee-growing region, which roughly coincides with the Zelaya-Matagalpa-Jinotega department lines, was also subject to frequent attack by the Contra forces. And within the heart of the coffee region, there were pockets of intense Contra activity. On several occasions, the Contras specifically threatened the *campesinos* with death if they went to the harvests (interview 124, private producer, February 23, 1984).[55] This strategy generated enough uncertainty and fear in some areas to keep people away from the harvests.[56]

An additional strategy pursued by the Contras was to target economically important locations. In the fall of 1983, a significant escalation in these operations occurred. Previously, isolated attacks on bridges, fishing boats, and the like had been carried out, but there did not appear to be a consistent pattern behind the incidents. In September and October 1983 the Contras launched attacks on Nicaragua's only international airport, its principal port, Corinto (which was critical for international trade), and Puerto Sandino, where the country's only offshore oil pipeline is located (see *New York Times*, 1983b, c, and d; Meislen, 1983). It also became clear during this period that another strategic target the Contras had decided to sabotage was the agroexport harvest (Eich and Rincón, 1985:113).

Contra efforts to sabotage Nicaragua's foreign exchange production through its agroexport harvests included air raids against hamlets in Chinandega, in the heart of the cotton-growing region. Several unsuccessful attacks on cotton, coffee, and sugarcane processing and storage facilities also occurred (Eich and Rincón, 1985:113; IHCA, 1983). In addition to the physical damage caused by the attacks, they also hampered the production process by creating the need for special security measures, which required that people be taken out of the work force to guard the laborers and facilities.

The tactic of dissuading workers from going to the harvest was most successful in the regions closest to the border. Thus labor shortages were more severe in Jinotega than Matagalpa, although both of these regions experienced increasing difficulty in attracting harvest workers after early

1983. This situation was in striking contrast with that of Nicaragua's other key coffee-growing region, Carazo, which, though safely removed from the war, also experienced harvest labor shortages. To the extent that the war affected labor availability there, it was in the mobilization of workers for the defense effort. Likewise, although much less dramatically, cotton harvest labor shortages resulting from Contra activity were more problematic in Chinandega than León.

The counterrevolutionaries chose a critical target when they decided to sabotage the agroexport harvests. Because over 50 percent of Nicaragua's foreign exchange earnings have traditionally come from coffee and cotton exports, the attacks threatened Nicaragua's economic lifeline. Although these operations did not succeed in damaging much agroexport infrastructure, they did disrupt the harvest in many areas of the country.

Whether the counterrevolution could continue to keep workers away from the agroexport harvests would be determined by whether the United States persisted in supporting the Contras. Yet even their disappearance would not completely resolve the problem of harvest labor shortages. Further advancement of the agrarian reform program in the succeeding years only reinforced the process of *campesinización* begun in 1979. As one high-level agrarian reform official stated in 1984, the development of various agrarian reform projects would increasingly absorb workers who had traditionally worked in the harvest (interview 131, MIDINRA, March 15, 1984). These projects ranged from the development of cooperative farming, to the installation of irrigation systems that facilitated year-round production, to several agroindustrial projects such as a milk processing plant and a major sugar refinery in Malacatoya. The various projects implemented as part of the agrarian reform provided alternative sources of employment to the rural poor, thereby alleviating the extreme need that had driven them to work in the agroexport harvests in the past.

Conclusion

The development of agroexport production in Nicaragua was made possible by a system of extremely exploitative relations of production. The heart of these production relations was a seasonal labor system that employed massive numbers of workers during three to four months of the year and then abandoned them to fend for themselves the rest of the year. The rural poor were driven to work in the agroexport harvests by economic necessity. The limitations of *minifundio* production, which developed alongside agroexport production, forced these *campesinos* to supplement their incomes with harvest labor. The instability of wages in the informal sector likewise ensured that many of those who formed this sector would offer their labor in the agroexport harvests. Without economic necessity, these people would no longer work in the harvest.

Yet it was precisely this economic exploitation that the Nicaraguan revolution sought to bring to an end. The agrarian reform was central to the new logic promoted by the revolution, "the logic of the majority." The reform brought about changes that went to the root of inequality in the countryside. These changes, as well as others produced by the revolutionary process more generally, led to a rupturing of the traditional labor system on which agroexport production depended.

While the revolution and the agrarian reform program in particular transformed the agrarian sector, Nicaragua continued to depend on agroexport production to generate foreign exchange earnings. An underdeveloped industrial sector and inadequate food crop production were among the legacies of the Somoza era. Somoza had also left behind a bankrupt economy and a huge foreign debt. These serious handicaps were compounded by a regional economic crisis, a trend toward a worsening in the terms of trade, a U.S. economic blockade, and the constant aggression of the U.S.-backed Contras on Nicaragua's borders.

This hostile panorama set severe limitations on the revolution's potential for experimentation with other means of capital accumulation. Agroexport production would remain the basis of the Nicaraguan economy for the foreseeable future. To prevent the tension between agrarian reform and agroexport production from impeding further reconstruction and development efforts, effective long-term policies had to be formulated that would facilitate both agricultural production and agrarian reform. The labor supply issue was but one example of the tensions that confronted the revolutionary government in its pursuit of economic development and social equity. It faced the challenge of finding solutions that would permit needed structural reforms while simultaneously maintaining the viability of the agroexport sector.

5

The Dilemmas of
Revolutionary Policy

Alternative Strategies for Resolution
of the Labor Supply Problem

The agrarian reform created new options for Nicaragua's rural poor, offering the landless and the land-poor the possibility of a better way of life based on greater access to key productive resources. For the first time, many agricultural workers and *campesinos* had the choice of working their own land year-round instead of having to rely on wages earned in the agroexport harvests to support them through the year.

At the same time, this reform process threatened to undermine the agroexport production that was the basis of agriculture in Nicaragua. The serious labor shortages that characterized the cotton and coffee harvests after 1979 showed that many agrarian reform beneficiaries had taken advantage of their new options and chosen not to work in the agroexport harvests. Thus it became imperative to prevent harvest labor shortages from undermining the efficiency of this sector. The losses resulting from unpicked crops and the cost of trying to find temporary solutions weakened the very accumulation process that was the agroexport sector's reason for being. Yet none of the alternatives that were experimented with during the first five years of the transformation process had provided the new government with an adequate solution.

Nicaragua was not alone in trying to cope with the dilemmas that arise in the process of attempting to transform an agrarian structure based on agroexport production (see Eckstein, 1981). Nicaragua's agrarian planners were able to learn much from the experience of other countries in dealing with this process. But the resolution of these dilemmas ultimately required a unique combination of solutions specifically designed to address the level of development of Nicaragua's productive forces, natural and human resources, foreign exchange situation, and other social, political, and economic characteristics. The problem continued to be more complex than efforts to bring about its resolution suggested.

The Alternatives

Nicaragua began experimenting with alternative strategies for resolving the harvest labor shortages in 1981. The strategies included using volunteer harvest workers, increasing the level of mechanization of the agroexport harvests, promoting several varieties of labor-sharing agreements, and forming cooperatives that specialized in agroexport production. Each of these alternatives had some potential for relieving the agroexport labor problem, but each also had drawbacks or limitations. More alternatives were still being considered several years later, such as the synchronization of crop production to stagger the harvests, but they remained at the hypothetical stage. Ultimately, resolution of the agroexport–agrarian reform dilemma would require the use of a combination of alternatives.

Voluntary Labor

Each fall beginning in 1981 a tremendous mobilization of volunteers to work in the cotton and coffee harvests was carried out.[1] The mobilization effort began to take form in September, two months before the harvest started. Volunteers were recruited from government ministries, workplaces, and schools. National attention was focused on the harvest until the volunteers returned in February, after most of the work had been completed.

University students formed the backbone of this volunteer labor force. Smaller numbers of high school students also participated. In the 1982/83 harvest approximately 15,000 students picked coffee, representing roughly one-third of the work force (*Barricada*, 1983j:1). Student volunteers numbered approximately 17,350 in the 1983/84 coffee harvest (*Barricada*, 1984f:3). Finally, an estimated 20,000 students were mobilized into the Batallones Estudiantiles de Producción (BEP) for the 1984/85 coffee harvest (*Barricada*, 1984a:3).

High school and university calendars were modified in 1980 to facilitate the participation of students in the agroexport harvests (PREALC-OIT,

1981). The students' summer break from classes coincided exactly with the key harvest months (December to March). Requirements for university admission also reflected the important role played by the student battalions. Although participation in the BEP was officially voluntary, unofficially most university students were expected to participate. In 1984 the National Council of Higher Education (CNES) required a certificate of participation in the student volunteer harvest battalions or completion of a series of civil defense courses for a student to be able to register for the next school year (CNES, 1984). Most full-time university students opted for the BEP. Before the 1984/85 harvest, Minister of Education Father Fernando Cardenal strongly urged students to participate, saying that those who stayed in Managua (therefore not participating in the harvest) did not love their country (interview 120, National Autonomous University student and BEP member, November 24, 1984). University registration requirements reinforced Cardenal's statement. By 1986 these requirements had been modified so that recruitment for the BEP was directed primarily at first- and second-year students. More advanced students were encouraged to find work in their field of study during this period (interview 200, student at the Central American University in Managua, August 25, 1987).

Peer pressure to choose the BEP option was great. Members of the Sandinista Youth organization (JS 19 de Julio) were the key BEP organizers within the universities. The combined effectiveness of their organizing and university requirements was evidenced in one informant's observation that in his class of thirty students only three did not join the BEP (interview 125, National Autonomous University student, January 22, 1984). This informant was one of the minority who did not work in the harvest. When asked about the consequences of his nonparticipation, he commented that though there had been many suggestions of a penalty for nonparticipation, as long as students committed themselves to participate in the next harvest, they were usually permitted to enroll in the next school year.[2] Nevertheless, concern about possible negative consequences probably did convince some students, who would not otherwise have participated in the harvest, to join the BEP. It is impossible to gauge the extent to which the potential for coercion inherent in university enrollment requirements was the fundamental motivating factor leading students to participate in the harvest. The question of coercion, however, should be considered in comparative terms. The measures adopted by the Nicaraguan government in mobilizing students to work in the harvest were mild when compared to the coercive pressures exerted in Cuba (Eckstein, 1981), Tanzania (Resnick, 1981; Deere, 1986), and other Third World countries attempting to transform their agricultural structures.

Students were paid for their participation in the harvest labor force. Their piece-rate wages were the same as those of the professional pickers. During the 1983/84 harvest, however, approximately 30 percent of that wage was deducted and allocated to the war effort. According to one BEP member, their remaining wages were also donated to the war effort (interview 120, National Autonomous University student, November 24, 1984). It remains unclear how voluntary this latter contribution was. The initial 30 percent deduction was not voluntary. That, according to this informant, contribution of the remaining 70 percent was unanimous suggests that BEP members felt under pressure to "donate" their wages.

Students were not the only participants in the volunteer harvest labor force. Volunteer mobilization for the harvest reached into all spheres of life, even government ministries. For example, several informants reported that up to 20 percent of the functionaries in their respective departments (in two separate ministries) had been sent to work in the harvest (interviews 126 and 127, Ministries of Labor and Planning, January 1984).[3] Volunteer participation in the harvest necessitated up to three months' absence from work. These functionaries received their regular salaries while they were mobilized.

The mass organizations also encouraged their members to participate in volunteer harvest brigades. Included in this organizing effort were the national women's organization (AMNLAE), the neighborhood organizations (CDSs), the national teachers' organization (ANDEN), and others. In the 1983/84 harvest more than two thousand foreigners formed international work brigades (interview 128, organizer of the international volunteer brigades, February 1984). The majority of these "internacionalistas" came to Nicaragua specifically to work in the harvest. Their numbers included approximately seven hundred North Americans.

The mobilization of volunteer labor had a very important function beyond its explicit purpose of ensuring that the agroexport harvests were completed. The volunteer labor battalions also served to build political identification and commitment.[4] The student volunteers came primarily from urban environments. Working in the harvest probably represented the first extended period of time they had spent in the *campo*. This experience may have given them their first clear look at the lives of the other half of Nicaragua's population, the rural poor.

This process of consciousness development was similar to that which took place during the literacy campaign in 1980. The campaign fostered a two-way learning process: that of the rural poor learning the fundamental principles of reading and writing and that of urban youth learning about life in the *campo*. BEP members lived with other temporary workers on the agroexport *fincas*. They shared the same eating, sleeping, and working arrangements. It would have been difficult for them to come back from the harvest untouched by the experience. They witnessed firsthand the poverty that still characterized the lives of the rural poor. It was hoped that through this exposure to rural poverty these youth would come to comprehend its relationship with the country's dependence on agroexport production and backward subsistence production. This understanding, in turn, would facilitate a more profound sense of the importance of the agrarian reform and the process of revolutionary transformation more generally. For many, as their social consciousness developed, pressure from peers and university requirements would carry less weight in making the decision to volunteer for the harvest in future years.

All volunteers who took part in the harvest underwent the same process of consciousness development. The only difference between the students and the other volunteers was that the former were younger and more impressionable. At the very least, the volunteers were confronted with the knowledge that most of the rural population lived very differently from the urban population.

The tremendous effort involved in the mobilization process also gave both participants and nonparticipants a greater sense of the importance of cotton and coffee in the nation's economy. The urgency of having a successful harvest was clear to anyone reading the newspaper, listening to the radio, talking with coworkers, or simply watching thousands of people being mobilized. In addition, the crucial role played by coffee and cotton pickers became more apparent.

Yet in spite of successful mobilization of large numbers of volunteers for the agroexport harvests, there were serious limitations, both political and economic, inherent in reliance on volunteer labor to resolve the harvest labor shortages. In the political sense, as the years passed it would become increasingly difficult to attract people to volunteer their labor. The revolutionary enthusiasm that typically characterizes the initial period of any transformation such as that experienced by Nicaragua could not be sustained indefinitely. In Cuba, volunteer mobilizations were organized during the late 1960s to resolve the labor shortages in the sugarcane harvests after the revolutionary process was initiated. In response to a number of factors, however, including "pressure from below" expressed in the form of absenteeism and low labor productivity, the Cuban government began reducing the number of labor mobilizations in 1970 (Eckstein, 1981:184). In Nicaragua, the reconstruction effort generated a strong willingness among the population to work harder during the first few years following Somoza's ouster. Later, the undeclared war imposed on Nicaragua by the United States rekindled the nationalist sentiment of many sectors of the population. This sense of nationalism stimulated a continuing willingness to sacrifice, including offering volunteer labor.[5]

A productive structure could not remain dependent on voluntary labor over the long run, however. Experience from other revolutions has shown that in the early stages of the transformation process the moral incentives that underlie voluntary labor need to be bolstered by material or economic incentives. The Cuban revolution provides much insight on this issue. In the early years of the Cuban revolution, too much reliance was placed on moral incentives in an effort to increase productivity and expand production (e.g., the 1970 sugarcane harvest). By the beginning of the 1970s an understanding had developed among the Cuban leadership of the need for a combination of moral and material incentives. It was concluded that "incentives must be viewed in the context of the development of the productive capacity, the economic organization and the political institutions of the country" (Karl, 1975:21). The shortages of consumer goods in Cuba during the 1960s and the historical underdevelopment of the productive capacity for consumer durables led to a tendency to rely too heavily on moral incentives. Following the unsuccessful sugar harvest in 1970, the Cuban leadership decided that in the short to medium run material incentives had to complement moral incentives if production and productivity were to be stimulated.[6]

Nicaragua's productive forces in the early 1980s were significantly less developed than were those of Cuba in the 1960s. Shortages of consumer goods in Nicaragua also encouraged a reliance on moral as opposed to material incentives. Yet the Cuban experience clearly pointed to the importance of using a variety of incentives in the initial stages of revolutionary transformation.

In addition to the difficulties involved in engendering a continued willingness on the part of the population to volunteer for harvest labor, there were economic limitations inherent in relying on a volunteer labor force. Because of the nature of the harvesting process, cotton was the only crop for which volunteer labor was even moderately efficient.

More volunteers were mobilized to pick coffee than cotton in Nicaragua. Yet the volunteer labor force was a mixed blessing for coffee production. Because coffee is a perennial crop, the way a plant is treated one year can affect its production the next year. This is particularly true of the harvesting process. Although volunteers may be very enthusiastic about participating in the harvest, they often lack the experience and training required to pick coffee correctly.[7] In spite of the fact that the picking procedure is relatively straightforward, coffee producers across the board complained about the damage to the trees caused by volunteer pickers. By picking the beans incorrectly, the volunteers often ruined the bud from which the next year's bean was to sprout. For many producers, the damage caused by inexperienced workers outweighed the potential benefit of having part of the coffee crop picked that would otherwise be lost. It was not uncommon for producers to say that they preferred to have the coffee beans go unpicked than to have volunteers come onto their farms.

Damage to trees was not the only aspect of volunteer labor that made it a less than desirable alternative to many coffee producers. The volunteers' productivity was significantly lower than that of traditional workers. Whereas a professional harvest worker might pick between six and eight *latas* a day, a typical student volunteer picking for the first time might average three *latas* a day (interview 133, volunteer coffee picker, March 1, 1985). One student volunteer working in her second harvest averaged four and a half *latas* a day and was designated a "vanguard" picker for her high level of productivity (interview 135, National Autonomous University student and BEP member, March 5, 1985). A study of volunteer participation in the coffee harvest on one state farm found that productivity varied according to the volunteer's normal occupation (Gieskes and Valkenet, 1986:39). When compared with traditional workers, productivity levels for volunteers on this farm were as follows: workers from state institutions, 91 percent; students, 76 percent; and international brigade participants, 51 percent. This study concluded that experience was the most important factor determining productivity differences. Reasons for participating in the harvest also affected productivity.

Private producers typically perceived the productivity of volunteers to be even lower than the above-mentioned estimates suggest (interview 129, private coffee producer, February 3, 1984). Moreover, expenses for maintaining this work force were the same if not more than for traditional pickers. With these two considerations in mind, many private producers concluded that there was little economic justification for using a volunteer work force. Consequently, most of the BEP worked on state-owned rather than private sector farms.

Disinterest in the private sector in incorporating volunteers into its harvest labor force was a result of more than just the lower productivity of these workers. The need for additional laborers was less pervasive in the private than the state sector because the former was able to attract more traditional workers. The state sector had been hardest hit by labor shortages and thus was more dependent on volunteers. Rudolf M. Buitelaar (1985) suggests that state farms had difficulty competing with the private and cooperative sectors in the labor market and little interest in doing so. Instead, they preferred to rely on volunteer labor. Clearly, further research is needed to develop a more comprehensive understanding of these labor force dynamics.

Low productivity was the chief complaint of cotton producers about volunteer pickers. Whereas traditional workers picked an average of 250 pounds of cotton a day, the BEP picked an average of 70 to 80 pounds a day during the 1984/85 harvest (interviews 138, *campesina*, March 19, 1985, and 136, state employee who worked as a volunteer picker, March 7, 1985). This was the BEP's second cotton harvest. The previous year these workers had averaged 40 pounds a day. Lack of experience with the picking process and the difficult working conditions were key reasons for the volunteers' lower productivity. As with volunteer coffee pickers, motivations for participating in the harvest also played a role in the lower productivity of volunteer cotton pickers. Professional pickers participated in the harvest out of economic necessity and were paid according to how much they picked. Many volunteers, by contrast, perceived their presence at the harvest rather than their productivity to be most important.[8]

The economic benefits derived from volunteer labor were significantly greater in cotton than in coffee production. Cotton is an annual plant so no damage could be caused to the next year's crop by inexperienced pickers. If the crop was not picked efficiently, the only consequence would be that there would be less cotton to export. The argument was also made that any amount of cotton picked by volunteers contributed to the generation of foreign exchange earnings for Nicaragua. Following this logic, even if expenses for maintaining volunteer cotton pickers were as high as those for professional pickers and their productivity was lower, their work produced dollars while their maintenance and wage expenses represented an expenditure in córdobas.

Nonetheless, the cost of volunteer labor was greater than was apparent at first glance. Although it is impossible to calculate the exact cost of the mobilization effort, it is possible to determine factors that would have to be included in any estimate of this figure. An advertising campaign that reached into every medium of mass communication was carried out to encourage people to volunteer for the harvest. Commissions to monitor the harvest labor shortages were established. The expense of transporting volunteers to the farms where they would work was another factor in the equation. For twenty thousand student volunteers, this represented a considerable expense. Professional pickers usually paid for their own transportation to the harvest. Finally, for government employees who worked in volunteer brigades, lost work time and payment of their normal wages (which continued while they participated in the harvest), must be included in any such calculation. These factors probably do not exhaust the costs of mobilizing the volunteer labor force. Table 5.1 gives a rough estimate of the costs, value produced, and net losses incurred in the use of volunteers for the 1984/85 coffee harvest (excluding expenditures associated with the media campaign, opportunity costs, and losses resulting from damage to coffee trees).

The net loss incurred in the use of volunteer labor was actually substantially greater than either the $144.76 or $239.33 shown in table 5.1. The price paid per pound of coffee is the amount of payment Nicaragua receives on delivery (*New York Times*, 1985). That is, labor costs are only one part of the equation in estimating production costs. These costs also include processing of the beans, transportation from *finca* to port, and transportation from Nicaragua to the purchasing country. The latter two costs are substantial. Labor should only represent a small part of production costs for a coffee-producing country like Nicaragua. The use of volunteer labor was clearly not economically feasible.

Table 5.1

Costs and Benefits of Volunteer Mobilization for the 1984/85
Coffee Harvest

Costs per Week per Worker[a]	10 × 1[b]	14.30 × 1[b]
Basic maintenance[c]	C$ 136.00	
Extras[d]	C$1,134.00	
Transportation	C$ 73.00	
Harvest wages (20.90 per *lata*)	C$ 302.00	
Subtotal in córdobas	C$1,645.00	
Subtotal in U.S. dollars	$ 164.50	$115.04
Salaries for government employees		
(Average monthly salary 6,000)	C$1,500.00	
Total in córdobas	C$3,145.00	
Total in U.S. dollars	$ 314.50	$219.93
Coffee picked		
Average number of *latas* picked	14.45	
Converted into roasted coffee		
(1 *lata* = 3.4 pounds roasted coffee)	49.13 lbs.	
Value of picked coffee		
(Calculated at $1.53 per pound)	$ 75.17	
Gross Loss	$ 239.33	$144.76

[a]Calculated from costs incurred by a private research institute for the volunteer harvest labor force it organized (Internal Document 120, March 1985).

[b]The official exchange rate in March 1985 was 10 córdobas per 1 U.S. dollar. A second exchange rate was used in transactions conducted in relation to agroexport producion, the "implicit exchange rate." This latter rate was 14.30 córdobas per 1 U.S. dollar in March 1985. These figures have been calculated for both exchange rates.

[c]Basic maintenance included three meals a day of rice (1 córdoba per serving), beans (2 córdobas per serving), a tortilla (1 córdoba per tortilla), coffee or juice (2 córdobas per serving), and meat, which was served once a week (10 córdobas per serving). Prices for these items varied somewhat according to what was produced on the farm. On some agroexport farms corn is grown so that tortillas could be made at a much lower cost than on a farm that had to purchase corn.

[d]This institute was especially generous in providing "extras" to its volunteers; however, some of these items are regularly provided to volunteers. The value of extras was as follows (a two-week supply for twenty-two people):

Cigarettes, candies, soap, juice, oats, candles	C$ 10,210
Toilet paper	1,217
Sanitary napkins	2,900
Blankets	5,601
Crackers	10,888

Table 5.1 (*continued*)

Rubber boots	8,668
Meals while en route	1,375
Batteries	600
Plastic ponchos	2,798
Miscellaneous	5,650
Total	C$ 49,907

In conclusion, the political benefits of mobilizing volunteers were un-questionably greater than the economic benefits. The importance of con-sciousness building early in the revolutionary process was a serious con-sideration. Volunteer labor played a key role in this effort. Yet as a solution to the economic problems caused by harvest labor shortages, its limitations were apparent. Volunteer labor, then, could be seen as a partial, short-term solution for labor shortages. Its value in the medium to long run was clearly limited.[9]

Increased Mechanization

A second alternative for solving the labor shortage problem was to increase the level of mechanization of the harvest so that fewer laborers would be needed. This alternative was already being implemented by 1981, and plans were made for further expanding the use of mechanical harvesters. There were some very serious limitations, however, in the extent to which the level of mechanization could be increased. Mechanization provided yet an-other partial answer, although its prospects for the medium to long run were brighter than those of volunteer labor.

A great variety of situations spur the impulse to resort to increased mech-anization when problems with the labor force arise. Labor unrest and a need to control the labor process were primary motivating factors behind the process of mechanization and technological innovation that accompanied industrial as well as agricultural development in the United States.[10] In Nicaragua, increases in the level of mechanization were usually related to labor shortages as occurred in cotton production during the early 1960s. By the late 1960s, however, the use of harvesters was declining because production was falling off and Salvadoran and Honduran workers were providing another source of labor. Increasing the level of mechanization was once again resorted to as a solution to labor shortages after 1979, and the use of mechanical harvesters in the cotton harvest expanded significantly after 1980. Yet this solution had severe limitations.

The most obvious limitation was that it was impossible to mechanize the harvest of Nicaragua's most important export crop, coffee, because of the terrain of the regions in which Nicaraguan coffee is grown and the methods of production employed. Attempts have been made in Brazil, the world's largest coffee-producing country, to increase the level of mechanization in coffee production. But the conditions of production characterizing the areas where machines have been employed in Brazil are so different from those in Nicaragua that parallels cannot be drawn. Coffee grown in Nicaragua will have to be hand-picked for the foreseeable future.

Consequently, increases in the level of mechanization were limited to cotton production. In the mid-1960s, when the use of mechanical harvesters took its first big jump, up to 17 percent of the cotton crop was harvested by machine.[11] By 1970, however, less than 5 percent of the crop was mechanically harvested. This figure dropped to less than 1 percent by 1975. Reliance on mechanical harvesters remained extremely limited through 1980. In 1981 Nicaragua began once again to import harvesters. The proportion of the cotton crop harvested by machine rose to 18 percent during the 1981/82 harvest. It increased to 29 percent in the 1983/84 harvest and continued increasing, reaching 39 percent in 1984/85.[12]

Several agrarian reform officials argued that the only solution for harvest labor shortages was to increase the level of mechanization of the harvest (interview 131, MIDINRA, March 15, 1984). According to their line of reasoning, as acreage planted with cotton expanded each year toward Nicaragua's average for the 1970s, two hundred thousand *manzanas*, a corresponding increase in the level of mechanization would be required. Yet the trend toward further mechanization would be hard to sustain because of the numerous limitations that confronted the Nicaraguan economy.

The most serious of these obstacles was the country's extreme foreign exchange crisis. All of the machinery used in the cotton harvest had to be imported. Consequently, its purchase required the expenditure of precious foreign exchange earnings. Increasing Nicaragua's reliance on imported machinery further strained the foreign exchange balance. Moreover, although Nicaragua's cotton acreage had expanded after 1979, it had not done so to the extent envisioned earlier (see table 3.4). By the mid-1980s the price of cotton in the international market had fallen significantly below the levels it had maintained since the early 1970s.[13] As a result, cotton production began to drop off in 1985. The reduction in the area planted lowered the amount of harvest labor needed. This trend is important for the present discussion because increased mechanization implied an investment of foreign exchange in a branch of the economy that was contracting rather than expanding. Moreover, even if the price of cotton increased once again and area expanded accordingly, this downturn underlined the instability of cotton production.[14] Furthermore, although some agricultural machinery can be adapted for a variety of purposes, cotton harvesting machines serve only one function. Therefore, increased mechanization of the cotton harvest represented an investment that was both considerable and risky.

Nicaragua's foreign exchange deficit had been its primary economic problem since the reconstruction process began in 1979. The value of Nicaragua's exports averaged between (U.S.) $400 and $500 million beginning in 1980, while its imports fluctuated around $800 million each year through 1984 (CEPAL, 1986b:32). This critical deficit was made more problematic by the U.S. economic blockade that was initiated in 1981. The blockade largely prevented Nicaragua from receiving multilateral aid. As the economic blockade deepened, resolution of Nicaragua's foreign exchange crisis became ever more remote.

Agricultural production was affected by the foreign exchange crisis along with the rest of the economy. Imports of capital goods for agriculture dropped by 17 percent in 1982 and 41 percent in 1983 as a result of the foreign exchange crisis (CEPAL, 1985:42).[15] Each cotton harvester cost Nicaragua approximately (U.S.) $55,000 (interview 146, technician at multinational agricultural inputs company, March 22, 1985). Unless the foreign exchange balance improved, it would be difficult for Nicaragua to continue importing harvesters. Spare parts for all agricultural equipment also had to be imported. Most of the country's agricultural machinery had been imported from the United States before 1985. Nicaragua had begun receiving equipment from Eastern Europe on more favorable terms than those received from the United States, but credits from Eastern Europe were of no use when replacement parts needed to keep equipment running had to come from the United States. Thus it was common to see agricultural equipment (and all other types of equipment) standing idle because of the lack of spare parts. Stephen Kinzer (1984) noted at this time that "in the rice-growing Malacatoya region, half the tractors are out of service because engine parts are unavailable." Cotton harvesters were no exception to this pattern.

Expanding the use of cotton harvesters also implied the adoption of related inputs that would upgrade the level of technology employed in the entire cotton production process. Harvesting cotton by machine requires the use of a specific variety of cottonseed. Cotton plants harvested by machine must be bred to be shorter and have a cotton boll that can be easily detached from the plant by the harvester. A special variety of cotton had been developed to meet these specifications and was made available by MIDINRA's Experimental Cotton Center for the same price as the seeds used on non-mechanized harvest acreage.

More problematic, however, was the fact that machine-harvested cotton must be defoliated before it can be picked or the leaves will stain the cotton boll as the machine harvests the cotton. The defoliants used in this process had to be imported. In 1984 Nicaragua paid approximately (U.S.) $1.10 for defoliants per *manzana* of cotton to be machine harvested (interview 146, technician at multinational agricultural inputs company, March 22, 1985). This increased strain on the foreign exchange balance was compounded because defoliants were traditionally applied by airplane, which required the expenditure of more foreign exchange and created additional spare parts problems.

A less apparent complication arising from the combination of using defoliants and mechanical harvesters was the time constraint it placed on the harvest. Defoliants accelerate the cotton maturation process so the harvest must be efficiently organized to get all of the cotton picked. Any problems that delayed this process were felt acutely because of the reduced harvest time.[16] Thus mechanizing the harvest introduced an array of technological and administrative problems.

The strain placed on the foreign exchange balance by increasing the level of mechanization of the cotton harvest was exacerbated because machine-picked cotton is of a lower quality than hand-picked cotton. One of the comparative advantages Central American cotton has had in the world market has been that it is hand-picked (Williams, 1986). Mechanical harvesters tear the fiber as they pull the cotton boll from the plant. The length of the cotton fiber is one of the key factors taken into account when assessing the value of cotton. The price paid for cotton varied according to its quality. One informant estimated that the value of machine-picked cotton was roughly 60 percent that of hand-picked cotton (interview 146, technician at multinational agricultural inputs company, March 22, 1985). Consequently, machine-picked cotton brought in fewer dollars for Nicaragua than hand-picked cotton.

For an agricultural country without a serious foreign exchange crisis there are obvious advantages to raising the level of technology employed in the production process. Mechanization facilitates the expansion of area under cultivation. The labor supply is also less important. Moreover, increased mechanization implies that tedious and difficult work can be done by machines instead of people. Theoretically, it frees the labor force to do less menial work. But employing greater levels of mechanization can also cause unemployment in both rural and urban areas if the labor force cannot be absorbed into other sectors of the economy. In sum, the planning of agricultural development strategies must take into account the efficient and equitable use of existing resources, which include land, labor, and capital.[17]

In the long run an expansion in the proportion of Nicaragua's cotton acreage harvested by machine would ease the pressure on the harvest labor supply, but in the short to medium run, the adoption of any process that placed increased strain on the foreign exchange balance was problematic. As the foreign exchange situation deteriorated (and it did each year after 1980), it became less likely that greater mechanization could be relied upon to resolve harvest labor shortages. Until the foreign exchange balance improved, which was unlikely in the near future, mechanical harvesters would continue to provide a limited solution to the agrarian reform–agroexport production dilemma.

Replacing the *Ajustador*

The limitations inherent in reliance on volunteer labor and increased mechanization required a shift in focus. A reevaluation of the potential for increased participation by the agricultural labor force provided perhaps the most reasonable solution to the harvest labor shortage. The remainder of this chapter will review several options stemming from an analysis of the agricultural labor supply.

Harvest labor shortages arose largely because the mechanisms that previously brought workers to the agroexport harvests were no longer operating. The agrarian reform had, in many cases, taken away the harsh economic necessity that forced *campesinos* to sell their labor during the harvest months. On a more specific level, it also reduced the role of the *ajustador* (the labor recruiter or intermediary paid by the large landowner) in the labor recruitment process. Because of the importance of the harvest labor force, it was widely felt that alternative mechanisms needed to be found that would facilitate mobilization of the agricultural labor force.

The first few years after the establishment of the revolutionary government the idea of developing a working relationship between the state, private, and cooperative sectors was discussed. Such a relationship would facilitate the flow of labor between basic grain production and the agroexport harvests. It was envisioned that the Rural Workers' Association would play a central role in this process (Deere and Marchetti, 1981). One of the goals of this coordinating effort was the organization of a body that would perform some of the tasks previously carried out by the *ajustador*. From the beginning, however, the ATC balked at the idea of serving as an intermediary (interviews 100, ATC, August 18, 1983, and 123, ATC, December 3, 1984). The ATC argued that it was first and foremost a labor union and that its primary duty was to act on behalf of the agricultural work force. Its concerns included improving living and working conditions and achieving higher salaries. Assuming the role of labor recruiter was seen by the ATC as contradictory to its role as protector of workers' rights.

In 1980 a national-level Production Commission was set up, composed of representatives from the ATC, MIDINRA, the ministries of Transportation (MITRANS), Labor (MITRAB), and Internal Commerce (MICOIN), and the National Council of Higher Education (CNES). The commission was charged with overseeing various aspects of agricultural production. One of its subcommittees was set up to study the issue of the labor force. This subcommittee's mandate included coordinating the mobilization of workers when labor shortages arose,[18] but this problem proved to be too complex for the subcommittee to solve.

In the fall of 1984, with the harvest only weeks away, a new National Commission on the Labor Force was formed with the specific responsibility of studying the issue. It was headed by former agrarian reform minister Jaime Wheelock and charged with finding a definitive answer to the labor shortage problem before the 1985/86 agroexport harvest. Resolution of the problem proved to be as elusive for this commission as it had been for its predecessor. Yet increased discussion stimulated the search for solutions in sectors previously resistant to participating in this effort.

Although the ATC had been unwilling to take on the role of *ajustador* in mobilizing the harvest labor force, it did begin to play an active role in the struggle to resolve the harvest labor shortages. The ATC believed that workers had to be provided with strong incentives to participate in the harvest. By organizing its members to demand an incentive system, the ATC succeeded in winning a significant wage increase for workers who participated in the 1984/85 harvest (see table 5.2).[19] Increased wages were the centerpiece of the incentive system. A reward system was also set up for workers whose productivity was high. The prizes to be awarded included clothing, furniture and other household items, and paid vacations. Similar incentives have been used with some success in Cuba (Karl, 1975; Benjamin et al., 1984). A realization that moral incentives had to be complemented by material incentives clearly underlay the development of this incentive system.

Wage and other material incentives were just one way of attracting agricultural workers to the harvests. The ATC argued that improved housing, provisions, and working conditions were all essential to making people more inclined to participate in the harvests.

Improved living and working conditions would surely make harvest labor more attractive to the rural poor, but there were clear limitations in the extent to which increased wages could resolve the labor shortage problem. The shortages of consumer goods in rural areas limited the impact of wage increases, both because there was not much to buy regardless of one's wages and because scarcity had driven up the prices of those goods that were still available. Prices of consumer goods nationwide increased steadily beginning in 1979 but were accentuated in rural areas because of the greater scarcity there. Wages, and particularly harvest wages, did not keep pace with these price increases. Table 5.2 illustrates the growing disparity between harvest wages and consumer prices.[20] The government pledged to try to make consumer goods more available (at controlled prices) in rural areas, but maintaining this pledge proved to be very difficult because of nationwide supply problems.

The *campesino* mentality also had to be considered in assessing the impact of higher wages on reducing harvest labor shortages. Many people involved in agricultural production have argued that the *campesino* has a certain concrete goal when entering the wage labor force. If wages are raised, the

Table 5.2

Shifts in Wage/Price Relationship, 1981–1987

Coffee Monthly	1981	1982	1983	1984	1985	1986	1987
Wages	1,399.44	1,612.80	1,680.00	2,016.00	3,511.20	8,442.00	28,560.00
Prices (March)	2,638.50	3,269.05	4,003.15	6,517.35	18,275.80	61,722.00	100,873.00
Percentage of coverage	53	49	42	31	19	14	28
Cotton Monthly	1981	1982	1983	1984	1985	1986	1987
Wages	588.00	1,218.00	1,260.00	1,680.00	2,526.44	13,860.00	23,100.00
Prices (March)	2,638.50	3,269.05	4,003.15	6,517.35	18,275.80	61,722.00	100,873.00
Percentage of coverage	22	37	32	26	14	23	23

Sources: Wages calculated from piece rate per *lata* of coffee picked and *quintal* of cotton picked (MITRAB, un-published data, 1987). Price data are from the Index for the Canasta Básica de Consumo Mínimo (Secretaría de Planificación y Presupuesto, unpublished data, 1986 and 1988).

result will not necessarily be greater productivity. Higher piece rates mean that the *campesino's* goal can be reached by working even fewer hours than in the past. Establishing a reward system to accompany higher piece rates could counter this tendency, but it, too, could fail to achieve higher productivity if the *campesino's* goals could be met without working long enough to receive a reward.

Moreover, the extent to which living and working conditions could be improved on agroexport estates was strongly influenced by factors that went beyond the willingness of producers (both state and private) to make the necessary changes in existing conditions. Nicaragua's insertion in the international market plays a central role in determining the conditions to which workers are subjected on agroexport estates. This is not to say that there is no margin for improvement in conditions. Producers do make a profit from the work of the agricultural labor force, but their margin for improving wages, housing, and so on is limited by what they can earn in the international market. Table 5.1 demonstrates the small margin that was open to agroexport producers (both state and private) to improve harvest conditions given international market prices for Nicaragua's export crops. In essence, Nicaragua's agroexport dependency limited the degree to which the living and working conditions of agricultural workers could be improved.

Within these constraints, the new government made significant investments in social services in Nicaragua's countryside in an effort to improve conditions there. In 1980, investments in social service infrastructure amounted to 33.6 percent of all investments (FNI, 1985). Expenditures in health, education, and housing represented almost two-thirds of these investments. Although other sectors later absorbed a greater percentage of investments, social services continued to capture between 20 and 30 percent of total investments through 1984.

These investments had a considerable impact on the standard of living of Nicaragua's population. The establishment of health care centers throughout the country (the number of which grew from 177 in 1977 to 463 in 1983), vaccination campaigns, nutrition programs, and the like reduced infant mortality from 120 per 1,000 live births in 1976 to 74 in 1982.[21] Similar strides were made in education: illiteracy was reduced from 50 to 12.9 percent through a national literacy campaign carried out in 1980; 17,000 adult education programs had been established by 1983 with 195,000 students and 22,000 teachers; and educational facilities expanded from 2,681 centers in 1979 to 5,377 in 1982.[22] Finally, between 1980 and

1983, the government constructed more than 10,000 new homes through-out the country (MINVAH, 1983). A special effort was made in all of these social programs to bring about a more equitable distribution of resources between urban and rural Nicaragua.

Conditions affecting the economy as a whole, and producers in particular, by the way Nicaragua was inserted into the international economy limited the extent to which individual monetary wages could be raised. Neverthe-less, life in the countryside could be improved through changes in the social wage. The government was acutely aware of the need to raise the rural standard of living. Increasing the social wage by offering more social ser-vices was one of the key means the government employed in its efforts to achieve this goal. Consequently, although monetary wages earned in the harvest did not keep pace with price increases for consumer goods, improve-ments in the social wage somewhat mediated their effect. Thus the process of breaking with the historic exploitation of the rural poor for their cheap labor in the interest of capital accumulation was begun.

Labor-Sharing Proposals

In the effort to find solutions for the harvest labor crisis based in the existing agricultural labor force, a number of promising labor-sharing proposals were developed. In 1981 a strategy involving the ATC was formulated in the hope of preventing labor shortages during the cotton, coffee, and sugarcane harvests. The proposal stipulated that those who received land through the agrarian reform would enter into a contractual agreement with the state. They would "spend eight months of the year on their own plots, producing basic grains for domestic consumption, and the other four as paid laborers on the state-owned and private farms" (*Latin American Regional Reports*, 1981). Once again, the ATC resisted being placed in the position of inter-mediary, arguing that it was the producer's responsibility to attract workers to the harvest. Furthermore, ATC organizers considered any contractual arrangement between the state and agricultural workers a form of coercion (interview 123, ATC, December 3, 1984). They argued that incentives rather than coercion should be used to attract workers to the harvest. Thus this proposal was never formally implemented.

The ATC's reaction to this proposal was symptomatic of the conflicting roles its initial composition imposed upon the organization. From its found-ing in 1978 until the establishment of the Unión de Agricultores y Ganaderos (UNAG) in April 1981, the ATC represented both agricultural wage laborers and producers. Before Somoza's overthrow, this mixed constituency did not present problems because the goal of all of the organization's members was to bring an end to the Somoza regime and begin the process of transforming the rural social structure. The ATC's experience during the first year of revolutionary change, however, revealed that the interests of workers and producers were often in conflict. The founding of UNAG, which was to represent small- and medium-sized producers, resolved the tensions that had been developing within the ATC because of the differing interests of these two sectors.

Whereas the ATC was unwilling to function as an intermediary between agroexport producers and workers, UNAG developed an informal arrangement that was similar to the strategy first proposed to the ATC in 1981. The *brigadas de producción* were the organizational form through which this mobilization effort was carried out.[23] Through the *brigadas*, UNAG sent an average of four thousand *campesino* volunteers to work in each harvest between 1983/84 and 1985/86 and a smaller contingent in 1982/83 (interviews 122, UNAG, November 29, 1984, and 225, UNAG, May 23, 1988; Barricada, 1983a). The *brigadas* were organized from among the organization's membership, which was largely composed of cooperative members (interview 122, UNAG, November 29, 1984). All *cooperativistas* had received some form of assistance through the agrarian reform. Although CAS members received greater benefits, members of CCS had also benefited.[24] Thus UNAG sought support in its efforts to organize production brigades for the agroexport harvests from all of the sectors that made up its membership.

UNAG did not formally require its members to participate in the *brigadas*. Rather, it relied upon convincing them of the need for volunteer labor and the importance of their participation in the success of the harvest. UNAG's goal was to channel *campesinos*, some of whom might otherwise have gone on their own to the harvest, into groups that would go to the areas most affected by labor shortages. Thus the organization coordinated the participation of a number of *campesino* battalions from the northern basic grain-growing region in the cotton harvest in León and Chinandega.

UNAG also organized its coffee harvest *brigadas* from among its members located within the coffee region. The danger the Contras posed to working in the north-central coffee region made traditional pickers from outside the region less inclined to go there. UNAG encouraged its members who lived in this region to participate in the harvest in their immediate locality. This strategy enabled the organization to avoid moving a large volunteer force through potentially dangerous areas and played on the consciences of the agrarian reform beneficiaries forming its membership in the coffee region.

Another variation on this relationship was carried out under the auspices of the ATC. In 1980 the ATC began urging the government to cede unused land in the state sector to seasonal workers. *Colectivos de trabajo* were then established on state farms, allowing temporary workers access to land during the off season. Basic grains were the primary crops grown by these work groups. The *colectivos* provided their members year-round employment so they did not have to look for work elsewhere during the eight to nine nonharvest months of the year.

In turn, the *colectivos* ensured the presence of their members in the harvest labor force. They were not stable organizations on a year-to-year basis. Land ceded to the seasonal work force one year was not always available the following year. The benefits received by these workers often had to be renegotiated each year. And members remained essentially wage laborers, although membership in a work group made them part of the permanent wage labor force.[25] But *colectivo* members would, in theory, still have had to go where work was offered, which meant participation in the harvest labor force. At least in the short run, however, work group members had more security than they would otherwise have had.

From the perspective of a farm administrator, there were advantages to be gained from the formation of a *colectivo* on the farm. Although the *colectivo* could not support all the workers that would be needed on the *finca* during the harvest, the farm would be guaranteed that at least part of its harvest labor requirements would be met. In a census of cooperatives that was conducted by several government agencies in 1982, it was found that sixty *colectivos de trabajo* were functioning with 614 members (CIERA, 1984b: 24).[26] According to several agrarian reform officials, the *colectivos de trabajo* were more prevalent during the first few years of the revolution than several years later (interviews 140, MIDINRA national level, February 7, 1985, and 141, MIDINRA, Region VI, February 11, 1985). They argued that throughout the areas where the *colectivos* had been heavily concentrated (particularly in Nueva Guinea) their numbers had dropped drastically by 1984 as a result of the increased emphasis placed on cooperative development, which encouraged *colectivo* members to form cooperatives rather than remain wage laborers. One agrarian reform official acknowledged that greater encouragement should have been given for temporary workers to form *colectivos* because of their potential for reducing labor shortages (interview 141, MID-INRA, Region VI, February 11, 1985).

Another agrarian reform effort that incorporated temporary workers in a year-round project was the Plan Contingente, a long-term project designed to increase Nicaragua's food crop production. Following the unsuccessful attempt to increase food crop production through the allocation of agricultural credits to small- and medium-sized farmers in 1980 and 1981, the GNR decided that a new strategy had to be devised if the country's growing population was to be fed. The Plan Contingente would reorganize agricultural production in western Nicaragua. While small- and medium-sized farmers would continue to receive credit to raise their standard of living, another sector would be relied upon for increased food crop production. The Pacific coastal plain, once the country's primary grain-producing region, would be the site for this massive effort.

The plan involved the use of irrigation to make food crop production possible during the period when Nicaragua's cotton land lay fallow. The project required a major investment and therefore was to take place over an extended period of time. During the 1984 crop cycle, 6,795 *manzanas* were cultivated with corn in the cotton-growing region (*Barricada*, 1984h). The goal was to reach 60,000 *manzanas* by the year 2000 (Swezey et al., 1984). Although the plan was heavily capital-intensive, the newly irrigated farms were already providing year-round employment to a small number of former seasonal workers by 1984. Employment of these workers in the off season ensured their availability at harvest time because as permanent wage laborers they could be sent where they were most needed.[27] Several cooperatives also participated in the project.

The development of a variety of production arrangements that provided year-round employment for agricultural workers helped ease the labor shortage. A sector of the labor force that previously had to be mobilized each year became readily available to meet part of the harvest requirements. The remainder of the harvest work force still had to be brought from elsewhere. Nevertheless, this new labor system was a definite step toward both raising the standard of living of the rural poor and reducing labor shortages.

Agroexport Cooperatives

Cooperative development in the agroexport sector was yet another alternative for resolving harvest labor shortages based on the potential inherent in the existing agricultural labor force. Agroexport cooperatives were usually formed on farms that had previously been part of the state sector. In other cases, cooperatives formed on land not previously cultivated with export crops, but production was then shifted to these crops. These cooperatives contrasted with the *colectivos de trabajo* insofar as cooperative members were responsible for the entire production process on a year-round, permanent basis.

In addition to providing land and year-round employment to their members, agroexport cooperatives had the potential of easing the labor shortage crisis. It was assumed that ownership of the land would provide the incentive needed to guarantee that the harvest would be completed in a thorough and timely manner. Membership in a cooperative would, in theory, give workers an interest in the harvest's success because it would ultimately be their responsibility. In contrast, workers who were simply wage laborers would probably not feel the same sense of responsibility toward the successful completion of the harvest.

Peer group pressure would help to ensure the harvest's success. Each member of a cooperative was dependent on the others. Any members who failed to meet their responsibilities would likely be pressured by the entire group because they all stood to lose. In addition, the relationship between the cooperative and each member's family was very different from that of normal capitalist enterprises owned by individual growers and the families of their workers. Cooperatives had privileged access to their members' labor time and that of their members' families (Lehman, 1983:31). Consequently, reliance on family labor was the norm in meeting harvest labor requirements in cooperatives. This privileged relationship would partially, if not completely, alleviate labor shortage problems.

The formation of agroexport cooperatives was already under way by 1982/83. The area cultivated with export crops that was controlled by the cooperative sector grew from 0.4 percent of the total in 1982/83 to 18 percent in 1984/85 (calculated from Spoor, 1987:Table 29). Likewise, the cooperative sector's participation in the production of export crops grew from 0.05 percent in 1982/83 to 13 percent in 1984/85. The weight of the cooperative sector was roughly the same in coffee and cotton production.

Critics of the strategy of forming agroexport cooperatives have argued that they are not an efficient organizational form for production. According to these critics, an "economies of scale" approach is crucial in agroexport production, and only the state or large private producers are capable of managing such enterprises.[28] Lack of administrative experience would probably make collectivization of large agroexport estates less economically efficient than already existing privately run production. The same would be true, however, of newly formed state enterprises on large agroexport farms. Large estates are usually characterized by a level of technology that requires skilled management. Nevertheless, collectivization of agroexport production on a smaller scale is feasible. A fair amount of agroexport production was already carried out on a small scale.[29] Thus formation of cooperatives did not necessarily require the subdivision of large-scale agroexport estates. Yields are usually lower in small-scale coffee and cotton production, but costs are also lower because less advanced levels of technology are used. In a capital-scarce economy such as that characterizing post-1979 Nicaragua, saving capital could outweigh the disadvantages of reduced yields.[30]

The formation of *brigadas de producción, colectivos de trabajo,* and agroexport cooperatives represented important alternatives for resolving the labor shortage crisis because they linked the benefits gained by the rural poor through the agrarian reform with an ongoing responsibility to the Nicaraguan state and society. Receiving a land title or access to land lying fallow on a larger estate became more than just one of the fruits of victory. Along with agrarian reform benefits came a responsibility to defend the revolution because only through its defense would the agrarian reform process continue. Ensuring the success of the harvest helped consolidate the revolution. All of these labor-sharing agreements represented an attempt to formalize this responsibility and foster the development of a new relationship between the state and the popular classes within the revolutionary process.

Conclusion

Nicaragua's Sandinista policy makers envisioned that a profound transformation would take place in the country's agricultural sector. Their vision went significantly beyond a simple redistribution of land to include a complete reorganization of agricultural production (see Wheelock, 1984a). It was hoped that this reorganization would foster a major expansion in agricultural production. These medium- to long-term plans emphasized the central role that agriculture was to play in Nicaragua's economy for the foreseeable future. Resolution of the labor shortage problem was essential if the country's agroexport production was to expand.

A number of possible solutions to the labor shortage crisis were experimented with after 1980. The mobilization of volunteer labor was carried out on a massive scale between 1981 and 1986 but could only provide a short-term, partial solution for this dilemma. Increased mechanization of the harvest offered a better solution for the labor shortages in cotton production but was viable only over the medium to long run because of the extreme foreign exchange crisis. Moreover, it provided no solution for labor short-ages in the coffee harvest.

The alternative with the greatest potential for resolving harvest labor shortages over the short, medium, and long run was the variety of labor-sharing and cooperative relationships that were developed. Together they offered an experienced, available labor force that could meet harvest labor requirements. The *brigadas de producción, colectivos de trabajo*, and collectiv-ization of agroexport production presented the possibility of extending the agrarian reform and, at the same time, reinforcing an awareness of the important role played by *campesinos* and agricultural workers in the nation's economy.

The various labor-sharing arrangements could not completely resolve the labor shortage crisis. They would have to be combined over the medium to long run with increased reliance on mechanical harvesters (at least for cotton) if cotton production was to be maintained or expanded. In the long run, the ideal situation would be that no one would have to carry out the arduous task of harvesting the country's export crops by hand. But until this ideal was reached, the various labor-sharing agreements would have to be relied upon, in conjunction with the other alternatives, to meet harvest labor supply requirements. In sum, the use of voluntary labor would have to be gradually phased out as quickly as labor-sharing arrangements could replace it. These arrangements would then be the mainstay until some point in the future when it would be possible to rely more heavily on mechaniza-tion.

As the transformation of agricultural production proceeded, human re-sources remained a key factor in government planning. The already difficult labor supply situation would be exacerbated if production expansions, par-ticularly in the agroexport sector, were not accompanied by solutions for the labor shortage crisis. These solutions did not need to be, and in fact could not be, purely technological in nature. Those benefiting from the agrarian reform offered a more comprehensive solution, for they had a responsibility to ensure the continued advancement of the revolutionary transformation.

6

Conclusion

The Sandinista revolution sought to transform the political and economic structure that emerged in Nicaragua with the development of dependent capitalism. Within the revolutionary process, the agrarian reform was designed to reorganize agricultural production. The goals of the reform were twofold: to move the country toward a new model of development and to improve the lives of the rural poor.

The agrarian reform was successful in meeting many of its short-term objectives. That success, however, created a new dilemma for agrarian reform policy makers. As the *campesinos'* standard of living improved, they increasingly chose *campesinización* over participation in the agroexport labor force. Thus labor shortages became a problem in the key agroexport harvests. The labor shortage threatened the very essence of agroexport production. Nicaragua's agroexport-based development has been dependent on the cheap labor of its *campesino* population. Yet the agrarian reform was specifically intended to better the lives of the rural poor, thereby lessening their willingness to provide cheap labor to the agroexport sector.

The agrarian reform was highly political in nature. The rural poor played an important role in the struggle to overthrow Somoza. Maintaining the political support of the *campesino* population required that its needs be addressed by the revolutionary government, but this political necessity came into conflict with the equally critical economic exigency of sustaining a viable agroexport sector.

The advantage Nicaragua has had in producing agricultural products for export has been its low labor costs, which have been kept to a minimum through a number of mechanisms, including the employment of workers for the shortest possible time period. A seasonal labor system has ensured that this goal was realized. Any increase in labor costs cut into the profits generated by agroexport production. Because prices for these products are determined by the international market and there are numerous intermediaries between the producer and the consumer, the former's profit margin is limited. If the producer is to make a profit, it must come from the cheap labor of those who make the production possible, the harvest workers. Ultimately, it is irrelevant whether the producer is an individual capitalist or the state. The principle is the same.

This agroexport–agrarian reform dilemma exemplifies the ways in which Nicaragua's legacy of dependent capitalism influenced its course of transformation and development. It was but one of the many obstacles that confronted the revolutionary process. Those obstacles, however, went beyond the economic realm. Political and ideological tensions and the interplay between these three realms also complicated the process of transition. Sandinista policy makers undoubtedly concluded, after a decade of revolution, that bringing an end to the old regime was infinitely easier than pushing forward social transformation.

Yet Nicaragua's revolutionary government was not alone in having encountered conflicts in these three realms. Indeed, the legacy of dependent development has affected the efforts of all who have attempted to carry out profound social transformation in the Third World, for many of the same factors that initially gave rise to revolutionary change in these peripheral societies are passed on directly to the new regime. Principal among the factors bequeathed from the prerevolutionary period is the role that has been assigned to each of these countries in the international economic order. Unlike the Soviet Union and China, the revolutionary movements that have gained power more recently have not had the alternative of opting out of the world economy. The changes in the international capitalist system in the post–World War II period have created a situation in which production, exchange, and mass communications operate at a worldwide level (Fagen et al., 1986). For a country to withdraw from that system requires a strength and self-sufficiency not possessed by even the most advanced capitalist nations. Furthermore, most of the Third World countries that have experienced revolutionary change in recent years have also been constrained by their small size. Their smallness presents an additional obstacle to withdrawal because their potential for self-sufficiency is even more limited than that of larger Third World countries.

Because they need to remain in the world economy, these revolutionary countries are confronted by the capitalist logic that is the driving force behind the system. That is, although the priorities guiding policy making in this new setting may vary significantly from those of most dependent capitalist countries, the world economy with which they interact remains capitalistic. Moreover, the rules of the international market still work to the advantage of the core countries and the disadvantage of those on the periphery.

Most of the peripheral countries in transition have been, and continue to be, price-takers, not price-setters. Only a tiny minority of these countries produce commodities that are in sufficient demand to provide them with bargaining power over prices.[1] Yet even those fortunate few remain dependent on foreign technology to make possible their primary production. The more advanced socialist countries have provided important material and technical assistance to many Third World revolutions. However, although the "multipolarity [represented by the advanced socialist countries] provides, in some cases, a secondary structure of opportunity, some political, military, and ideological leverage on occasion . . . it is not the fundamental architecture within which development on the periphery is played out" (Fagen et al., 1986). That architecture is the capitalist world system.

Continued participation in the international division of labor means that the export sector of each of these economies remains pivotal, even as the revolutionary transformation proceeds. This, in turn, implies that many of the conditions previously characterizing export dependency are still predominant, at least in the early stages of transformation. For example, export production is still concentrated on a small number of primary goods whose market in the core countries is inherently unstable. Yet a profound process of change has been initiated in the relations of production. The case study developed in the preceding chapters provides an example of the dilemmas that arise as these two circumstances collide. In essence, the relative advantage of each of these countries in the world economy is threatened because excess profits can no longer be extracted through the cheap labor of the harvest workers. The very viability of their economies is thus called into question.

At the same time, the transition process creates a general need for increased financial resources. The cost of reconstruction following the overthrow of the old regime is only the beginning. The revolutionary process itself also contributes to this need "because of the low productivity resulting from the transformation of social relations and the need for rapid accumulation to overcome underdevelopment" (FitzGerald, 1986:35). Moreover, the need for greater financial resources is not simply an economic issue but a political issue as well. The revolutionary process gives rise to expectations of improvements in the standard of living that if not met could prove to be fertile ground for counterrevolutionary organizing. Nonetheless, though projects that develop and transform the economy are crucial for the legitimacy of the revolutionary regime, internal financing is extremely limited. Thus revolutions in the Third World are even more dependent on export earnings and foreign assistance than are their capitalist counterparts.

Economic constraints are not, however, all that condition the course of revolutionary transformation in peripheral societies. The political structure that prevailed in the prerevolutionary period may have been dismantled with the overthrow of the old regime, but the previously existing social structure does not disappear overnight. This is particularly the case in those societies in which a mixed economy strategy is pursued, although it also affects the process of change where the economy has been largely nationalized. Given the myriad of forms under which production is carried out in dependent capitalism, it is logical that the new productive structure will reflect a continuation of this diversity.[2] Because class relations in peripheral societies cannot usually be reduced to a capitalist-worker relationship, the revolutionary period will of necessity require a variety of forms of production relations.

In revolutionary societies previously characterized by a more advanced stage of dependent development, nationalization of a greater proportion of the economy is possible.[3] That is, where precapitalist production relations have been largely subsumed by capitalist relations, it becomes possible to nationalize production and move toward worker management of the newly formed state enterprises.[4] In contrast, in peripheral societies in which precapitalist relations still characterize a significant part of production, the transformation process must allow for individual or gradually collectivized production. Nicaragua fell into this latter category. First, the adoption of a mixed economy meant that the private sector continued to participate in production, although the nature of this sector changed. Second, petty commodity production, which carried great weight in the prerevolutionary economy, also had a place in the new productive structure.[5] Nonetheless, the formation of small-producer cooperatives was promoted in both industry and agriculture as a way of beginning the process of transforming this latter sector through its gradual collectivization.

The case study developed in this book, however, has shown that although the transformation of precapitalist production relations is possible, the process is often fraught with difficulties, in part because, to some degree, prerevolutionary production relations and the economic system they sustained worked "in the sense of being an integrated and functioning system of accumulation" (Fagen et al., 1986:15). The process of social change disrupts, as it is intended to do, that previously functioning system, without automatically replacing it with an alternative system. This is the essence of the dilemma described here. It is a problem experienced in all facets of social life in a revolutionary society immediately following the overthrow of the previous regime. The establishment of a new internal equilibrium, which facilitates the functioning of the system following the initiation of revolutionary change, takes time. A system of social relations that developed over several centuries cannot be instantly replaced.

The process of achieving equilibrium within the transitional society is made more difficult because there are no models for revolutionary change. Although much has been written about the problems and contradictions of capitalism, particularly in the periphery, little work has been completed on the actual transition to socialism. Experience has been accumulated during several decades of revolutionary change in the USSR and China. Yet the differences between these two countries and the more recent Third World revolutions, in terms of size, prerevolutionary level of development, and the historical moment at which the transformation was begun, limit the lessons that the latter can derive.

Revolutions in the periphery can look to each other, however, for guidance in pushing forward the transformation process. Although the experience of these countries is less extensive than that of their predecessors, it is nonetheless useful as they inevitably face obstacles arising from a shared history of dependent capitalist development. For example, Nicaraguan policy makers benefited from analyzing Cuba's experience with carrying out a revolution while under siege. At the same time, those planning Nicaragua's future had to look inward at the country's class structure, history, and so on in forging the course of social change there.

In addition to the lack of models that sketch the process of transformation, revolutionary policy makers are confronted with the difficulties inherent in the planning process itself. Planning during the prerevolutionary period was designed to bring state policies in line with the developmental needs of the dominant capitalist class. Development planning was not, and is not, a neutral process. Rather, it reflects the goals of a specific class: "The basic issues of development—what to produce, how, for whom—have no answer outside of class projects" (Vilas, 1986:31). In the transitional setting, redefinition of the class project and its translation into specific policy measures must be carried out by revolutionary planners. Resolution of such issues as whether the mechanisms of the market, which had previously facilitated the accumulation of productive resources in a few hands, will be replaced by a more just system of distribution depends on the active intervention of the revolutionary state. That intervention is hindered, however, by lack of information about the concrete reality to be transformed, the still unconsolidated nature of the revolutionary state, and the limited supply of human resources capable of carrying out the planning process.[6] Planning proves even more complicated in a mixed economy because actors with diverse class interests are called upon to work together in pushing the country's economic development forward. Yet contradictions exist in these actors' definitions of development.

At the same time, the planning process cannot remain the domain of only those trained in the technical skills of planning. In the prerevolutionary period, those with influence on the planning process are few in number. Within a revolutionary society, if planning is to have any success, the perspective of those whose lives it affects must be taken into account. This means that "the popular forces, who in this case make up the fundamental social base of the revolutionary project, must be organized to participate in the development and implementation of the state's economic [and other] policies" (Coraggio, 1986:146). Yet these are precisely the same sectors that were excluded from the decision-making process under the previous regime. Revolutionary transformation thus has as an essential feature the establishment of numerous channels that make possible a dialogue between those in the government charged with policy making and other sectors of society.

These peripheral societies in transition typically have inherited little in the way of formal democracy and so must undertake a major restructuring of state and civil society relations. Facilitating the popular classes' access to the planning process is only part of the more general process of democratization that the revolution must set in motion. The vision of this process extends much further than periodically holding elections. Historically, the right to participate in electoral politics has not been sufficient in peripheral societies to eliminate poverty and exploitation. The organization of a revolutionary movement leads to a broadening of the definition of democracy to include social and economic democracy in addition to representative democracy.[7] That is, although elections must be held to choose those who will govern, the revolutionary project is not only political but social and economic as well.[8] In Nicaragua, the concepts of social and economic democracy were translated into the logic that guided the revolutionary project, the logic of the majority. It was the responsibility of those elected to govern both to ensure that this logic prevailed in policy making and to facilitate the creation of channels to broaden the participation of the popular sectors in the governing process.

Yet the issue of democracy is a delicate one, given the lack of consolidation characterizing the revolutionary state (Fagen, 1986). Although legitimacy will be maintained by the new regime only to the degree that it follows the logic of the majority in pushing forth the revolutionary project, the democratic openings it creates can, and will, be manipulated by those who are opposed to that project. The opposition has its base in the minority who benefited from the policies of the previous regime (i.e., the propertied classes). If an alliance had been formed between this sector and the revolutionary movement at the moment the latter gained power, its existence would almost of necessity be brief. A break is practically unavoidable because of the differing natures of the propertied class's project for the future and that of the popular classes, who are to be represented by the revolutionary regime. The historical relationship between the bourgeoisie and the functioning of "democratic" participation during the prerevolutionary period has given this sector much greater experience than the newly emancipated in calling attention to its concerns. Although initially it may genuinely seek recourse within the nascent political system, the propertied class's political participation will gradually be transformed so that its main goal is to block the advancement of the revolutionary project. This class will almost undoubtedly look to former allies for assistance in its efforts. Not surprisingly, it is particularly in the international realm that these "counterrevolutionary" voices find their echo, among those who are preoccupied with maintaining peripheral capitalist societies within their hegemony.

Post–World War II history suggests that revolutionary governments in the Third World will inevitably be confronted by counterrevolutionary forces. The face these forces show the world is that of the previously dominant local bourgeoisie. But their real strength is based in the advanced capitalist nations, particularly the United States. Thirteen of the fourteen revolutionary regimes that were established in peripheral societies between 1974 and 1980 encountered the active opposition of the United States in their efforts to push forward social transformation.[9] Nicaragua was subjected to continuous attack by U.S.-organized, armed, and trained counterrevolutionary forces throughout the period between early 1982 and the electoral defeat of the Sandinista government in 1990. It was also the victim of a financial and commercial blockade orchestrated by the United States and an international campaign to delegitimate the revolution. In sum, the Nicaraguan revolution had to contend with U.S. intervention almost since its inception, but it was only one more peripheral country in transition to experience the wrath of the United States.[10]

Intervention by the United States and its allies must therefore be understood as another given affecting the process of revolutionary change in the Third World. It has been argued that "the first step in the analysis of socialist transition is to recognize that socialism develops in dialectic with its imperialist enemy and the first phase of this dialectic is military . . . new social institutions must be built in the midst of protracted war" (Marchetti, 1986:304). The context of counterrevolutionary war thus comes to complement these peripheral societies' heritage of dependent capitalist development in conditioning the transformation process. The two become intertwined and mutually reinforcing. Hence all of the tensions described above which arise in the course of this transformation process are compounded by material, financial, and human resource limitations resulting from counterrevolutionary warfare.

As a consequence, the war constricts the space for experimenting with solutions to the numerous dilemmas that arise in the peripheral society in transition. Yet precisely because the very survival of the revolutionary regime is, thus, eventually called into question, policy makers must become ever more creative in their problem-solving efforts. While the luxury of peace may allow a revolutionary government to move cautiously in pushing forward profound societal changes, the pressure of war may require dramatic responses to the same need for change.[11] In sum, the counterrevolution often accelerates the very process of transformation it seeks to reverse.

The issue of the effects of counterrevolutionary war on the process of social change in the periphery, however, inevitably leads to a much larger question: Will not the advancement of revolutionary transformation in the Third World ultimately require social change in the advanced capitalist world as well? Experience suggests that the answer is affirmative. Without such change, the United States and its allies will persist in undermining these revolutionary movements. The space for Third World revolutions will become more and more constricted, and the problems for those countries that have already begun this process will increase. The social tensions gener-

ated by dependent capitalist development in the periphery will, in all likelihood, continue to foster the call for revolutionary transformation. But social
change must extend beyond the Third World for these countries to break the
bonds of dependent capitalist development.

Postscript

In the foregoing chapters one of the numerous dilemmas that confronted the Nicaraguan revolution during the first few years of its development was described. The case study presented above illustrated the manner in which conflicts in resource requirements arose as the process of restructuring agriculture was carried out. The production of coffee and cotton, formerly the country's two key generators of foreign exchange, was called into question as severe labor shortages affected the harvests of both crops. What happened after the 1983/84 agroexport harvest? Was this dilemma resolved, or did it become intractable? Did the agrarian reform continue to undermine production in a sector of the economy whose importance grew increasingly each year? The following pages will address these questions, as well as situate this dilemma within the context of the ongoing process of agrarian reform and the Contra war that characterized Nicaragua through February 1990.

The Context

As we saw in Chapter 4, many factors contributed to the breakdown of the previously existing labor system. This breakdown led, in turn, to the labor shortages that were experienced in the agroexport harvests in 1980/81 and the years thereafter. Only two of these factors were potentially of a lasting nature, the agrarian reform and the Contra war, both of which consistently affected the availability of labor for the cotton and coffee harvests after that time.

The process of agrarian reform that was begun immediately following Somoza's overthrow in 1979 continued unabated in the years succeeding the 1983/84 harvest. The redistribution of land, in particular, benefited more and more of the rural population. In 1986 more land was redistributed than in any other year during the 1979–88 period (see table 4.1). For the first time, individual farmers received a notable percentage of this land: individuals received 110,652 *manzanas* (35 percent), and cooperatives received 192,257 *manzanas* (61 percent).[1] The land titling program, which affected those producers who had previously been farming their land without legal recognition, dropped off after 1984 (CIERA, 1989:Table 3) but still operated on a reduced scale in the following years. By the end of 1988, approximately 108,765 *campesino* families had benefited from the land redistribution and titling programs, 71 percent of whom had received land that had been affected by the agrarian reform law and 29 percent of whom were able to legalize the ownership of their land (CIERA, 1989:Tables 6 and 18).

In early 1986 the Agrarian Reform Law was revised to expand the area potentially subject to confiscation.[2] The original law had specified that only farms larger than five hundred *manzanas* in the Pacific region and coffee-growing regions of Matagalpa and Jinotega and one thousand *manzanas* in the rest of the country were subject to confiscation if left idle or abandoned. The revised law allowed for farms of any size to be affected if they were not being used efficiently. In addition, the conditions of compensation were altered so that, unless reduced productivity was caused by circumstances beyond the control of the landowner, the confiscation of idle farms would no longer be compensated (i.e., they would be treated the same as abandoned farms). Finally, even farms that were being used in a productive fashion could be subject to confiscation if the minister of agrarian reform determined that exceptional circumstances applied. Those circumstances included social emergencies in which it became imperative to establish special agricultural programs designed for displaced *campesino* families; areas characterized by a high concentration of *minifundios* in which larger rural properties existed that impeded efforts to bring about a more just distribution of land; and areas that the state had designated for agricultural development and agrarian reform projects (see *Barricada*, 1986a:4).

What triggered these revisions in the 1981 Agrarian Reform Law? There were two central reasons for the law's revision: the ongoing Contra war and the continued existence of a landless sector of the rural population. The Contra war had come to affect much of Nicaragua's central region by 1985, reaching from the Matagalpa-Jinotega area, clear down to south-central Zelaya (particularly Chontales). Beginning early that year a resettlement plan was set in motion that was supposed to eliminate potential bases of support for the Contras and provide a viable alternative for displaced *campesino* families, including those "resettled" by the government and those who relocated on their own. In 1985 alone, 204,057 *manzanas* were organized into 228 cooperatives, which incorporated 13,022 displaced *campesino* families (MIDINRA, 1986a:7). The revised Agrarian Reform Law would facilitate the organization of additional agricultural cooperatives, where necessary, for those displaced by the war.

The second reason for changes in the Agrarian Reform Law was the continued existence of a sector of landless *campesinos* within the rural population. An awareness of the implications of this phenomenon emerged in the aftermath of the 1984 general elections. Studies undertaken at that time showed that support for the FSLN was lower in areas where an important part of the *campesinado* still remained landless or land-poor five years after the Sandinista government had come to power. This issue was most pressing in the regions affected by the war, but it seemed urgent to respond to this sector of the population in other areas of the country as well. In addition, the escalation in rural-urban migration in the Pacific region, which reached a peak at this time, contributed to the growing concern about the problem of *minifundismo* and landlessness. Because land that could easily be affected by agrarian reform had, in large part, already been redistributed by 1985, it was felt that new areas had to be opened up for the *campesino* sector.

The decision to make more land subject to confiscation was also a product of the redefinition of state–private sector relations that occurred at this time. The deterioration in state–capitalist producer relations had by the 1985–86 period reached an all-time low. Ilja Luciak (1987) points out that the revised law was meant to enable the government to confiscate the land of those medium-sized producers who provided support for the Contras. Thus the size limit for farms that were potentially subject to confiscation was reduced. Yet the law also signaled the adoption of a new definition of the private sector, emphasizing the inclusion of small- and medium-sized *campesino* producers in this concept. The goal of this change was to form an alliance between private producers of all sizes, who supported the revolutionary project, and cooperative members. This alliance would serve to counterbalance the part of the traditionally recognized private sector that opposed the government.[3]

Following through on the effort to respond to the needs of the rural poor and to strengthen its base in the countryside, the government designated 1987 the year to consolidate the cooperative movement. The cooperative movement had continued to expand after its founding and initial development. By the end of 1988, 3,151 cooperatives existed, with 76,715 members (CIERA, 1989:Table 24). Of this total, Sandinista Agricultural Cooperatives represented 37 percent, while the Credit and Service Cooperatives made up 48 percent. Thus the promotion of cooperative organization on redistributed land and throughout the *campesino* sector more generally had been successful.

Although the number of people participating in cooperatives had grown each year, certain weaknesses persisted within the movement. High dropout rates among members, lack of internal democracy, excessive hiring of agricultural laborers, and inefficient use of profits were some of the problems that had emerged within the cooperative movement (see Porras, 1987). It was not surprising that these and other problems had arisen, considering the underdevelopment characterizing Nicaragua's countryside and the newness of the movement. Nonetheless, government policy makers felt that it was important to try to resolve them before they further impeded the movement's development.

A related effort, which was combined with the project of consolidating the cooperative movement, was to form territorial cooperatives or cooperative unions (Unión de Cooperativas Agrícolas, UCA) (see INIES, 1987:32– 33). These cooperative unions were promoted on the assumption that it would prove more economically feasible to provide a group of cooperatives, as opposed to a number of individual cooperatives, with technical assistance and inputs such as machinery. Whereas a cooperative with twenty members probably would not have the resources to purchase a tractor and the government could not justify providing it with one, a union of six cooperatives with a total of one hundred members might be able to make such an investment. It was also envisioned that the development of this kind of organization in the countryside might lead to collective efforts to obtain other benefits for the rural communities where they were based.[4]

A final goal behind the cooperative consolidation drive was to increase the membership in already existing cooperatives with landless and land-poor *campesinos*. Thus appropriate land/person ratios were calculated, and membership openings were established accordingly. Work toward this goal simultaneously helped to strengthen the existing cooperatives, while providing a partial response to the issue of landlessness.

Related projects were also undertaken to address the continuing problem of *minifundismo*.[5] Special agrarian reform programs were implemented that targeted specific *minifundio* populations for land redistribution. In areas where further distribution was not feasible, crop diversification, the adoption of new technologies, or both were promoted with the goal of improving the income level of those participating. Nonetheless, the problem had yet to be completely resolved (interview 220, MIDINRA, Region IV, January 14, 1988). Thus it was foreseen that efforts would persist in the coming years to find ways of providing the rural poor with land or other means of overcoming the poverty that continued to engulf them.

At the same time that these efforts were being made to improve the lives of the rural poor, life in the Nicaraguan countryside (as well as in urban areas) was made increasingly difficult by the ongoing Contra war. By the end of 1988, the war had claimed 29,513 victims, including 8,173 dead, 13,865 injured, and 7,475 kidnapped (INEC, 1989:57).[6] The war had also forced the relocation of 250,000 *campesinos* (CNPPDH, 1988:17, 20–21). In addition, 2,305 homes, 64 schools, and 32 health centers had been destroyed. Contra activity between 1980 and 1988 was estimated by INEC (1989:58) to have caused Nicaragua (U.S.) $1,998 million in losses, 82 percent of which resulted from lost production and 18 percent from infrastructural damages. In addition, losses for the same period resulting from the commercial and credit blockade mounted by the U.S. reached (U.S.) $1,102 million.[7]

In addition to a general worsening of conditions in the countryside, the agroexport harvests remained a target of the Contras. Their efforts to sabotage the harvest were part of a larger strategy of undermining the revolutionary government by damaging the economy. The primary coffee-growing region (Matagalpa and Jinotega) was still one of the areas most affected by the war. Coffee production in some pockets within this region proved impossible to maintain because of the ongoing presence of the Contras. The Contras also continued to keep people away from the harvest, out of fear of their attacks. The fear was not unfounded: at the height of the 1987/88 coffee harvest, two volunteer coffee pickers were killed in a Contra attack in Jinotega (*Barricada*, 1988a:2). Moreover, the coffee harvest was affected by reduced worker productivity resulting from participation in the twenty-four-hour vigilance required to protect the farms from the Contras (interview 219, state employee and volunteer coffee picker, January 13, 1988, who described the tension throughout the 1987/88 harvest on the state farm where she worked).

The war also continued to affect the national economy. An average of 35 percent of the national budget was devoted to defense spending between 1984 and 1987,[8] diverting funds from other key sectors of the economy. As a consequence, in some areas of the economy the process of reconstruction and development remained stagnant at the levels reached in 1982, while in others the advances that were made between 1979 and 1982 were reversed. The war also continued to aggravate Nicaragua's foreign exchange situation, primarily through production losses that reduced exports and led to the need for greater imports. Between 1983 and 1988 alone the foreign debt grew by 91 percent (calculated from CEPAL, 1989:39).

This general economic deterioration, especially the worsening in the balance of foreign exchange, made agroexport production even more important in the years following the 1983/84 harvest. As production throughout the economy fell off, more and more attention was focused on guaranteeing the success of production in the agroexport sector. This was clearly illustrated during Nicaragua's severe energy crisis in early 1988. Drastic measures designed to reduce energy consumption were adopted, including a reduction in the workweek from 42.5 to 25 hours in government ministries, as well as selected private agencies; the closure of several heavy energy-consuming factories; and a severe rationing of electricity.[9] The announcement of these measures was accompanied by an explanation that because of the need to reduce national consumption of electricity, all sectors except the agroexport sector would experience rationing. The agroexport sector was excepted from rationing because of its potential to generate foreign exchange. Thus sugar refineries, cotton ginning facilities, and coffee *beneficios* were to be provided with the resources necessary to get the harvest processed and to port.

Post-1983/84 Coffee and Cotton Harvests

One of the most significant changes that took place in the agroexport sector after 1984 was a major reduction in cotton production. Whereas cotton acreage increased from 1980 to 1983, by 1985 the area under cultivation was decreasing (see table 3.4). Among the reasons for this drop were the virtual disintegration of the cotton production system, which resulted from import limitations caused by Nicaragua's economic crisis and the U.S. economic blockade; continuing difficulties in ensuring a sufficient supply of labor for both preharvest and harvest work, but particularly the latter; a growing preference among producers for basic grain cultivation instead of cotton, as a consequence of the first two factors; and a drastic drop in the price of cotton in the international market.

The cotton production system had begun to fall apart several years before the drop in production became evident in 1985. As Nicaragua's economic situation worsened in the early 1980s, imports of agricultural inputs were interrupted. Cotton cultivation is extremely delicate—timing is of the essence—and input shortages increasingly disrupted the production process. The U.S. trade embargo imposed on Nicaragua in 1985 multiplied the problems that had begun to develop in previous years. Ultimately, it became impossible to ensure an adequate and opportune supply of imported inputs for the extensive cotton-producing area, and MIDINRA recommended to the government's national-level planning commission (the Consejo de Planificación) that the area planted with cotton be restricted to the most ecologically appropriate zones (interview 228, MIDINRA, June 6, 1988). This strategy would enable the government to focus its efforts on providing inputs to producers in the prioritized areas.

Labor supply problems also continued to plague the cotton production system. In the early 1970s, when the area cultivated with cotton was approximately equivalent to that in the 1982–84 period, the harvest labor force was composed of around one hundred thousand workers (see tables 3.2 and 3.4). Yet in 1984/85 only an estimated sixty thousand workers participated in the harvest (interview 228, MIDINRA, June 6, 1988). This figure dropped to forty thousand in 1985/86, thirty thousand in 1986/87, and fifteen to seventeen thousand in 1987/88. Although the impact of this dramatic reduction in the number of harvest workers was somewhat alleviated by a heavier reliance on mechanical harvesters, the persistent shortage of traditional pickers contributed significantly to the crisis experienced in the cotton production system.

In response to the increasingly problematic input and labor situations in the cotton sector, producers began shifting their acreage into other crops. Sorghum was the first alternative crop to be adopted. Sorghum production proved less complicated for growers because it was less dependent on imported inputs than cotton. In addition, the larger growers were able to mechanize the harvest completely, thereby eliminating the need for an extensive labor supply. Later, the liberalization of the basic grain market resulted in corn also being adopted as an alternative to cotton production.

Finally, the price of cotton on the international market plunged in the mid-1980s. Between 1984/85 and 1985/86 the price Nicaragua received for its cotton fell from (U.S.) $62.15 to $38.38 (ENAL, unpublished data, 1988). Although this price decline proved to be temporary, when combined with the other difficulties in cotton production, it provided the impetus to reduce the area planted with cotton. By early 1988, MIDINRA had concluded that if inputs and labor requirements were to be met, cotton acreage could not exceed one hundred thousand *manzanas* during the following few years (interview 228, MIDINRA, June 6, 1988). Yet Nicaragua would need to continue producing this minimum amount of cotton to satisfy local demand, particularly for cottonseed oil.

The significant reduction in cotton acreage after 1985 resulted in a corresponding decrease in the demand for labor. At the same time, the area harvested by machines expanded, further diminishing labor requirements. Nonetheless, in all of the cotton harvests after 1983/84 there was a deficit in the number of workers available to pick the crop.

Coffee production also continued to suffer from both absolute and relative labor shortages during its yearly harvest. That is, the absolute number of pickers who worked in the harvest was smaller than the number required, and the productivity level of those who participated was less than it needed to be.[10]

A recent study of the agricultural labor force, carried out by CIERA, found that the absolute shortages of harvest laborers for coffee and cotton were caused by (in descending order of importance) mobilizations related to the defense effort, land redistribution, the existence of alternative (informal) sources of employment, and migration out of the areas where agroexport production was concentrated.[11] Thus the absolute labor shortages continued to be caused by the incorporation of potential harvest workers into the various branches of the military and the new possibilities created for the *campesino* population through the agrarian reform.

The Sandinistas had few options for diminishing the influence of these two factors on the harvest labor supply. Mobilization for the defense effort would continue as long as the Contra war went on. Although the U.S. Congress voted to suspend official U.S. funding (i.e., of a "military" nature) for the Contras in February 1988, it appeared that the U.S. administration was loath to allow the Contra forces to disintegrate. Without that certainty, the Nicaraguan government felt compelled to maintain the strength of its defense forces. Thus recruitment for the military would continue to absorb an important part of the potential harvest labor force.

Moreover, the Sandinistas' intention to maintain the agrarian reform as an ongoing effort implied that the size of the population it benefited would grow with each additional year of its implementation. The process of cooperative formation and land redistribution would persist as long as there was a land-poor and landless sector of the rural population. Far from lessening its influence on the harvest labor force, the agrarian reform would reach further and further into that labor force, offering it a much more attractive alternative through *campesinización*.

The other source of harvest labor problems, reduced labor productivity, also remained an issue. Another recent study of the coffee harvest labor force found that women made up 56 percent of the 275 harvest workers sampled during the 1986/87 harvest.[12] If similar sampling techniques were used in the various surveys that have been carried out thus far on the harvest labor force (e.g., Wheelock, 1980; INCAE, 1982b; CIERA, 1984a; Aznar, 1986; and CIERA et al., 1987), this finding signals a continuing pattern of increased participation of women in the harvest labor force. The expanded presence of women in the labor force would, in turn, imply a further reduction in the average productivity per picker because of the general tendency for women to pick less than men. But because statistics describing labor productivity more generally are unavailable, it is impossible to make definitive statements about this issue.[13] Nonetheless, efforts to improve labor productivity, even as late as 1988, suggested that problems in this area still existed.

The CIERA study referred to above described an additional aspect of harvest labor shortages—instability within the work force that did participate in the harvest.[14] That is, workers spent less time on a specific farm than they formerly did. This instability was attributed to several factors, including problems with the wage scale, the availability of provisions on agroexport farms, the social conditions on the farms, and competition for workers between the private, cooperative, and state sectors. In sum, labor shortages in the agroexport harvests still remained an issue of concern after a decade of revolutionary transformation. The limited success of efforts to resolve the labor shortages underlined the profound nature of this dilemma.

The Ongoing Search for Solutions to the Harvest Labor Dilemma

Each agroexport harvest since 1983/84 has been characterized by shortages in the labor force available to pick these critical crops. The Sandinista government continued to rely on a combination of alternatives in its efforts to lessen the impact of the shortages on coffee and cotton production.

The mobilization of volunteer labor for the agroexport harvests became a tradition after eight years of implementation, but the nature of the volunteer labor force changed and its weight in the overall labor force diminished beginning in 1986/87. The participation of students, in particular, was dramatically reduced. Between 1982 and 1985 the number of students mobilized for the harvest each year grew from fifteen thousand to twenty thousand. Although approximately twenty thousand student volunteers worked in the 1985/86 harvest, the following year (1986/87) their number dropped to about three thousand (interview 215, MIDINRA, October 13, 1987). Only about one hundred students participated in the 1987/88 coffee harvest (interview 226, student at the UCA and member of Brigada XXV Aniversario in 1987/88, May 25, 1988). Instead, university students were encouraged to work in projects related to their area of study during the three-month semester break when they had previously gone to the harvest.

The mobilization of government functionaries into the harvest labor force also continued, though on a lesser scale than in previous years. In 1983/84 between twenty-five hundred and three thousand members of the Unión Nacional de Empleados (which represented state employees) were mobilized for the coffee harvest, and more than five thousand went in 1985/86, but only approximately fifteen hundred state employees were mobilized in 1987/88.[15] Likewise, the number of CDS members participating in the agroexport harvests decreased after the early years of volunteer mobilizations. Finally, the presence of international volunteer brigades also diminished. Whereas more than two thousand foreigners participated in volunteer brigades in 1983/84 (see Chapter 5), their number was down to between three and four hundred in 1986/87 (interview 215, MIDINRA, October 13, 1987).

The changes that occurred in volunteer participation in the harvest labor force were the result of a decision made by the Comisión Nacional de la Cosecha. This commission, which was headed by Jaime Wheelock (former minister of MIDINRA), concluded that the use of large numbers of inexperienced pickers had severe drawbacks (interview 225, UNAG, May 23, 1988). That is, although the political impact of volunteer participation in the harvest had a positive effect in raising the volunteers' level of political consciousness, its economic impact was negative. Because of their inexperience, the volunteers frequently damaged the trees, thereby affecting future yields of coffee beans; the use of volunteers was costly because they had to be transported to and from the harvest and provided with supplies; and the volunteers' productivity was notably less than that of traditional pickers. The losses resulting from this combination of factors far outweighed the benefits produced by the coffee the volunteers were able to pick. Thus as was prognosticated in Chapter 5, the employment of a volunteer labor force in resolving the harvest labor shortage dilemma would prove useful only in the short run.

The use of volunteer labor in the cotton and coffee harvests was not eliminated entirely, however. Two special brigades continued to be organized each year to participate in the harvest. The first, the Brigada XXV Aniversario, was composed of students and government functionaries who had gained experience picking coffee by working in previous harvests.[16] Its members were also required to be more productive than the average volunteer.

The second special volunteer brigade participating in the coffee harvest, the Contingente Bernardino Díaz Ochoa, was organized by UNAG. *Campesinos* who had both harvesting and military experience formed the Contingente. In contrast to the UNAG's earlier strategy of organizing *brigadas de producción* from within a region (especially in the northern coffee-growing region) to work in that region's harvest, the Contingente brought together *campesinos* from throughout the country to work in Matagalpa and Jinotega. The Contingente was sent to the areas that were made most problematic by the war. Thus its members often spend as much time defending the coffee farms where they were sent as they did picking coffee. In 1986/87, five hundred *campesinos* formed the Contingente; in 1987/88, two thousand (interview 225, UNAG, May 23, 1988). These *campesinos* were selected by their cooperative or community to join the Contingente.

Brigada and Contingente members received the same piece-rate salary as traditional pickers, but their multiple responsibilities of harvesting and defending the coffee farms typically resulted in their not being able to pick as much coffee as most of the others working in the harvest. For those forming the Contingente, the need for supplemental income that drove them to the harvest in the past was replaced by a sense of duty to defend what they had gained through the revolution by ensuring the success of the harvest. Likewise, those who composed the Brigada XXV Aniversario were not motivated to participate in the harvest because of coercive factors such as university enrollment requirements. Instead, they joined out of an understanding of the harvest's importance for the country.

An additional reason for the reduction in the volunteer labor force was the lessening in the severity of harvest labor shortages that began in 1985. This was a result of the fact that the demand for cotton harvest laborers had diminished in part because the area cultivated with cotton contracted in 1985 and still had not increased by the end of the decade. In addition, an increase in the use of harvesting machines began in 1981/82. By 1983/84, 29 percent of the crop was mechanically harvested, surpassing the historical levels of the late 1960s. Mechanization reached 42 percent of the area harvested in 1985/86 (calculated from unpublished MIDINRA data, 1986). Even as cotton acreage began to level off and then fall, the number of harvesting machines operating in the country was growing. Whereas in 1975/76 there were thirteen active mechanical harvesters in Nicaragua and twenty-one the following year, this figure had grown to two hundred by 1985.[17] Though mechanical harvesters did not completely replace human harvest workers, their importance grew enormously in the post-1979 period.

Although increased mechanization of the cotton harvest helped to alleviate the impact of harvest labor shortages, its widespread adoption was not problem-free. Problems inherent in mechanizing the cotton harvest stemmed primarily from the costs that were incurred. The purchase of harvesting machines required the expenditure of scarce foreign exchange earnings at a time when Nicaragua's foreign exchange balance could only be described as dismal. The dramatic vacillations that the international cotton market underwent in the 1980s and the increased expense entailed in the purchase of harvesting machines stemming from the U.S. trade embargo of Nicaragua were also drawbacks in relying on mechanical harvesters.

The decline in the price of cotton in the international market in the mid-1980s led MIDINRA officials to suggest a shift to producing other crops instead of cotton (*Barricada*, 1986d; interview 205, private producer, July 20, 1987). As planting season approached in 1987, the price of cotton rose once again in the international market, making it more attractive to continue producing cotton. Beyond the serious planning difficulties that these price fluctuations provoked, they also amplified the dangers inherent in increasing Nicaragua's dependence on a mechanized harvest. In the short term, as prices dropped, so did production levels, compounding the already significant falloff in foreign exchange earnings resulting from the lower prices. The employment of mechanical harvesters, to say nothing of their purchase, required the use of imported inputs. Thus permitting cotton's import dependence to increase, when the quantity of foreign exchange earnings generated by the crop was unstable, was an extremely questionable strategy. Much more problematic, however, was the very real possibility that at some point in the near future it might prove more economically efficient to replace cotton with other crops. Further investments of scarce foreign exchange earnings in imported machinery that was suitable only for harvesting cotton, when its production for export could be discontinued, was simply not justifiable.

The importation of cotton harvesting machines was further compounded by the U.S. trade embargo. The United States had previously been Nicaragua's primary source for agricultural machinery and its only source for cotton harvesters. The trade embargo necessitated the search for new markets for both sale of the country's produce and its foreign purchases. But Nicaragua did not have the option of purchasing harvesters in alternative markets because only those made in the United States were appropriate for the conditions under which its cotton was grown. Thus Nicaragua was forced to purchase U.S.-made harvesters through third countries. Although these triangular arrangements helped to resolve the immediate problem of obtaining the machines and their replacement parts, purchase costs were significantly higher because of the intermediaries' charges and increased transportation fees.

Finally, the difficulties inherent in organizing all aspects of the production process when the harvest was mechanized multiplied after the 1983/84 harvest. Maintaining a sufficient supply of the many accessory inputs required in the use of mechanical harvesters became more problematic with each successive year (see *Barricada*, 1986d, 1988e). In conclusion, if cotton continued to be an important export crop, the increased employment of harvesting machines would be desirable over the medium to long run, but its feasibility in the short run remained extremely limited.

A final area in which it had been hypothesized that solutions to the labor shortage might be found was in developing mechanisms to reincorporate those who had previously worked in the harvest. The possibilities in this area ranged from making harvest labor more attractive to traditional pickers, to creating permanent employment on or in the vicinity of export estates, to promoting the collectivization of export agriculture. The following discussion will briefly review the changes that occurred regarding each of these alternatives in the latter part of the 1980s.

Early on in the revolutionary process it became clear that the Rural Workers' Association was unwilling to act as an intermediary between the agricultural labor force and agroexport producers. Instead, the ATC argued that its role in the resolution of this dilemma was to represent rural workers in articulating the wage levels and working conditions that would be required to bring them to the agroexport harvests. That is, the ATC insisted that employment in the harvest had to be made more attractive if traditional pickers were to participate in it once again. In the several years following the 1983/84 harvest, wages did increase for cotton and coffee pickers (see table 5.2). Unfortunately, inflation significantly undercut the effect of the wage hikes.[18]

On the other hand, an important effort was made to guarantee the availability of basic provisions for those who participated in the harvest.[19] Needed supplies included food, clothing, and household items. Moreover, workers were provided with all of their meals while they worked in the harvest. Increasingly, this meant that traditional pickers received priority over those who lived in the area of the export farms in the distribution of scarce goods.[20] At a time when even basic food items were difficult to obtain, the provision of meals and the possibility of purchasing extra quantities of scarce goods proved to be attractive incentives to many.[21]

In addition to the goods that were made available to the pickers through commissaries located in the vicinity of the *finca* (if not on the *finca* itself), country fairs were organized for them. Many basic items that were otherwise inaccessible or could be purchased elsewhere only at exorbitant prices were offered for sale there at government-set prices. Thus the adoption of one of the mechanisms that attracted workers to the harvest in prerevolutionary years, the country fair (or its equivalent, in the form of workers arriving with goods for sale at reasonable prices), served to ensure the participation of workers who might not have come in the previous few years.

While the ATC struggled to convince the government that conditions on agroexport *fincas* had to improve if pickers were to be attracted to the harvest, it also worked to persuade the pickers that their productivity in the harvest had to increase. Reduced productivity among workers who had participated in the harvests in the early 1980s also contributed to the labor shortages. Whereas the workday had historically lasted six to eight hours, it dropped to two and a half hours in the few years following Somoza's overthrow (interviews 227, ATC, May 27, 1988, and 228, MIDINRA, June 6, 1988). After two years of organizing efforts, the ATC succeeded in lengthening the workday to five hours in 1986 and improving the quality and quantity of work accomplished during that time. An incentive system, in which the piece rate was doubled for each additional quota picked after the norm was met, facilitated this process. Thus the ATC helped reduce both absolute and relative labor shortages by gaining more material incentives for harvest workers and implicitly linking these to improvements in labor productivity.

The ATC also directed its organizing efforts toward the *colectivos de trabajo*. The *colectivos*, which first emerged in 1980, were envisioned as an ideal way of providing permanent employment for those who had previously had access only to seasonal employment, increasing the food security of these workers, and ensuring the participation of *colectivo* members in the harvest labor force. By 1987/88 there were two hundred *colectivos* with approximately fifteen thousand workers (interview 227, ATC, May 27, 1988).[22] The *colectivos* were thus successful in extending permanent employment to many who had formerly not had it. They also served to provide these workers with an improved level of food security. But the *colectivos* did not function as intended in guaranteeing the availability of these workers for the agroexport harvests.

Ironically, participation in a *colectivo* provided landless workers with sufficient economic security to permit them to choose not to join the harvest labor force. Two factors combined to cause this situation: in certain areas the bean harvest of the *colectivo* coincided with the coffee harvest, and the workers prioritized their own harvest over that of the agroexport estates; and the *colectivos* had become so successful that they produced enough to market a portion of the crop, further ensuring their economic security. As had occurred with the *campesino* population who had previously participated in the agroexport harvests, when other opportunities for economic survival arose, these workers typically opted for farming their own land instead of working as wage laborers.

Following the 1987/88 harvest (and the several before it), the ATC adopted a new position vis-à-vis the *colectivos de trabajo*. It began to promote the replacement of *colectivos* by *huertos empresariales* (food crop plots located on the export farms). In essence, each large export estate would be required to have a small area dedicated to food crop production. The workers' food self-sufficiency would thereby be guaranteed. Permanent employment possibilities would also increase. And perhaps most important the workers would be employed by the farm for their work both in the *huerto* and in the coffee or cotton harvest. The *huerto* would be run by the farm enterprise as a whole, not only by those who worked in it. Thus those who worked in the *huerto* would not have the independence necessary to opt out of participation in the agroexport sector. Several years would have to pass, however, before it would be clear whether the *huertos* had ensured an adequate supply of both food and labor for the export sector.

Another project carried out under the auspices of the agrarian reform, the Plan Contingente, was also designed to increase food crop production and provide permanent employment to former seasonal workers. The plan relied on an irrigation scheme to make basic grain production possible during the dry season in the cotton-growing region. It was capital- rather than labor-intensive. Nonetheless, it was expected that several thousand workers would obtain employment through the project. By 1985/86, almost twenty-two thousand *manzanas* were planted with corn, sorghum, and beans through the plan (as opposed to 6,795 in 1984/85).[23] This figure declined somewhat in the following agricultural cycle because of difficulties in maintaining the project's relatively sophisticated irrigation equipment. Nevertheless, it represented a significant advance over the first year's acreage and demonstrated the government's seriousness about the need to increase food crop production. Moreover, an estimated five thousand workers had gained permanent employment through the plan by 1987/88 (interview 227, ATC, May 27, 1988). Thus, although the plan did not incorporate enough workers to provide an adequate labor supply for the cotton harvest, it did contribute to the effort by maintaining these workers in the region when they would otherwise have had to find employment elsewhere during the dead time.

The last labor-sharing alternative was that of collectivizing agroexport production. It was argued that the combination of two phenomena that had emerged in cooperatives would ensure the arrival of a sufficient number of pickers to complete the harvest successfully: the sense of landownership implied in cooperative membership and the privileged access cooperatives had to their members' labor time and that of their families. In sum, cooperative members would have an interest in guaranteeing that all of the crop was harvested because (as opposed to workers in either the private or state sectors) their livelihood would depend on it.

The participation of cooperatives in the agroexport sector increased notably in the several years following the 1983/84 harvest. Whereas cooperatives were responsible for 13 percent of agroexport production in the 1984/85 agricultural cycle, they accounted for 21 percent of the production by the end of 1986.[24] Most of the agroexport *fincas* that were turned over to the cooperative sector during this period had previously been within the domain of the state sector.[25]

Several patterns arose that differentiated the labor force in the cooperative sector from that in both the state and private sectors. First, the cooperative sector's harvest labor force was much more locally based than that of either of the other two sectors. In a study of the labor force employed in coffee production in the Matagalpa-Jinotega region, Pablo Aznar (1986:72) found that 98 percent of the pickers working on cooperatives lived within the same municipality in which the cooperatives were located; the figure for those working on state farms was 72 percent and for those on private farms, 85 percent.

Even more striking was the difference between the three sectors in their reliance on relatives of those in the permanent labor force (or, in the case of the cooperative sector, its members) to fulfill their harvest labor needs: approximately 45 percent of those employed by cooperatives were relatives, as opposed to 31.6 percent in the state sector and 29.7 percent in the private sector.[26] Both of these tendencies point to the cooperative sector's greater ability to draw on the available labor force located near the farm. Their members' integration in the local community, in contrast to that of state and private sector farm managers, was in all likelihood the source of their success in this effort. In sum, integration in the community and their members' interest in ensuring an adequate labor force for the cooperatives proved to be decisive factors in the success of their labor recruitment.

Finally, labor recruitment for the agroexport harvests in the cooperative sector was also facilitated by the unwritten labor-sharing agreement that existed between cooperatives in a given area. UNAG promoted these relationships among cooperatives throughout the country, but it placed a special emphasis on mutual assistance between cooperatives in the agroexport regions less affected by the war (interview 225, UNAG, May 23, 1988).[27] In this way, many cooperatives that would otherwise have difficulty fulfilling their labor requirements were able to overcome this potential dilemma.

Although many changes took place in Nicaragua's agroexport sector in the latter half of the 1980s, the implications of these changes did not call into question the accuracy of the prognoses set forth in Chapters 4 and 5. Labor shortages continued to affect coffee and cotton production, and their eventual resolution would depend on a combination of measures. The conceptual significance of one alternative that was implemented on a small but

growing scale, however, remains to be highlighted. The agroexport cooperatives had great potential for contributing to the resolution of harvest labor
shortages. Their contribution also suggested that the relationship between
agrarian reform and agroexport harvest labor shortages could be modified
depending on the type of reform implemented. Where agrarian reform beneficiaries are encouraged to grow crops oriented to their own consumption
needs, this relationship will be overwhelmingly negative. *Campesinos* will
almost always prefer to guarantee the success of their own basic grain crop
rather than that of someone else's export crop. Nonetheless, if the primary
crop grown on land ceded to agrarian reform beneficiaries is oriented toward the export market and its production is encouraged, the agrarian
reform–harvest labor shortage relationship will be weakened, if not eliminated.

In early 1990, most of Nicaragua's agrarian reform beneficiaries still remained outside of the agroexport sector. Thus the thesis developed throughout this study, that the restructuring of agriculture entailed in the implementation of the agrarian reform would undermine the basis of the country's
export agriculture, remained intact. Yet an expansion of the agrarian reform
into the export sector of agriculture might very well have countered this
process and offered a means of both fulfilling the goals of the agrarian
reform and contributing to the success of production in this vital sector of
Nicaragua's economy.

Conclusion: After the 1990 Elections

On February 25, 1990, Nicaraguan voters surprised the world by voting the
FSLN out of office. In what were probably the most closely monitored
elections in the hemisphere's history, the candidate of the National Opposition Union (UNO), Violeta Barrios de Chamorro, was elected to be the
country's next president, beating the FSLN's candidate, Daniel Ortega, with
a 14 percentage point advantage. UNO also won an absolute majority in
Nicaragua's legislative body, the National Assembly, obtaining fifty-one of its
ninety-two seats.[28] Among other issues put in question, the electoral defeat
of the Sandinistas created great uncertainty as to the future of the decade-
old agrarian reform program.

The new ruling alliance, UNO, had been formed in mid-1989 by fourteen
political parties that ranged from Nicaragua's Communist and Socialist par-

ties to parties on the far right of the spectrum. The only common ground these groups shared was their opposition to the FSLN, yet it was also clear that the dominating force within the coalition was the bourgeoisie, which included both the more liberal capitalist sector and the traditional oligarchy. At various stages in the process leading up to the election, it appeared that the alliance would disintegrate. The selection of the presidential and vice-presidential ticket and the drawing up of the alliance's platform were two such moments. Not surprisingly, the platform remained extremely vague because of the tremendous divergences within UNO. Nevertheless, it was apparent that UNO's victory represented the resurgence of a capitalist social project, as opposed to the Sandinista social project, whose guiding logic had been to meet the needs of the majority of Nicaragua's population.

One of the issues that was sure to prove particularly contentious for the UNO government was agrarian reform. During the campaign, the contradictory positions within UNO vis-à-vis the agrarian reform came to the fore, as Chamorro attempted to dispel the concerns of the reform's beneficiary population that if she were to win they would lose their land.[29] Yet some of UNO's strongest backers were large landowners who had lost their property to the agrarian reform. The difficulty of placating the concerns of both of these sectors and the differing positions on the issue within the newly elected alliance became evident in the first statements made by its members following their electoral victory. Whereas Chamorro's economic adviser, Francisco Mayorga, promised the large landowner sector the return of their land (*Barricada*, 1990b), her campaign manager, Antonio Lacayo, took a more moderate position, stating that the gains that had been made by the revolution would be respected (*La Prensa*, 1990b).

UNO leaders had, however, reached a consensus on several key policy measures that they would implement in the agrarian sector. These measures included providing individual land titles to CAS cooperative members (in contrast to the collective title that they had previously held); legalizing the sale of land received through the agrarian reform (until this time agrarian reform beneficiaries had had lifetime use rights but could not sell the land); and privatizing the properties held in the state farm sector (the APP).[30] Nonetheless, the pace with which these changes would take place and their implications remained unclear early in UNO's governing period.

A number of alternative scenarios were possible within the framework suggested by these policy changes. The most optimistic of these included the possibility that the sector of the rural population that remained landless and land-poor in early 1990 would share the benefits to be derived from the subdivision of the state farms with those large landowners who had been affected by the agrarian reform. At the same time, the latter group would be able to ensure employment to the laborers who had previously worked in the state farm sector. Within this scenario there would be no need to take back land from those who had received it from the Sandinista government. Furthermore, with the country's newly achieved peace and economic assistance, agricultural production would begin to increase, as it had in the early 1980s, and thereby contribute to the process of economic recovery.

There were, however, several aspects of this scenario that remained in doubt. It was doubtful that the property held by the state farm sector alone would be sufficient to meet the needs of the estimated twenty-five to sixty thousand peasant families who still needed land[31] and the landowners who might demand compensation in the form of new farms for the properties they had lost. An alternative solution might have been to provide monetary payment to the expropriated landowners in lieu of land, but the limited amount of U.S. funds that were authorized for Nicaragua following the UNO victory eliminated that possibility. It was also doubtful that all of these landowners would be satisfied with receiving land other than that which they had lost to the agrarian reform.[32] And it was extremely unlikely that if state farm land was divided between these two groups, employment possibilities for former APP workers would remain the same.

A more likely scenario would entail transformation of the Nicaraguan agrarian reform into a program whose results were similar to reforms implemented in nonrevolutionary contexts (see de Janvry, 1981). That is, with the newly gained right to sell their land, agrarian reform beneficiaries would increasingly do so when confronted with the economic hardships that were bound to prevail for some time to come. Moreover, the generalized economic crisis that had affected all of Nicaragua's population during the latter half of the 1980s was sure to be compounded for certain sectors following the implementation of UNO's economic program. That program promised tougher agricultural credit policies, with the implication that farmers who were unable to pay back their debt (typically the smaller producers and cooperatives) would be forced to sell their land to those who had the means to purchase it (the agricultural bourgeoisie). As one representative of the largeholder sector summed up the situation, there was no need to resort to the politically explosive measure of taking land away from those who had received it through the reform because, in all likelihood, former landowners would be able to purchase back their land over the next few years from the economically strapped beneficiaries (interview conducted by Rose J. Spalding with a member of COSEP [Consejo Superior de la Empresa Privada], March 7, 1990). Thus the pre-1979 status quo of significant disparity in the distribution of agricultural land could be restored within half a decade.

Ultimately, the future of the agrarian reform would be determined by an interplay between Nicaragua's key sociopolitical forces. Those forces consisted of UNO, the FSLN, and the *desmovilizados* (the former Contra forces). Because the UNO coalition was politically diverse and a number of its leaders had personal ambitions, the alliance was tenuous. The potential for instability within UNO consequently made it difficult to predict the policy orientation that would finally prevail toward the agrarian sector.

At the same time, although the FSLN lost control over the executive branch of government and did not have a majority in the National Assembly, it remained the largest and best-organized party in Nicaragua. Its strength extended beyond party membership (and a cohesive voting bloc in the new assembly) to include the mass organizations that had been developed during the FSLN's tenure in power. Those organizations represented most of the organized work force and small- and medium-sized agricultural producers. The FSLN's strength would limit UNO's freedom of movement in policy making because it would have to avoid direct confrontation with this important force. The Sandinistas have stated their intention to defend the changes brought about during ten years of revolutionary change (*Barricada*, 1990a). If the peaceful process of seeking negotiated settlements to political differences that developed during the electoral process continued, the interplay between these two forces could buffer the tendency of UNO's open market/privatization approach to bring about the complete reversal of the agrarian reform.

There was, however, another actor in the Nicaraguan drama, the newly demobilized Contra forces. Although the Contras were formally disbanded as an army in June 1990, it was common knowledge that they remained a military and political force to be reckoned with even after that time. The *desmovilizados'* desire for a complete dismantling of Sandinismo logarithmically heightened the potential for violent resolution of the differences between UNO and the FSLN. They perceived the agrarian reform to be one of the key vestiges of the Sandinista era, thus suggesting that they would push for its rollback. Moreover, by mid-1990 the existence of strong links between the more extremist sectors in UNO and the *desmovilizados* was accepted by most as a reality. The consolidation of this alliance, and the implicit, if not explicit, support it received from the U.S. administration, pointed to the very real danger of a civil war breaking out.

In conclusion, the agrarian reform was a key issue in the extremely delicate process of transition that was set in motion on February 25, 1990, just as it was perhaps the most important program implemented by the revolutionary government. The status of the agrarian reform after UNO's tenure in the government would suggest the extent to which it is possible to push forward social change, designed to ensure a more just distribution of a country's resources, in the context of a regime that did not have as its objective breaking with dependent development.

Appendix

Some Methodological Notes

Several methodological issues have particular relevance for the case study presented in this book. The first is the definition and subsequent quantification of the various classes that composed the rural social structure. These provide the underpinning for the description of Nicaraguan agriculture presented in Chapters 1 to 3. Second, within this delineation of the rural social structure, further specification of the categories peasant, semiproletariat, and proletariat sets the stage for presentation of the issue of *campesinización* (see Chapters 3 to 4). A number of competing definitions of the rural class structure were developed during the past ten years. The following discussion will describe their relative strengths and weaknesses.

The traditional measure used to define the rural class structure has been access to land. (The class categories described in Chapter 1 were established using this key criterion.) Yet this model has several important limitations, including the arbitrariness of the standard size specifications mentioned in the text. That is, other factors such as crop, region, and soil fertility should also be taken into account. For example, in the Matagalpa-Jinotega region (where land has been relatively abundant and larger farms more common) it may be reasonable to consider a medium-sized capitalist producer as one having more than fifty *manzanas* planted to coffee. In Carazo, however, it probably makes sense to lower the minimum size in this category to fifteen or twenty *manzanas* because land is much scarcer and ground rent is greater there (see, e.g., Gariazzo, 1984). Likewise, a producer who owns one hundred *manzanas* of prime coffee land has a more sizable enterprise than one with one hundred *manzanas* of undeveloped pasture land.

What is important here is the complexity of developing a system for categorizing the rural population. Recent studies have only begun this difficult task, but each proposed system has some limitations. For example, *Pensamiento Propio* (1983:27) set forth a model of Nicaragua's class structure (both urban and rural) for 1980 that takes into account the importance of differences among crops when setting size specifications. This model is limited, however, because it does not consider differences between regions and existing information such as pre-1979 census data describing crop production and acreage and land tenure patterns cannot be fit into its categories.

A more recent effort to modify the standard categories of the class structure for rural Nicaragua is presented in Zalkin (1988). This model adds another key factor to the definition of each size category, namely, the "social relations of production" (or a person's relation to the wage labor market and the means of production). Zalkin measures this factor by taking into account the number of days informants sold their labor or employed someone else. Yet the model does not provide categories for all of the rural EAP (e.g., the medium- and large-sized capitalist producers were excluded), it does not specify by crop or region, and it does not allow for a comparison of available data on crop production and acreage to social class category.

In conclusion, all of the existing models of the rural class structure have important limitations. Given the nature of the limitations characterizing the various alternative conceptions, and in the interest of making some general statements about Nicaraguan agriculture, I have opted to use the commonly accepted size specifications delineated in Chapter 1 to define the overall rural class structure.

A second, more specific issue related to the characterization of Nicaragua's rural class structure is the need for a further refinement of the categories "peasants" and "proletariat." As was discussed at length in Chapters 1 to 3, it is clear that most of Nicaragua's rural population does not fit neatly into either the peasant or the proletariat category. Rather, most fall on a continuum between the two. This issue is important because it influences, to a considerable extent, policy making in the agrarian sector. In other words, how government policy makers define the vast majority of the rural population (as peasant, worker, or some combination of the two) affects their conceptions of how policies should be oriented to achieve desired outcomes.

The labor shortage issue gets at the essence of this definitional dilemma. On one hand, if the rural population is conceived of as being largely semi-proletarian in nature and the harvest labor force is seen as its primary (and, in most cases, only) point of entry into the wage labor force, policies that improve its status as *campesinos* (such as land redistribution and the provision of agricultural credit) should reduce its participation in the labor force. On the other hand, if it is seen as being largely proletarian in nature, pro-peasant policies should not affect the size of the harvest labor force. Rather, wage policies and other "worker" issues should be the key variables affecting participation in the harvest labor force. (Kaimowitz [1986] discusses this definitional dilemma at great length. He concludes that the latter position is largely correct, relying on a study reported upon by Havens and Baumeister [1982] to reach his conclusions.)

In 1981 and 1982, studies describing the cotton and coffee harvest labor force were completed that reached strikingly different conclusions as to its nature. The first (CIERA, 1981), which provides the more quantitative evidence for this case study, was conducted by literacy workers during the literacy campaign in early 1980. A total of 51,400 rural dwellers were included in this survey. It was not a study of harvest workers per se, but rather was addressed to the rural population in general. But it did include extensive information about those members of the rural population who had participated in the cotton and coffee harvests before and after 1979. That is, it also included the population who had dropped out of the harvest labor force after 1979, thus avoiding a critical weakness of subsequent surveys of the harvest labor force. Later studies included only the population of workers still participating in the harvest, thus providing only limited information about why others dropped out of this labor force.

One of these later studies, which was conducted by CIERA during the 1980/81 cotton and coffee harvests, focused specifically on the harvest workers. It found (in contrast to the data described in Chapter 3 for the first study) that 45 percent of coffee and 55 percent of cotton harvest workers had no access to land at that time and had not in the past (see Havens and Baumeister, 1982:47–72). In an analysis of the survey data, Havens and Baumeister argue that the harvest labor force is not composed primarily of semiproletarians: rather, that group composed only 17 percent of coffee harvest workers and 12 percent of cotton harvest workers. An additional 16 percent of the coffee harvest labor force is composed of "peasants" and "middle peasants," thus bringing the overall percentage of *campesinos* participating in the harvest to 33 percent (ibid.). Likewise, peasants and middle peasants composed an additional 10 percent of the cotton harvest labor force, thus increasing the overall percentage of *campesino* participation to 22 percent.

Instead, Havens and Baumeister assert, fully proletarianized workers formed the better part of this labor force: 50 percent in coffee and 58 percent in cotton. This conclusion was reached by defining the household as semiproletarianized or fully proletarianized according to how household labor was distributed, instead of access to land, the traditional measure for rural class relations and the one used in the earlier CIERA study (also the one used herein). Accordingly, a proletarian household was one in which "at least 12 person months [per household] were spent working in the agroexport sector." In contrast, a semiproletarian household was one in which "family labor was distributed to the land and to wage labor but less than twelve months a year to both." This alternative measurement system adds a critical new element to the definition of rural classes—the distribution of household labor. Yet it also suffers from limitations in its descriptive capacity. For example, if four members of a household (all of whom are above ten years of age, as prescribed by their study) participated in an agroexport harvest for three months in a given year, the household is considered proletarian. Yet the family may have worked the entire remainder of the year on its own farm. Clearly, a combination of the variables "access to land" and "participation in the wage labor force" is required to achieve a more accurate understanding of the rural population. Moreover, this study did not reach the population of rural dwellers who had participated in the past but had opted out of this work force by the time of the survey's implementation, which particularly limits its usefulness in providing information about why these people no longer sell their labor in the harvests.

Finally, in order to refine the definitions of peasants and workers, Zalkin (1988) returned to the first CIERA (1981) study and reclassified the data further, specifying the variables "access to land" and "participation in the wage labor market" (both the buying and selling of labor). This reclassification of the data did not lead to a substantial shift in the distribution of the informant population from the category of peasant to that of proletariat (Zalkin, 1988:9). (The largest shift that occurred was between the poor peasant and middle peasant categories.) A follow-up analysis of the data remains to be completed that uses Zalkin's new categories to describe the nature of the harvest labor force.

These weaknesses in existing definitions and data point to the clear need to continue efforts further to refine the model of the rural class structure. The issues raised here are only a few examples of the methodological dilemmas one encounters in conducting research in Nicaragua today. The base of information that is required to conduct systematic research on that country is only beginning to solidify. In the meantime, thoughtful research requires a combination of methodologies so that weaknesses in the body of existing statistical information do not undermine efforts to expand our understanding of the processes of change under way in contemporary Nicaragua.

Notes

Chapter 1

1. The term *cheap labor* is used here to refer to several facets of the labor system in these small agroexport economies. First, and most important, the organization of work is such that capital is responsible for the reproduction of the labor force (through wages) for only three to four months of the year. Second, even within this three- to four-month period, capital provides for only the absolute minimum in reproduction costs because of the lack of legislation concerning wages and working conditions for rural workers (or where it does exist, it is not enforced). In addition, the use of a piece rate to determine most agricultural wages reinforces the exploitativeness of this system by forcing laborers to work at an accelerated speed to earn minimal subsistence wages. (This is not to say that a piece rate itself implies exploitation. Rather it is the context of capitalist production relations that determines that piece rates be used to speed up the production process.)

These conditions are extraordinary in comparison with labor systems found in the advanced capitalist countries, where capital is most frequently responsible for the year-round maintenance of the wage labor force. The labor force in these countries usually has no, or very restricted, access to the means of production. Therefore, it is entirely dependent on wages for its reproduction. In addition, labor legislation prescribes wages, working conditions, and so on. This legislation is commonly a product of labor unrest; the state has stepped in to mediate between capital and labor and redefined the rules so that capitalist production can continue. The response of the state in Third World countries is most frequently to repress labor unrest, thereby requiring workers to accept their marginalized condition (see Casanova, 1985).

One final difference between capitalist production in the most industrialized countries and that in the Third World is the source of profit. In the former countries, the industrial revolution began a process of increasing capital's reliance on relative surplus value to raise profit levels. In the Third World, where the level of technology is much less developed, larger profits come primarily from increasing the production of absolute surplus value. Torres Rivas (1983:16) summarizes capitalist production in Central America saying, "This is the paradise of absolute surplus value."

2. Evans (1979) describes this relative advantage in primary goods production for Latin America as a whole. FitzGerald (1986) suggests some of the implications for peripheral countries in transition to socialism.

3. Torres Rivas (1980b) provides a detailed analysis of the development of dependent capitalism in Central America. See also Wheelock (1980) and Biderman (1982) for descriptions of this process in Nicaragua.

4. FitzGerald (1984a) uses these elements to describe the peripheral socialist economy (PSE). He argues that these structural elements, the first two of which were inherited from the previous regime, constrain the process of constructing socialism.

The final element describes the state structure in the PSE. The state is less than fully consolidated because, to some extent, the overthrow of the previous government eliminated the existing structure. A new state must be formed that reflects the change in overall orientation. Yet "the legacy of the past continues to condition the politics of the present in profound ways" (Fagen, 1986:250).

The prerevolutionary state played an important role in the development of dependent capitalism in Nicaragua. The process of revolutionary transformation required that the state represent interests distinct from those of its predecessor. To understand the dilemmas raised by the lack of consolidation of the state in the PSE, it is important to grasp the nature of the prerevolutionary state. Thus, the following discussion outlines the latter, in addition to sketching the other structural legacies confronted by Nicaragua's revolution: the incompleteness of the economy and the continued existence of a large peasant sector.

5. The local bourgeoisie undeniably played an important role in the development of capitalism in Nicaragua. Yet external factors consistently triggered any dramatic growth in the economy. See Williams (1986) and Biderman (1982).

6. The system created by the CACM was also dependent on external markets. See, for example, Weeks (1985a).

7. Thomas (1974) also provides an informative discussion of the relationship between a nation's size and underdevelopment.

The CACM represented an effort to overcome the limitations caused by the small size of each of the Central American republics. Its logic was to combine, and thereby expand, the markets and resources of each country, but its success was short-lived because it quickly encountered major economic and political obstacles. See further Torres Rivas (1980a).

8. See Evans (1979:28) and de Janvry (1981) with regard to this problem defining all of Latin America. FitzGerald (1986) argues that for socialism to develop in the periphery of the world capitalist system, the position these countries occupy in the international division of labor must change or labor will continue to be subject to exceptionally low wages.

9. This is the case for almost all peripheral countries. See Fagen et al. (1986:12–13).

10. Discussion of these factors is beyond the scope of this study. For a discussion of the vicissitudes of international commodity pricing see the special issue of *World*

Development (vol. 15, no. 5, May 1987) entitled "Primary Commodities in the World Economy: Problems and Policies."

11. FitzGerald (1984a:30) argues that a nation's "insertion into the international division of labor is a (or perhaps the) crucial determinant of the model of growth and distribution." This is also true of countries that have a more developed industrial base. Both Brazil and Mexico have capital goods sectors, yet both clearly represent cases of dependent capitalist development (see Evans, 1979; and Gereffi and Evans, 1981).

12. In Central America, only Costa Rica remained untouched by deteriorating terms of trade between 1980 and 1985 (CEPAL, 1986a:20). In 1986 this trend was reversed for Honduras, Guatemala, and El Salvador, but for Nicaragua the terms of trade continued to deteriorate. CEPAL (1987b:38; and 1989:34) describes the drop in the purchasing power of Nicaragua's exports between 1980 and 1988.

13. It may be argued that 1977 should not be used as a base year when analyzing terms of trade in Central America because prices for the region's exports reached a peak that year (Weeks, 1985a:180). The general trend in the purchasing power of Nicaragua's exports since 1980 has been one of steady decline even when using a significantly lower base year, 1970 (see CEPAL, 1986b:24).

14. See CEPAL (1987b:44). Torres Rivas (1982a) provides a comprehensive discussion of the numerous aspects of the economic crisis. For more recent data see CEPAL (1987a and 1989:38).

In addition to these general factors, Nicaragua's foreign exchange crisis has been affected by production losses experienced during the war against Somoza and against the Nicaraguan counterrevolutionaries, the economic blockade launched by the United States against Nicaragua in 1981, lack of cooperation from the private sector resulting in reduced production, and errors in the economic planning process of the new government. For further information on Nicaragua's foreign exchange crisis see Stahler-Sholk (1987); FitzGerald (1987); Weeks (1987); and Pizarro (1987).

15. Repayment of the foreign debt has become an increasingly critical issue for all of Latin America and has the potential for creating a political alliance between debtor countries that questions the economic order that led to the contemporary debt crisis. For key Latin American positions on the debt crisis see Castro (1985) and García (1985).

16. The delineation of Nicaragua's rural class structure described in this chapter must be understood as an "ideal type" that captures the essence of social relations in the countryside. The reality of life in the *campo* is much more complex and varied and will be discussed in greater detail in the following chapters. See the Appendix for some caveats that should be noted vis-à-vis this description.

17. The percentages given in the text are from a study completed by MIDINRA in 1983, as cited in Deere et al. (1985:78). An earlier analysis (MIDINRA, n.d.:Table 5)

of the agricultural EAP in 1980 produced slightly different results. According to this second study, the Nicaraguan rural class structure was composed as follows: large bourgeoisie, 0.7 percent; medium bourgeoisie, 4.4 percent; medium and rich peasants, 27.5 percent; poor peasants and semiproletariat, 36.5 percent; permanent agricultural workers, 13.5 percent; and seasonal agricultural workers, 17.4 percent.

18. In contrast to the rest of Central America, the medium-sized bourgeoisie in Nicaragua is more important in export crop production than the large bourgeoisie. For example, whereas 60 percent of Nicaragua's cotton was produced on medium-sized farms, as opposed to 31 percent on large farms in the early 1960s, 52 percent of El Salvador's cotton production occurred on large farms and 28 percent on medium-sized farms (calculated from CEPAL et al., 1980:159, 162). Data cited in a later study on Nicaraguan agriculture (Baumeister, 1985:17) indicate that by 1971 the importance of medium-sized cotton producers had declined and large-scale production had increased: 52 percent of cotton production was carried out by the medium-sized sector and 42 percent by large producers.

19. See de Janvry (1981) for a summary of the debates concerning the appropriate definition of the peasantry in underdeveloped countries. De Janvry (1981:102) himself argues that the peasantry forms "a transitory fraction of a class within capitalism," as opposed to the key actor in a separate mode of production.

20. The development of this specialization in Nicaraguan agriculture was not as complete as elsewhere in Central America (see Baumeister, 1985). De Janvry (1981) describes the process of specialization for Latin America as a whole. See also Dorner and Quiros (1973), who analyze this problem focusing specifically on Central America.

21. Spalding (1987) provides a rich description of the development of the Nicaraguan agricultural bourgeoisie as a class. See Winson (1978) for further discussion of the class structure that developed with agrarian capitalism throughout Central America.

22. The one exception to this pattern of stagnating food crop production was rice cultivation. While corn and especially bean production became more and more marginalized, rice was adopted for large-scale capitalist production (see Biderman, 1982; Baumeister, 1985; and Dorner and Quiros, 1973). Once again the state assisted this process, providing loans for infrastructure and other improvements. Large-scale rice production quickly became heavily capital-intensive, with irrigated cultivation the norm for large capitalist producers. Although some peasant producers continued to cultivate rice, their production became increasingly marginalized. This pattern was more extreme in the other Central American countries than in Nicaragua (Baumeister, 1984).

23. I recognize that there has been debate concerning the use of this term, although those writing about Latin American agriculture generally agree that an important relationship exists between peasant agriculture and agroexport production.

For that reason, and for the sake of brevity, I will only discuss the generally agreed-upon aspects of the concept. Furthermore, the relationship described herein must be seen as a model. Nicaraguan reality only approximates the model and does so much less closely than, for example, Guatemala (Schmid, 1967).

24. Production for a product's use value is production of a product for use rather than sale. Production for a product's exchange value means the opposite.

The term *wage labor* refers to labor performed by workers who are paid wages for their services rather than being obligated in some way to a member of the landed classes (e.g., a tribute, as was the case for the indigenous population during the colonial era).

25. The development of state structures in Latin America following independence varied in different regions. The process of nation-state formation in Central America was slow in comparison to the rest of Latin America. It reflected the delayed development of agroexport capitalism. See Torres Rivas (1980b) and Torres Rivas and Pinto (1983).

26. Speaking of Latin America as a whole, Roxborough (1979:107) argues that "which form of state occurred was to a great degree a function of the degree of integration of the landowning class."

27. The term *marginalization* is used here to refer to the increasingly limited access to a variety of resources, but most especially to productive resources (fertile land, credit, inputs, infrastructure) that characterized the situation of the peasantry as a consequence of the expansion of agrarian capitalism.

28. The term *relations of production* refers to the Marxian concept of the social relationships that compose a society. Within the Marxist tradition, human society is considered to be "fundamentally a society of production, a set of 'social relations' that men enter in the activity of producing" (Tucker, 1970:12). Capitalist relations of production, for example, are those which characterize people's social relations in a capitalist society. More specifically, within capitalism, society is divided between those who produce but do not own the means of production (e.g., land, oxen, factories), and those who own or control the means of production and appropriate the surplus produced by the former group. The former group is composed of the workers or proletariat and the latter of capitalists.

29. According to Spalding (1987), the relationship between the Somocista state and agroexport elites was not always harmonious. Somoza favored certain agroexport capitalists over others. Moreover, toward the end of Somoza's tenure in power the level of intrabourgeois conflict regarding Somoza's representation of its class interests reached a critical level. Nonetheless, these nuances in state–private sector relations did not contradict the general model described herein.

30. Throughout the Third World, states have had much less autonomy than in more developed countries because they have had to "respond to specific exchange conditions with both the world economy and the peasant sector, through the external and

internal terms of trade" (FitzGerald, 1984a:30). See also Hamilton (1982) with regard to the issue of state autonomy in the periphery.

See Offe (1974; 1975) and Poulantzas (1978) for a discussion of the "relative autonomy" of the state in the context of the more industrialized nations.

31. One consequence of the lack of state autonomy has been the weakening of the state in a number of Latin American countries in the past decade in part because of the deepening economic crisis. In Central America, regimes hitherto relatively stable have been seriously weakened by the economic crisis affecting the whole region (Torres Rivas, 1982a). Although each of these regimes contains its own internal contradictions that threaten the status quo, the regional economic crisis has greatly exacerbated existing social tensions. The very ability of the Central American regimes to overcome this "final crisis of the agroexport model" has been called into question (Torres Rivas, 1982a). Yet the social conditions inherent in the agroexport model form the critical factor in this equation of social change.

32. Once Central America was found to be mineral-poor in comparison with Mexico and Peru, land became the key to wealth. By the early 1960s land concentration in the region was such that "subfamily units represent[ed] 78 percent of all farms and account[ed] for 60 percent of the rural labor force, [while] they occup[ied] only 11 percent of the farmland. At the other extreme, 6 percent of all farms [were] multifamily units. They control[led] 72 percent of the farmland but employ[ed] only 28 percent of the rural labor force" (Dorner and Quiros, 1973:218).

33. In the early 1960s, the large landowners, who made up 1 percent of the rural population, earned an estimated 81 percent of the income. At the other extreme, those who had very little land or were landless (and made up 66 percent of the rural population) earned an estimated 5 percent of the income. Income distribution figures were calculated from CEPAL et al. (1980:72), which also discusses the relationship between the agrarian structure and income distribution in Nicaragua and the rest of Central America. This relationship still held true in the mid-1970s and described Central America as a whole (see SIECA, 1975a).

34. Data describing the poverty of the Nicaraguan poor will be presented in Chapter 2. Nicaragua did not differ dramatically from the rest of Latin America in this regard. INIES/CRIES (1983a:21) quotes the United Nations Economic Commission for Latin America as stating that "62 percent of the region's people live in poverty (lacking the minimum basic necessities) or in absolute poverty" (see also Altimir, 1979). Another UN study (CEPAL, 1979a:85) states that 40 percent of the population of Latin America lived in absolute poverty in 1970. It appears that the measures for poverty employed in the latter study were significantly more narrowly defined. Nonetheless, the level of poverty is alarming even if one relies on the lower of the two figures.

35. Nicaragua's rural class differentiation was less extreme than that of El Salvador or Guatemala (see Baumeister, 1984) because of the importance of the medium-sized

bourgeoisie in the former. Furthermore, the capitalist class in Nicaragua was less integrated than those of El Salvador and Guatemala. Whereas Nicaragua's medium-sized bourgeoisie was more involved and carried greater weight than the large bourgeoisie in direct production, the latter concentrated its control in processing and commercialization. Nonetheless, the medium and large bourgeoisie together represented only 5 percent of the rural EAP. Thus, even with these caveats, it is clear that the bourgeoisie (both medium and large) composed the elite sector of rural society and, indeed, of Nicaraguan society as a whole.

36. The program promoted by the Instituto de Bienestar Campesino (INVIERNO), in particular, was supposed to reduce growing unrest in rural Nicaragua. Somoza's two agrarian reform programs will be discussed at greater length in Chapter 2.

37. An illuminating example is that the military component of the Alliance for Progress aid, which flowed into the region during the 1960s, exceeded the economic development component (LaFeber, 1983). The same has proved true for U.S. aid to Central America since 1980, when the United States once again realized that social unrest threatened its interests in the region (see Fagen, 1987:147–50).

38. See Vilas (1986) for an informative discussion of the interplay of factors that led to Somoza's overthrow and the initiation of the revolutionary process in Nicaragua.

39. For further discussion of this "logic of the majority," see Gorostiaga (1983) and Fagen et al. (1986).

40. Reinhardt (1987) argues that reliance on certain key export crops severely limited the course of the Nicaraguan agrarian reform during the 1979–84 period.

41. Cuba was confronted by this dilemma during the 1960s and early 1970s as new sources of employment became available to rural laborers who had previously been drawn to work in the sugarcane harvest. See Pollitt (1982) and Eckstein (1981).

Chapter 2

1. The debates about the nature of capitalism in Latin America, beginning with the colonial period and extending through the present, are described in the issue of *Latin American Perspectives* entitled "Dependency and Marxism" (issues 30 and 31, vol. 8, [Summer and Fall, 1981]).

2. See Radell (1969) for further discussion of Nicaragua's shipbuilding and lumber industries.

3. Ayón (1977) provides a detailed description of the development of both the *encomienda* and the *repartimiento*, beginning with the land distribution carried out by Christopher Columbus in 1499.

4. Squier (1972) and Levy (1976) described the relative scarcity of labor and its effect on the development of agriculture in their classic writings on Nicaragua.

5. Wheelock (1980:60) notes that the use of cacao as money until the end of the nineteenth century indicates the underdevelopment that characterized rural Nicaragua.

6. Although Radell (1969) argues that relatively little labor was needed in cacao cultivation, MacLeod (1973:71–72) asserts that large numbers of workers, including semiskilled laborers, were required. The fact that labor shortages contributed to the decline of cacao production in Nicaragua and elsewhere (see Browning [1971] with respect to this phenomenon in El Salvador) seems to support the latter's position.

7. The merchant class in Guatemala City had managed to use Spain's regulations to its advantage, at the expense of those from the rest of the Central American region. Thus it was particularly the rural landed classes who opposed Spain's extensive regulations—especially the indigo and cattle producers (see, e.g., Romero Vargas [1988]).

8. For a complete account of the troubled years following independence in Central America see Torres Rivas (1980b).

9. Weber (1981:3) described these civil wars as being like "wars between clans of rival nobles."

10. For informative descriptions of the William Walker affair see Scroggs (1969) and Rosengarten (1976).

11. The regions in which the cattle *hacienda* predominated were Chontales, León, and Chinandega (Granada had been included in this list during certain periods of the colonial era).

12. See Lanuza (1976) and Romero Vargas (1988) for further discussion of the *ejidos* and other communal landholdings.

13. According to Haarer (1969:27), coffee was introduced to several of the Central American republics in the mid- to late 1700s. Nicaragua adopted its cultivation somewhat later.

14. In 1885 El Salvador produced 17.1 million pounds of coffee; Guatemala, 39.3 million pounds; and Costa Rica, 24.5 million pounds (FAO, *The World's Coffee*, 1947, cited in Torres Rivas, 1980b:Statistical Appendix). In contrast, Nicaragua produced only 9.2 million pounds that same year.

15. Lanuza (1976) describes the series of laws that were passed beginning in 1841 to guarantee land and labor for the *latifundistas*. The legislation enacted by the Zelaya regime was almost identical to that decreed half a century earlier. The difference was that Zelaya had the strength to guarantee its implementation.

16. See República de Nicaragua (1943:37–38). This pattern was to change again following World War II. Even before the U.S. embargo on trade with Nicaragua was enacted in 1985, Western Europe had once again become Nicaragua's most important market for coffee, purchasing over half of its crop (*Barricada*, 1983d:3).

17. Torres Rivas (1980b:62) argues that Central American coffee production never

fully recovered from this first bust, which affected the rest of the region even earlier than it affected Nicaragua.

18. Wheelock (1980) describes at length the chicanery used to compound the indebtedness of the peasantry, thereby ensuring their participation in the harvest labor force. For example, because of the isolation characterizing these rural areas, peasant families often had no alternative to the plantation commissary for the purchase of supplies. Prices were high in the commissary, and these families often built up a sizable debt to the landowner. Their only recourse was to work in the harvest to pay off their debt.

19. Biderman (1982:55–56) suggests that even describing this process as the development of capitalism may be an exaggeration. Rather, it may have been the continuation of primitive accumulation. This suggestion is based on the fact that many of the mechanisms relied upon for surplus extraction in this period were precapitalist in nature. Numerous characteristics of coffee plantation production were holdovers from the cattle *hacienda*. In fact, it was (and still is) common for coffee production to be combined with cattle raising.

20. In a study conducted for the U.S. State Department in 1928, Cumberland (1980:21) argues that one of the primary difficulties coffee producers encountered in expanding their production was that the "native population" was still too tied to its land and insisted on returning to it for a part of each year. Yet it was precisely those small plots of land that allowed for the survival of the *campesino* population. The *latifundio/minifundio* relationship was a central part of coffee production.

21. Cumberland (1980:33) says that continuous political turmoil in the two decades following Zelaya's overthrow was "distracting [to] those who should be business leaders." But he does not distinguish between the different sectors engaged in these political struggles and makes no suggestion of the U.S. role in Nicaragua's economic stagnation.

22. This partial list of the components of Sandino's platform is taken from a compilation of Sandino's writings (Fonseca, 1981:10–12). See also Macaulay (1971), Selser (1979), and Ramírez (1981).

23. Gold was an important export commodity for Nicaragua at this time; between 1935 and 1943, coffee, gold, and bananas constituted the crux of the export economy. During five of these nine years, gold was the most important of Nicaragua's export products (República de Nicaragua, 1935–43). Furthermore, the mining industry was essentially a foreign concern. Gold mining in this region was largely Canadian- and U.S.-owned.

24. Somoza's early years in power were characterized by what Weber (1981) termed his "primitive accumulation of capital."

25. The term *social division of labor* refers to the division of society into two separate populations. In this case, Nicaraguan society was increasingly divided into those who

owned the means of production and those who did not and as a consequence were forced to work for the first group.

26. The area planted with cotton rose from 23,945 *manzanas* in 1950/51, to 66,767 *manzanas* in 1951/52, to 123,616 *manzanas* in 1954/55 (CONAL, 1973:Table I-1).

27. Its yield increases were also phenomenal: Nicaragua was 35 percent above world yield in 1951/52 and 236 percent in 1966/67 (Belli, 1968:59).

28. The exchange rate in the 1950s was (U.S.) $1 = C$7 (Nicaraguan).

29. In contrast with several other studies of Nicaragua's cotton production (e.g., Williams, 1986; and Biderman, 1982), my analysis of various CONAL studies does not substantiate the argument that the percentages represented by insecticides and fertilizers in cotton's production costs grew significantly in the 1960s: in 1962/63 fertilizers and insecticides and their application amounted to 34.5 percent of production costs; in 1964/65, 38.4 percent; in 1966/67, 38 percent; in 1968/69, 40.5 percent; but by 1973/74 this figure had dropped to 33.6 percent. For information on insecticide and fertilizer use in cotton production see CONAL (1973:Tables IV-29, IV-30, IV-31; and 1975:69).

30. Much of the cotton cultivation took place on rented land. When the world market price for cotton was good, the large producers rented more land. Because cotton is an annual plant, cotton producers could move in and out of the market on a yearly basis. Large landowners controlled the crops their land was used for by varying rental fees and implementing cash rentals, which excluded the peasant sector from access.

31. Calculated from Ministerio de Economía (1966:Table 31). The agricultural census of 1963 provides a wealth of information about agricultural production in the early 1960s. Although a similar census was conducted in 1953, the raw data from it are not available. Some of the data from this earlier census, however, can be found in two studies of it (Blandón, 1962; Porras Mendieta, 1962). Likewise, an agricultural census that was conducted in 1971 was never published in its entirety, but Warnken (1975) provides some of the data from this later census.

32. Jarquín (1975) and Programa Centroamericano de Ciencias Sociales (1978) provide detailed analyses of migration patterns as they relate to changes in Nicaragua's agrarian structure.

33. See Jarquín (1975:121–23) for a discussion of the regional specificity of this process of proletarianization.

34. Even though the lengthy maturation process of coffee trees implies that a considerable investment must be made over a several-year period, and consequently within the coffee-growing regions one would expect that the municipalities where most of the coffee was grown might have a higher percentage of legal ownership of farms than the region as a whole, this was not the case. For example, in the department of Jinotega, 87 percent of the coffee was grown in the municipality of Jinotega

in 1963 (calculated from Ministerio de Economía, 1966:Tables 12 and 3). Yet only 40 percent of the farms in that municipality had legal land titles. And in the department of Matagalpa, the municipalities of Matagalpa and Matiguas together produced 66 percent of the department's coffee, yet only 27 percent of the farms in those two municipalities had legal land titles (ibid.).

35. The Nicaraguan cattle herd grew from 1.3 million head in 1963 to 1.8 million head in 1971 (Ministerio de Economía, 1971:Table 4). Beef exports expanded from 5.7 million pounds in 1963 to 11.3 million pounds in 1971 (República de Nicaragua, 1963, 1971).

36. For more extensive analyses of this cattle-raising expansion/*campesino* displacement dynamic see Williams (1986) and FIDA (1980). FIDA (1980:21) also describes the expansion of the agricultural frontier: the colonization process of the last twenty years resulted in the agricultural frontier "covering 31 percent of Nicaragua's surface area and accounting for 20 percent of its agricultural population."

37. Williams (1986) describes this process in an analysis of the transformation of agricultural production in the municipality of Matiguas (in the Department of Matagalpa) in north-central Nicaragua. By the early 1960s Matiguas had become the most important corn-producing and the second most important bean-producing municipality in the country. By 1976, however, cattle *latifundios* had displaced most of the corn and bean producers in Matiguas, sending them further east into the agricultural frontier.

38. See Consejo Nacional de Economía (1965:Table 17). The first five years (1950–55) of the cotton boom saw an even more dramatic average growth rate: 8.4 percent annually.

39. The following discussion will be limited to the issues most relevant to this study. One further problem that emerged with CACM industrialization, however, was that the new industrial sector was characterized by a high concentration of productive resources, also a key problem in Central American agriculture (see Weeks, 1985a; and Williams, 1986).

40. This figure does not include the import content for petroleum refining. See Weeks (1985a:137).

41. Only 40 percent of Nicaragua's total volume of exports of manufactured goods was sent to CACM countries in 1970 (calculated from SIECA, 1981:Tables 141 and 206).

42. Baumeister (1982:16) noted that "with an agricultural area, at the end of the Somoza era, of approximately 6–7 million manzanas, the heart of export agriculture only absorbed approximately 500,000 manzanas (130,000 for coffee, 60,000 for sugar cane, and 250,000 for cotton, etc.) . . . [that is,] . . . less than 10 percent of the farmland, yet given its labor intensive character (fundamentally seasonal labor), it controlled approximately 54 percent of the rural labor force." Baumeister's noninclu-

sion of cattle-grazing land in these calculations of acreage dedicated to export agriculture land probably accounts for the discrepancy between these two sources of data.

43. According to Porras Mendieta (1962:105, 111), 58 percent of the acreage planted with beans and 55 percent of the acreage planted with corn was located on subfamily and family farms in 1952 (i.e., farms smaller than fifty *manzanas*). In 1963, 66 percent of bean production and 53 percent of corn production was carried out on these small farms (calculated from Ministerio de Economía, 1966:Tables 29 and 30). Although "acreage sown" and "percentage of production" are not identical, in the absence of production data categorized by farm size for 1952, I have opted to use these figures to highlight the importance of small- and medium-sized grain producers suggested by both variables.

The available data for 1971 suggest that some changes were under way in this pattern: 58 percent of the nation's bean crop and 41 percent of the corn crop came from these farms. This latter figure suggests that the *campesino* sector had diminished in importance in corn production. The data for 1971 are partial, however, because they do not include information for the department of Zelaya (i.e., the entire Atlantic coast region). Therefore, though the data can be used to point to possible tendencies, they are not complete enough to conclude that a major change had taken place in the traditional sectoral specialization in crop production.

44. A comparison of census data from 1952, 1963, and 1971 illuminates both of these trends (see Blandón, 1962; Ministerio de Economía, 1966; and Warnken, 1975).

45. See Biderman (1982:131) regarding food imports. According to data presented in SIECA (1981:126–31), imports of corn and beans increased significantly in the early 1970s, coinciding with the development of several new export crops in the wake of the cotton boom and the continuing expansion in coffee cultivation. Weeks (1985a:107) calculated that per capita consumption of corn, rice, and beans dropped by approximately 25 percent between the 1960s and 1970s.

The exception to this pattern was rice production, which expanded throughout the 1960s and 1970s. Rice producers, however, were from a different social sector than those producing other basic grains. They were primarily large producers, and they shared with the cotton producers a capitalist orientation toward agricultural production. That is, they grew rice for its exchange value, not for its use value. They received extensive support from the state in developing the required infrastructure. By contrast, corn and beans were produced by the *campesino* sector, primarily for their use value. Their production was carried out in much less fertile regions of the country, with little or no support from the state. See Biderman (1982) for further discussion of the development of rice production. Williams (1986) argues that capitalist-oriented corn and bean production also spread at this time.

46. Calculated from the agricultural census figures cited in Blandón (1962:43) and

Ministerio de Economía (1966:xiv). The 1952 agricultural census, in contrast to the 1963 census, did not include farms smaller than one *manzana*. Porras Mendieta (1962) argued that the 1952 census consequently ignores a significant sector of agricultural producers whose number he estimated to be 44,612 (of a total of agricultural producers he placed at 96,193). Because it is impossible to verify this estimation, the above calculation disregards this size category for both 1952 and 1963. The 1971 agricultural census was never published in complete form so it is not possible to bring these data up to the 1970s. Partial findings for the census are available in Ministerio de Economía (1971) and Warnken (1975).

47. According to Biderman (1982:139), "77 percent of . . . [rural families] . . . had annual incomes of less than $700 in the early 1970s." This figure fell far short of meeting the minimum nutritional requirements estimated to be $150 per person, thus $900 per family (assuming six members per family). See also CEPAL et al. (1980) for further information on rural incomes.

48. Moreover, 55 percent of the diseases diagnosed in infants were nutrition-related. See AID (1976b:10–14) and INCAP (1969).

49. Only 13.5 percent of Nicaragua's rural population had access to potable water (Ministerio de Salud Pública, n.d.:II-53).

50. Figures for the rural population were taken from FIDA (1980) and Banco Central de Nicaragua–Ministerio de Economía, Industria y Comercio (1974:v). Data on educational services were calculated from MED (1980:30). This situation prevailed even though 69 percent of the primary schools were located in rural areas, suggesting that classes in the countryside were very large.

Wheelock (1980:68) argued that one reason for the lack of educational services offered to the rural poor was the need to maintain a submissive work force on the agroexport estates. Education would make these *campesinos* more resistant to working and living under the deplorable conditions characteristic of the agroexport *latifundios*. This rural-urban disparity probably also occurred because teachers and doctors were less inclined to go into rural areas to work. They preferred the advantages of living and working in urban areas to the isolation and dismal conditions of the *campo*.

51. Williams (1986:129–34) illuminates this dynamic in an analysis of the relationship between the displacement of the *campesino* population by cattle ranching and the development of guerrilla warfare in the area of Pancasan (municipality of Matiguas) in 1967.

52. Several other agrarian reform projects were promoted by the Somoza government after the enactment of the Agrarian Reform Law in 1963, including an agricultural credit program for small farmers.

53. The departments affected by the land titling program were Nueva Segovia, Jinotega, Matagalpa, Chontales, Rio San Juan, and Zelaya (Núñez, 1981:77).

54. The Rigoberto Cabezas project in Nueva Guinea alone established twenty-four of the sixty-three colonies, incorporating 2,384 families (IAN, 1974b:9).

55. Furthermore, this program did not seriously attempt to incorporate *campesinos* formerly outside of the credit system: "In INVIERNO's first year, it served 571 clients who had previously received loans through the Rural Credit Program," which had been established in 1959 (Enríquez and Spalding, 1987:111).

Chapter 3

1. Capital flight during the Somozas' last eighteen months in power was estimated to be on the order of (U.S.) $535 million (CEPAL, 1979a:14, 45). In addition to the foreign debt and the empty treasury, a tremendous amount of damage was done to Nicaragua's infrastructure: the United Nations estimated that the material damages alone caused by two years of generalized warfare amounted to (U.S.) $481 million.

2. In an early report on Nicaragua's development potential in the post-Somoza era, FIDA (1980:145) concluded that agriculture (and more specifically, export agriculture) would have to be the axis of development for the next few years. See also Wheelock (1984b).

3. These investments and pursuit of this strategy in general were subject to growing criticism beginning in 1985 because of the role the government's investments played in deepening Nicaragua's economic crisis. See, for example, FNI (1985).

4. Moreover, the need for extensive growth in the agroexport sector (5 percent annually through the year 2000) was seen as essential for the generation of required foreign exchange earnings (*Barricada*, 1983f).

The composition of the agroexport sector, however, would change in the coming years. By late 1986 the price of cotton in the international market had dropped so low that the government began to consider phasing out its production for export. Yet by mid-1987, prices for cotton had once again risen in the world market in a pattern that echoed the centuries-old boom-and-bust cycle of agroexport production.

5. This description of Nicaragua's agroexport production focuses on coffee and cotton, to the exclusion of sugarcane, because of the relative importance of the former two crops historically, both as generators of foreign exchange earnings and as employers of harvest labor. For example, coffee and cotton together generated 54 percent of Nicaragua's foreign exchange earnings in 1977, as opposed to just under 5 percent from sugarcane (calculated from MIDINRA, 1983:51). The percentage of exchange earnings derived from sugarcane grew in 1981, but it was still slightly less than 10 percent, as opposed to approximately 52 percent for coffee and cotton.

Coffee and cotton have also been, by far, the most important source of employment for harvest laborers. Together they absorbed 86 percent of the total harvest labor force (INCAE, 1982a:9).

6. Definitions of producer size differ dramatically in the literature on Nicaraguan agriculture. Gariazzo (1984) describes the various criteria used to distinguish pro-

ducer size and the consequent stratifications in coffee production. For the purpose of consistency, this study relies on the size categories developed in CEPAL et al.'s classic work on land tenure in Central America (1980:47, 162). Their findings show that medium (from fifty to five hundred *manzanas*) and large (more than five hundred *manzanas*) capitalist farms together produced approximately 78 percent of Nicaragua's coffee. Medium-sized capitalist farms were the most important producers, growing 58 percent of the country's coffee. An INCAE (1982a:20) study defines coffee producer size as follows: small producers are those whose total annual production is one hundredweight or less; medium producers are those whose annual production is between one hundredweight and five hundredweight; large producers are those who produce more than five hundredweight annually.

7. Although more recent data on employment of chemical inputs are unavailable, no evidence exists to suggest their more widespread adoption since that time.

8. The fungicide that is used to control *la Roya* is composed of copper compounds. These materials are not available in Nicaragua and must be imported. In 1988 it cost Nicaragua approximately (U.S.) $36.25 to treat each *manzana* of coffee affected by *la Roya* (calculated from data provided to me in interview 229, Empresa Mauricio Duarte, June 24, 1988). This informant (and many of my other informants) asked that his anonymity be maintained. Other informants who provided access to internal ministerial documents requested that the documents not be cited. Therefore, these sources will be cited by interview number, ministry or occupation, and date.

9. Gariazzo (1984:88) states that following official termination of the CONARCA program, an additional two thousand *manzanas* of coffee were renovated through the program. This figure confirms an estimate given to me that a total of approximately twelve thousand *manzanas* were renovated under the auspices of CONARCA (interview 229, Empresa Mauricio Duarte, June 24, 1988).

10. Nicaragua has a rainy season and a dry season. During the harvest months, one is especially aware of the disastrous effects that unpredictable climatological conditions can have on the year's coffee yield. Unexpected rains throughout the 1983/84 coffee harvest speeded up the maturation process of the beans. This put pressure on coffee producers to begin the harvest earlier than usual, complicating an already problematic labor situation.

11. The coffee bean turns bright red when it is ready to be picked. For this reason, the mature bean is commonly called "el rojito," the little red one. In earlier stages of maturation, the bean is green.

12. In general, medium- and large-sized producers complete at least part of the processing on their *finca*. In areas of greater rainfall the final stage of processing, the drying of the beans, is carried out at a second *beneficio*. The first type of *beneficio* is called a *beneficio humedo*, or wet processing plant; the second type is called a *beneficio seco*, or dry processing plant. In describing prerevolutionary coffee production, Kaimowitz (1980:9) commented that "the approximately 65 coffee processing plants in

Nicaragua vary greatly in size and degree of vertical integration. While some are small operations run on individual coffee plantations, others such as the Calley Dagnall and Commercial International, S.A. (CISA), are veritable agro-complexes including everything from coffee farms to processing plants, exporting houses, and banks."

13. ENCAFE was also responsible for categorizing the quality of the coffee. Lower qualities were usually designated for domestic consumption.

14. Coffee requires 242 person/days per *manzana* compared to 45 for cotton and 36 for corn (Sociedad Cooperativa Anónima de Cafetaleros de Nicaragua, as cited in Kaimowitz, 1980:24).

15. Forty-six percent of Nicaragua's coffee acreage was located in Matagalpa and Jinotega alone (Gariazzo, 1984:151).

16. The last figure, 90,000 people, was calculated using the estimation that 50 percent of the beans reached their maturation point, thus need to be picked, between mid-December and mid-January (roughly 30 days). Hence, $(5,400,000 \div 2) \div 30 = 90,000$. MITRAB (1984) developed coefficients for labor requirements in the 1984/85 coffee harvest cycle that take into account the level of technology employed on the *finca*. They were as follows per *manzana*: traditional production, 26.42 person/days; semitechnical production, 79.25 person/days; and high-technology production, 132.66 person/days. These coefficients express the relationship between the level of technology employed on the *finca* and yield levels. As can be seen from the coefficients, higher-yielding trees require more laborers. These coefficients must be understood as estimates.

17. The average number of coffee pickers per family was 3.46 in 1980, as opposed to 2.57 for cotton pickers (INCAE, 1982b:Table 2).

18. See Swezey and Daxl (1983) and Brader (1979) for informative discussions of pest problems in cotton production and innovative means to control them.

19. The cotton production process corresponds to Nicaragua's two seasons in that harvesting and subsequent preparation of the soil take place during the dry season (November to April), while planting and cultivation occur during the rainy season (May to October). Unusual weather conditions such as a delay in the beginning of the rainy season or unexpected rain in the dry season affect the production process.

20. Medium- and large-sized capitalist growers produced 91 percent of Nicaragua's cotton in 1963 (calculated from CEPAL et al., 1980:162). This figure had grown to 95 percent by 1971, when the next agricultural census was conducted (calculated from data cited in Warnken, 1975:Table 67).

21. Wheelock's estimate of a 90/10 labor requirement differential for coffee is larger than most other estimates. My fieldwork tends to confirm Biderman's estimate of a 80/20 differential. Though the accuracy of this specific estimate might be questioned, in general Wheelock's characterization of the coffee *latifundio* captures the essence of Nicaraguan coffee production.

22. For example, during the 1983/84 cotton cycle, unexpected winds threatened to damage the cotton left on the plants too long. By the end of February 1984, only 40 percent of the cotton had been harvested (Radio Sandino, Nicaragua, February 29, 1984). These winds threatened to blow the remaining cotton to the ground.

23. At this point cotton collected from the ground requires extra cleaning, but it does not usually achieve the same quality rating as cotton picked while still on the plant.

24. Calculated from IRCT (1982:Table 1). As of 1982, there were twenty-five ginning facilities in operation in Nicaragua.

25. See INCAE (1982a:Table 14). These statistics refer to the percentage of producers in each size category who relied on foreign labor, not the percentage of their labor force that was imported.

26. Murray (1984:9) cites an ICAITI study showing that "more than 80 percent of the cotton workers live within 100 meters of the fields in which they work." He goes on to state that studies of aerial drift from pesticide spraying have shown that "50 percent of the pesticide landed outside the target area due to wind turbulence, temperature conditions and the types of application equipment used. Measuring devices set up at intervals beyond the edge of the fields found between 5 and 10 percent of the total application drifted at least 100 meters from the fields (the same area occupied by the agricultural labor force)."

27. See CONAL (1977:3). Tenure in the harvest varied according to the size of the farm, with employment lasting longer on larger farms: employment on farms of three hundred *manzanas* or more averaged 105.52 days; on farms between fifty and three hundred *manzanas*, 73.32 days; and on farms smaller than fifty *manzanas*, 29.05 days.

28. It is not uncommon in Nicaragua to see corn and beans being farmed on the sides of hills with a forty-five-degree angle. Cultivation under these conditions can be done only by hand. Furthermore, a PREALC-OIT (1981:Annex 2, p. 17) study found that "59.5 percent of the semiproletarian *campesinos* (those *campesinos* who sold their labor during part of the year in the agroexport harvests) had less than five *manzanas*."

29. According to CEPAL (1966:122), small farmers had access to only 4 to 5 percent of the agricultural credit offered by the banking system in the early 1960s. Enríquez and Spalding (1987:111) estimated that approximately 11 percent of the peasantry (including poor, middle, and rich peasants) had access to agricultural credit at the height of the Rural Credit Program in 1978. This program was specifically designed to open up this sector's access to credit.

30. See the Appendix for a discussion of the strengths and weaknesses of the other surveys that have been conducted on this topic.

31. The concentration of land that occurred with the most recent expansion of coffee production following World War II was more extreme in Carazo than in Matagalpa and Jinotega. Thus more people were pushed off the land and into other

sectors of the economy there. As Gariazzo (1984:78) points out, only 45 percent of the EAP in Carazo was involved in primary sector activities in 1977, in contrast to 71.7 percent in Matagalpa.

The term *informal sector* refers to all businesses and industries with five employees or less. They range from market women with fruit and vegetable stalls to a tailor working out of his home and employing four assistants. This economic sector plays an extremely important role throughout Latin America because formal industry is insufficiently developed to employ a significant part of the urban population and provide the necessary range of goods and services. The nature and scope of the informal sector in Nicaragua are not well understood. See DeFranco (1979) for an analysis of Nicaragua's informal sector before the revolution. Although the term usually refers specifically to the urban population, it is used more broadly here to include the large population of artisans who reside in Carazo, as well as those who participate in commerce (both in nearby cities and in rural communities) but live in this area.

32. Traditionally this equation had a third factor: the intermediaries (with their profit margins), who purchased the crop from producers and sold it on the international market. In 1979 this third factor was replaced by the state, which became the intermediary. The international market, however, continued to determine much of the economics of production.

33. Calculated from INCAE (1982b:Tables 35 and 39). These percentages were arrived at by averaging the figures for the occupation in which harvest workers were employed during the seven months of the year when they were not involved in the harvest: for cotton harvest workers, data for April to October were averaged, and for coffee harvest workers, data for March to September were averaged.

34. Reliance on imported labor is a common feature of agricultural production in developed countries as well. Even in areas such as the southwestern United States, where mechanization was well under way by the turn of the century, relying on cheap imported labor instead of promoting technological innovation and mechanization remained the prevalent pattern. See further McWilliams, 1971; Galarza, 1964; and Majka, 1978.

35. The bracero program was the most developed in a series of U.S.-Mexico temporary worker agreements. Legislation opening the way for the bracero program arose in response to labor shortages. See Galarza (1964) for an interesting account of the role of temporary workers in the struggle to organize California farm labor.

Núñez (1981:74) discusses the role of foreign laborers in reducing Nicaragua's harvest labor deficits. He also describes the political purposes these foreign laborers served: "In this case economic needs and political needs complemented each other; customs officials permitted the entry of Honduran and Salvadoran laborers on the condition that these workers submit themselves to the requirements of officials of the party in power, that is, to vote for the liberal-somocista party, to pay certain taxes, etc."

Chapter 4

1. Coffee acreage increased in 1979, following a significant expansion between 1977/78 and 1978/79. Information describing both acreage and yields during the 1977–82 period were taken from unpublished data, PAN-MIDINRA (1986). See also table 3.4.

2. Buitelaar (1985) provides data from four coffee farms describing the relative weight of permanent versus temporary labor in the post-Somoza period. The average ratio for these farms was thirty permanent workers to one hundred temporary workers (for the harvest). This ratio is significantly higher than that characterizing the pre-1979 period (see Chapter 3).

3. The 1980/81 coffee harvest also experienced a labor shortage, although not as severe as the cotton harvest (Programa Centroamericano de Ciencias de la Salud, 1983; and Deere and Marchetti, 1981). A PREALC study carried out in 1981 concluded that there was a greater tendency in general for harvest labor shortages in cotton than in coffee. PREALC (1981:4) cited the following as some of the reasons for this difference: "the existence of more than 20,000 small coffee producers, the extension of coffee production over several regions, the relatively longer harvest period, and the existence of other agricultural activities on the medium- and large-sized fincas which allow[ed] for a larger permanent workforce."

4. Internal Ministerial Document 113, MIDINRA, 1982.

5. Ibid.

6. Decree 3 was ratified on August 22, 1979 (*La Gaceta*, 1979a). Decree 38 was ratified on September 3, 1979 (*La Gaceta*, 1979b).

7. Reinhardt (1987) argues that the land redistribution policy of the Nicaraguan agrarian reform did not differ significantly from El Salvador's reform in the first few years of its implementation. That is, only a limited quantity of land was redistributed because of the revolutionary government's perception that agroexport crop production could not be carried out efficiently on anything other than large-scale estates. She thus concludes that the impact of Nicaragua's agrarian reform (read land distribution) was limited before 1985, when the government adopted a more propeasant policy.

8. The figure for CAS included precoops and work collectives (CT). These data are based on PROCAMPO and BND reports, as cited in Deere and Marchetti (1981:56).

9. The development of a mixed economy was one of the basic tenets of the Nicaraguan revolution. In the agrarian sector this meant the coexistence of capitalist

agroexport growers, small- and medium-sized individual peasant farmers, cooperatives, and the state sector. But the relationship between the large agroexport producers and the government deteriorated to the point that Collins (1982) described it as a "failed partnership" only three years after the revolutionary process had been initiated. According to Collins, the failure was largely the result of these capitalists' continued opposition to economic and social reform. A significant expression of this opposition was the economic sabotage carried out by this sector in the form of decapitalization. Decapitalization was brought about by reducing the area under cultivation, laying off necessary workers, selling machinery and livestock, and the funneling of government loans to foreign banks instead of investing in production expansions. For further discussion of the difficulties encountered by the new government in the implementation of policies based on a mixed economy strategy, see Weeks (1987).

10. See CIERA (1982b:128–30). Eighty-seven percent of this land was either uncultivated (62.5 percent) or abandoned/insufficiently exploited (24.3 percent).

11. There was frequently a time lag between when *campesinos* were actually given the land and when they received title to it. In the case of these early land grants, however, titles were quickly extended to the beneficiaries.

12. See further Censo Nacional de Cooperativas (1982) cited in CIERA (1984a:Table 6). These figures do not include Zelaya Norte or Sur (Zonas Especiales I and II).

13. Havens and Baumeister (1982:47) also found that cotton harvest workers had gained more access to land than had coffee harvest workers, but their overall findings for how much of the harvest labor force had greater access to land after 1979 contrast strikingly with those of INCAE. According to Havens and Baumeister, only 13 percent of the cotton pickers had greater access to land in 1980/81 and only 5 percent of the coffee pickers. Although it is unclear why the findings of these two studies are so different, what is important is that less than eighteen months after Somoza's ouster (and before the official initiation of land redistribution, which came in July 1981) this sector of the work force had greater access to land than it had before July 1979.

14. I have explored the role of credits in the agrarian transformation more extensively in Enríquez and Spalding (1987).

15. Interest rates for agricultural credit encouraged the channeling of credit through cooperatives: whereas the rate for small, individual producers was 13 percent, CCS members paid 10 percent interest and CAS members, 8 percent.

16. Repayment rates for corn and beans were 16 percent and 28 percent respectively, for the 1980/81 cycle (CIERA, 1982b:110).

17. Following the first increase in the distribution of Rural Credit in 1980, 972 million córdobas were allotted in 1981; 1,129 million córdobas in 1982; 1,555 million in 1983; and 2,353 million córdobas in 1984 (CIERA et al., 1984, for 1980–81; BCN unpublished data for 1982–84).

18. Collins (1982:53) mentions another way in which the harvest was affected by

the credit "piñata": "Because of the logistical difficulties of getting credit to tens of thousands of farmers, often in remote areas, some *campesinos* received credit so late that they were still harvesting their corn and beans when the season arrived when their labor was desperately needed on the export crop farms."

19. Both of these figures are the yearly rate. See further Gaceta 5 (*La Gaceta*, 1980a) and Gaceta 28 (*La Gaceta*, 1980b). According to CIERA (1982b:121–22), cotton land had rented for the equivalent of (U.S.) $300 per *manzana* and basic grain land for the equivalent of (U.S.) $70 per *manzana* before the ratification of these two laws.

20. FIDA (1980:46) states that INCEI's storage facilities were capable of handling 40 percent of national grain production, although they were never used to full capacity. Thus intermediaries were still responsible for marketing at least 60 percent of the nation's basic grains. But even this 35 to 40 percent control over the market affected basic grain prices.

21. Calculated from unpublished data (PAN-MIDINRA, 1987). ENABAS's purchases of rice were even more discouraging this first year: 9.6 percent. Its rice purchases improved significantly after 1980, reaching 58 percent in 1981 and 64 percent in 1982, only to fall again to 43 percent in 1983, 40 percent in 1984, and 27 percent in 1985. Government-purchased rice came primarily from large-scale producers, operating on highly capital-intensive farms. In contrast, corn and bean purchases came primarily from the *campesino* sector. Interestingly, increases in the government-set price for rice were more than double what they were for corn and beans in 1980 (CIERA, 1982b:135). Likewise, in 1981 price increases for rice were significantly greater than those for corn and beans.

22. See CIERA (1982b:135) for data on government-set producer prices for basic grains and CEPAL (1983:30–31) for data on inflation.

23. See CIERA (1983a:69) for a discussion of subsidies through 1982. Utting (1987) provides information about later changes in subsidization policies.

24. See Collins (1982:70). Colburn (1984:112) cites the following as the percentages of wage increases beginning in 1979: 48.2 percent for 1979/80, 31.6 percent for 1980/81, and 0.0 percent for 1981/82. The point here is not to emphasize these differences in data. Rather, what is important is to highlight the wage increase that occurred between 1979 and 1980.

25. Internal Ministerial Document 115, 1982. Accounts of this preharvest/harvest wage relationship differ. Some claim that the average daily wage during the harvest was between 50 to 100 percent higher than the average preharvest daily wage (see, e.g., INIES/CRIES, 1983b:Section 3.4; and CIERA, 1984b:8). What is most important here is that harvest wages were at least equal to preharvest wages.

26. Colburn (1984) argues that wage increases for all agricultural workers were undercut by inflation.

27. The Comisión Nacional de la Fuerza de Trabajo and its regional counterparts was composed of representatives from the Rural Workers' Association (ATC), the

small- and medium-sized producers' association (UNAG), MIDINRA, MITRAB, and the ministries of Planning, Health, Transportation, and Internal Commerce.

28. These conclusions were reached through a quantitative analysis of the relationship between variations in the participation of traditional workers in the coffee harvest and changes in the wage scale during the 1985/86 harvest (Aznar, 1986: 125–27). Policy makers at MITRAB shared this perspective, arguing that wage scales were not the key determinant in attracting harvest laborers. Likewise, low harvest wages could not account for the shortages of laborers in the harvest (interview 193, MITRAB, June 8, 1987).

29. The debate was also referred to in a PREALC-OIT study of labor availability for the 1981/82 crop cycle: "On the one hand, some documents argue that there is a direct relationship between salary levels and labor availability. On the other hand, there are those who argue that salary scale increases reduce the amount of time that the labor force will work" (PREALC-OIT, 1981:Annex 2, p. 1).

30. This is especially true of those from El Salvador, where the ratio of land to laborer is much lower than in the rest of Central America and the concentration of landownership is extreme: the population density (*manzanas*/inhabitants) of El Salvador was 0.7; Nicaragua, 7.6; Costa Rica, 3.4; Honduras, 4.7; and Guatemala, 2.4 (CIERA, 1982c:22). See also CEPAL et al. (1980) and Deere (1982).

31. Internal Ministerial Document 115, MIDINRA, 1982.

32. The first figure is from Internal Ministerial Document 115, MIDINRA, 1982. The second set of figures was calculated from Aznar (1986:18) and table 3.3.

33. For example, interviews 97, MIDINRA, August 8, 1983; 80, MIDINRA, April 18, 1983; 66, MIDINRA, October 22, 1982. One informant who held this position in 1983 still argued that salaries were the key issue in these early harvests in an interview conducted in 1987 (interview 190, MIDINRA, May 28, 1987).

34. For a sampling of the articles that discuss harvest labor shortages, see *Barricada* (1983b, 1983c, 1983i, 1983k, 1984e), *Nuevo Diario* (1984), and *La Prensa* (1982a).

35. See, for example, *Barricada* (1983h, 1984d) and *Nuevo Diario* (1983). Deere et al. (1985:97) also describe "the need to mobilize massive brigades of urban students and other volunteers for the 1981–82 coffee harvest."

36. Bean production increased by 19 percent and corn production by 18 percent between the 1982/83 and 1983/84 crop cycles (calculated from unpublished data, PAN-MIDINRA, 1986).

37. For example, DeFranco and Cantarero (1984:23–24) found that whereas workers had traditionally participated in the harvest an average of seventy-four days, in 1981/82 the average number of days worked was fifty-six, a drop of 24 percent.

38. The word *appears* is used here because it is possible that rather than an actual increase in the number of women and children working in the harvest, they were included in the statistics gathered in more recent studies and were not in the past. For example, it was common in the past for only the male head of household to be listed

in farm records on employees. Following this logic, the head of household collected the family's wages, and other family members' work was not necessarily recorded.

39. CIERA's estimate of the participation of children between the ages of eight and fourteen in the cotton harvest in 1977/78 (4 percent) and 1980/81 (4.2 percent) is significantly below the figure estimated by INCAE (1982b:Table 6) for children aged ten to fourteen in 1980/81 (17.3 to 17.8 percent). The reason for the significant difference in findings is unclear. CIERA's findings for the 1981/82 harvest (16.9 percent) more closely approximate those of INCAE.

40. INCAE (1982b:Table 7) estimated that the participation of children between the ages of ten and fourteen represented 21.7 to 22.7 percent of the coffee harvest labor force in 1980/81.

41. Although INCAE (1982b:Tables 7 and 8) found that women composed 34.1 percent of the coffee harvest labor force and 28 percent of the cotton harvest labor force, figures that vary slightly from those cited by CIERA et al. (1987), the point is their overall pattern of increased participation.

42. CIERA et al.'s (1987:21) findings confirm this difference between the state and private sectors, although its magnitude in the latter study was less extreme: 48 percent in the state sector, as opposed to 39 percent in the private sector.

43. See CIERA et al. (1987) for a discussion of some of the reasons for these differences.

44. INCAE's (1982b:Tables 32 and 33) data substantiate Gleskes and Valkenet's estimates of men/children ratio for productivity.

45. Vilas (1986) provides a short discussion of dropping labor productivity in the industrial sector after 1979. Wheelock (1984a) addresses the issue of labor productivity in agriculture.

46. Buitelaar (1985) suggests that an additional factor in reduced labor productivity on state farms was the workers' lack of identification with the farm, which stemmed from an absence of the paternalistic relationship that had typified private farms and the lack of a direct ownership relation as existed, for example, in the cooperative sector.

47. According to Buitelaar (1985) and interview 194, MIDINRA, June 16, 1987, relatives also served as a source of labor in the private sector. Aznar (1986:87) found, however, that the state sector's harvest labor force was composed, even more heavily than the other two sectors, of relatives of permanent workers: relatives made up 54 percent of the harvest labor force in the state sector, 44 percent in the cooperative sector, and 45 percent in the private sector.

48. See, for example, an editorial entitled "Ahorro, eficiencia y productividad" in *Informaciones Agropecuarias*, MIDINRA, División de Comunicaciones, vol. 2, no. 14 (1986). For a more general discussion of the issue of labor productivity in revolutionary Nicaragua see García Gallardo (1987) and García Gallardo and Delgado Silva (1987).

49. For further information about the situation of formal sector industry in post-Somoza Nicaragua see Weeks (1985b) and Brundenius (1987). For the impact inflation has had on informal sector activity, see Alemán et al. (1986) and Olivares (1987).

50. In a study of four small urban communities located in cotton- and coffee-growing regions, DeFranco and Cantarero (1984:22) found that 47 percent of their sample had previously participated in the harvest labor force, but only 35 percent did so in 1982.

51. See, for example, *New York Times* (1982, 1983a) and *Washington Post* (1982a, 1982b).

52. See Black and Butler (1982:34) for this early characterization of the Contras. By the mid-1980s, even high-level U.S. government officials began to admit that the Contras were incapable of overthrowing the Sandinistas (see U.S. House of Representatives, Permanent Select Committee on Intelligence, *Adverse Report*, March 12, 1986; Nordland, 1987).

53. This region continued to be under constant attack through the end of the decade. See the Postscript for more recent information on the war.

54. See, for example, Americas Watch Committee (1985); Eich and Rincón (1985); and Kornbluh (1987).

55. See also the interview with a captured member of the Contras, who described his efforts to sabotage the coffee harvest (Eich and Rincón, 1985:112–19).

56. One large coffee producer told me that many workers who had previously worked during the harvest on her *finca* had not returned in 1983/84 out of fear of the Contras (interview 129, private producer, February 3, 1984). Another informant, who worked as a volunteer in the 1983/84 harvest, told me of being forced to flee into the coffee trees in the middle of the night by a Contra attack. This informant was on that particular *finca* three or four days.

Chapter 5

1. Small numbers of volunteers were sent to the harvest as early as the 1980/81 crop cycle. See, for example, *Barricada* (1980a:9, 1980b:8). Nonetheless, the number of people mobilized this first year was minuscule compared to later years.

2. This informant is a foreigner, which may have played a role in the leniency displayed by university officials in spite of his not joining the BEP.

3. Government functionaries were also mobilized for defense purposes. In these same two divisions up to one-third of the total work force was mobilized into defense units at the same time that the mobilization for the harvest occurred. In one of these two divisions a full 45 percent of the staff had been mobilized into either defense units or harvest brigades.

4. This process of consciousness development was the primary goal of a similar program of sending students into the countryside that has been carried out for many years in Cuba. According to Benjamin et al. (1984:175), "an awareness and appreciation of manual work is considered an essential part of the student's education." In Cuba, the students' role in reducing labor shortages was secondary to consciousness development.

5. Karl (1975) notes that a similar process occurred in Cuba following the Bay of Pigs invasion and the Cuban missile crisis.

6. Benjamin et al. (1984) show that even as recently as 1981 the Cuban government was adjusting salary scales to productivity in the agrarian sector to improve productivity rates. That is, it was still striving to achieve a better balance between material and moral incentives.

7. An informant who participated in one "rojo y negro" (volunteer day) during the 1982/83 coffee harvest told me that he had been picking coffee for three to four hours before he was informed that only the bright red beans were to be picked. The informant then told the "responsable" that that might be a problem because he was color-blind (interview 116, volunteer coffee picker, September 28, 1983).

Another informant mentioned that his volunteer brigade had been picking coffee for a week before being told that it was important not to break off the stem from which the next season's beans would sprout (interview 133, volunteer coffee picker, March 1, 1985)

8. One BEP member mentioned that some of the less motivated volunteers in the coffee harvest had been found sleeping in the groves (interview 135, National Autonomous University student, March 5, 1985).

9. These time periods were roughly defined by Sandinista policy makers as follows. The short term was less than four years and corresponded to the immediate crisis period and the second term of the Reagan administration (assuming that a change in administration might bring an end to the Contra war). The medium term was between four and ten years. The government estimated that by the end of this period most of its agroindustrial projects would be operational. The long term was more than ten years.

10. See O'Connor (1984) for a provocative discussion of the role of workers' struggle as "an engine of accumulation" in Western capitalism. For descriptions of the relationship between labor relations and industrial development, see Gutman (1966) and Stone (1974). Friedland and Barton (1975), Hightower (1973), and McWilliams (1971) similarly address agricultural development.

11. See CONAL (1976:37). The figure for 1981 is from IRCT (1982:Table 2).

12. The figure for 1983/84 is from *Barricada* (1984b:10), and the figure for 1984/85 is from unpublished MIDINRA data (1986).

13. In 1968/69 the price of cotton dropped to (U.S.) $23.05 on the international market (BCN, 1979:75). By the mid-1970s the price was once again above $50.00,

reaching $75.59 in 1980/81 (ENAL, unpublished data, 1988). It remained in this range through 1985/86, when it dropped to $38.38.

14. The price of cotton in the international market rose once again in mid-1987 to (U.S.) $67.70 (ENAL, unpublished data, 1988).

15. In 1984 this pattern reversed itself and imports of capital goods for agriculture increased by 65 percent (CEPAL, 1987b:43). By 1985, however, these imports were once again on the decline, dropping 11 percent.

16. Among many others, problems frequently experienced in the cotton harvest after 1979 included tire shortages for the trailers that carried harvested cotton from the field to the gin, gas shortages that made the use of vehicles difficult, and organizational problems that meant that mechanical cotton harvesters were not at the right place at the right time.

17. For further discussion of the need for development strategies appropriate to the specific resource context of each country, see Dorner and Kanel (1971).

18. The Ministry of Labor was to play the key role in this subcommittee's efforts to mobilize labor (interview 123, ATC, December 3, 1984).

19. For example, the piece rate per *lata* for coffee was increased from 12.00 córdobas in the 1983/84 harvest to 20.90 córdobas for the 1984/85 harvest (MITRAB, unpublished data, 1987).

20. Table 5.2 is meant to illustrate a trend rather than to offer precise statistical information. The figures shown should be interpreted as rough approximations for several reasons. First, data on consumer prices were collected in urban areas. No nationwide survey of consumer prices had been conducted at the time of this study's publication. Consequently, these figures do not describe with exactitude consumer prices in the countryside. In addition, the rural "consumer basket" differs from that of urban areas because many basic food items are produced by the rural population. Thus the consumer basket would contain different, if not a reduced number of, items. Finally, harvest laborers receive food and housing while working in the harvest. Wages earned in the harvest are primarily intended to supplement other sources of income earned during nonharvest months. To counterbalance the weaknesses of the national-level "Canasta Básica" data, I analyzed prices in the department of Matagalpa for a selected number of products used by the *campesino* population (including cooking oil, salt, sugar, cigarettes, and alcohol) for the 1981–86 period (using unpublished INEC data). The average increase annually for these five products was 119.7 percent, as opposed to the 105 percent increase annually for the Canasta Básica. Thus table 5.2 provides an approximate picture of the wage/price problem.

21. Information about health care centers and the rate of infant mortality in 1982 was taken from *Barricada* (1984g); the figure for infant mortality in 1976 is from AID (1976a:22).

22. See *Barricada* (1984g) for further information about the reduction in illiteracy and adult education programs. The data describing educational facilities are from MED (1983:56).

23. UNAG would not, under any circumstances, describe the *brigadas de producción* as fulfilling an agreement made by agrarian reform beneficiaries before they received land. Yet in an informal sense, that was what they represented.

24. Until late 1983 CAS members were the primary recipients of land titles given out by MIDINRA. As of November 1983, CAS members had received 79 percent of the land redistributed by the agrarian reform, as opposed to 10 percent for CCS members and 10.5 percent for individual *campesinos* (calculated from *Barricada*, 1983g). CCS members benefited from the agrarian reform primarily through agricultural credits and technical assistance.

25. See Slutzky (1982) for an explanation of the *colectivos de trabajo*.

26. Several years later UNAG organized its own *colectivos de trabajo*. But the *colectivos* organized by UNAG were composed of groups of *campesinos* who had either received land through the agrarian reform or pooled their own land and worked it collectively. UNAG's *colectivos* differed from cooperatives only in that their membership numbered less than ten. In essence they were precooperatives. By the end of 1987, UNAG had organized 362 *colectivos*, which included 3,617 members (unpublished data, UNAG, 1988).

27. An increase in the labor supply was already evident on farms participating in the Plan Contingente during the 1984/85 harvest (interview 136, MIPLAN Region II, March 7, 1985).

28. Peek (1982) discusses some of the difficulties that have arisen with the expansion of cooperatives into agroexport production. Putterman (1985) and Carter (1987) analyze the intrinsic and extrinsic problems in cooperatives more generally.

29. According to Baumeister and Neira Cuadra (N.d.:37), 30 percent of Nicaragua's agroexport production was undertaken by *campesino* producers in 1983.

30. Dorner and Kanel (1971) argue that in a land- and capital-poor but labor-abundant context such as that characterizing most of Latin America, agricultural development strategies should promote the organization of labor-intensive rather than capital-intensive production units. Although Nicaragua cannot be characterized as land-poor (in fact, it is land-rich in comparison to most of Latin America), it is certainly capital-poor.

Chapter 6

1. Munslow (1983:29) describes the relative economic strength that Angola's oil reserves provided its revolutionary government. He points out, however, that the country continues to be dependent on transnational companies for the technology and expertise required to extract and process the oil.

2. A particularly rich description of Nicaragua's prerevolutionary social structure and its influence on the process of social transformation is provided in Vilas (1986).

3. Fagen et al. (1986:19) also include the extent of foreign economic penetration as

a decisive factor in determining the degree of nationalization that is possible in the revolutionary period.

4. The nature of the Cuban agrarian reform illustrates this phenomenon. In pre-revolutionary Cuba the sugar industry had succeeded in proletarianizing the agricultural labor force to such a degree that worker-managed state farms, rather than cooperative or individual farming, became the primary goal of the agrarian reform. Deere (1986) compares the agrarian reform process in thirteen "transitional" societies and describes the relationship between the previously existing social structure and the nature of the agrarian reform each government pursued.

5. The extent to which Nicaragua's pre-1979 agricultural structure has determined post-1979 agrarian policy making is the focus of a study by Baumeister (1985).

6. See FitzGerald (1986) and Coraggio (1986) on the role of planning in the process of transition.

7. For example, for Nicaragua's new leadership, democracy was characterized as "the economic regime assures men and women their basic necessities in food, work, housing, education, and food; the governmental institutions are designed to improve the flow of communication between the apparatus of power and the popular majorities; the government rests the defense of Popular Power on the armed population; it counts on organized popular participation for the realization of economic, political, and social plans; there exist the political will, the legislation and the mechanisms to effect and guarantee the political, social and cultural rights of the majority; power is held by the working masses" (Carlos Núñez, as cited in Vilas, 1986:250).

8. See Coraggio (1985) on the subject of revolutionary democracy.

9. See Burbach (1986:79) for further discussion of this dynamic. The one exception was Zimbabwe, which has had to contend with intervention by South Africa since its revolutionary government was elected in 1979.

10. For a discussion of why the United States consistently opposes these young socialist regimes, see Burbach (1986).

11. Marchetti (1986) provides examples of this process for the case of the Nicaraguan revolution.

Postscript

1. See Luciak (1987) for an analysis of the political motivations behind the increase in land distributed to individual farmers beginning in 1985.

2. The Agrarian Reform Law was revised by law No. 14, entitled "Reforma a la Ley de Reforma Agraria" (see *La Gaceta*, 1986:57–61).

3. Baumeister (1986) provides a further analysis of the revisions in the Agrarian Reform Law.

4. This proved to be the case in several areas I visited where UCAs were formed.

Additional services such as potable water and rural commissaries were made possible through the community organizing that resulted from the establishment of a UCA.

5. Two such projects, Plan Masaya and Los Patios, are the subject of my current research. Both projects were designed to address the problem of the large *minifundio* sector that still existed in the agricultural belt surrounding Managua several years into the agrarian reform process. See Enríquez and Llanes (1988) and Enríquez (1989).

6. In 1988 the government began adding the Contra casualties to its calculations of "victims of the Contra war" (which previously had included only non-Contra victims). Thus if both groups are taken into account, the total number of victims of the Contra war was 57,731 by the end of 1988, including 29,270 dead, 18,012 wounded, and 10,449 kidnapped or captured (INEC, 1989:57).

7. See INEC (1989:58). The methodology employed in making this calculation was developed by CEPAL. See FitzGerald (1987) for a discussion of all of the factors that must be taken into account in evaluating the cost of the Contra war.

8. See CEPAL (1988:56). CNPPDH (1988:21) and the Secretaría de Planificación y Presupuesto (unpublished data, 1988) say that 50 percent of the national budget was devoted to defense spending during this period. A reduction in defense-related spending in 1989 was the result of an overall cut in government spending caused by the severe economic crisis Nicaragua experienced at that time.

9. These measures were announced in a press conference held by former Vice-President Sergio Ramírez, which was transmitted on public television and radio ("Noticiero Sandinista," February 1, 1988). See also *Barricada* (1988c:1).

10. Aznar (1986:139) found the absolute deficit of workers in the 1985/86 coffee harvest (in the Matagalpa-Jinotega region) to be on the order of 38 percent. See also unpublished data, "Producers Survey," Departamento de Economía Agrícola (DEA), Universidad Nacional Autónoma de Nicaragua (UNAN) (1987).

11. Internal Ministerial Document 120, CIERA-MIDINRA, 1987.

12. See the unpublished results of the harvest worker survey carried out by the DEA, UNAN (1987). The sample used in this survey did not include anyone under the age of fifteen.

13. I have seen references to several studies of labor productivity among agricultural workers, but access to their findings is extremely restricted.

14. Internal Ministerial Document 120, CIERA-MIDINRA, 1987.

15. The figure for 1983/84 is from *Barricada* (1984c:12), for 1985/86, *El Nuevo Diario* (1986a:1), and for 1987/88, interview 219, state employee and volunteer coffee picker, January 13, 1988.

16. The Brigada XXV Aniversario was so named before the 1986/87 harvest in commemoration of the founding of the FSLN in 1961.

17. There were 215 mechanical harvesters registered in the country in 1987. The figures for 1975/76 and 1976/77 are from CONAL (1976:37) and IRCT (1982:Table

2), respectively. Those for the 1980s were obtained from MIDINRA (unpublished data, 1988). The IRCT study states that provisional data for 1981/82 showed there to be 150 cotton harvesters in Nicaragua that year.

18. The percentage of the "Canasta Básica" covered by harvest wages did improve for cotton pickers in 1986 and for coffee pickers in 1987, but these figures were still alarmingly low.

19. See *Barricada* (1986b, 1986c), *Nuevo Diario* (1986b), and interview 227, ATC, May 27, 1988.

20. I found this to be the case on several coffee cooperatives in Carazo during the 1987/88 coffee harvest. Cooperative members were provided with these basic goods only after all the workers from outside of the cooperative had received their quotas of the scarce items.

21. One high-level ATC representative argued that the provision of meals and access to the workplace commissary were the two key factors that had brought workers to the harvest in the previous several years, irrespective of wage increases (interview 227, ATC, May 27, 1988).

22. It remained unclear whether the *colectivos* went through a renaissance after the 1984/85 harvest or whether their impermanent nature had simply led to an erroneous conclusion.

23. The figures for 1985/86 and 1986/87 are from MIDINRA (unpublished data, 1986 and 1987). The figure for 1984/85 is from *Barricada* (1984h).

24. The figure for 1984/85 is from Chapter 5 and that for 1986 from Porras (1987:17). The latter figure was calculated from the most recent census that has been conducted of the cooperative movement (1986).

25. On a number of agroexport *fincas* I visited, this transfer in ownership was a result of both the severe problem of *minifundismo* or landlessness prevailing in the region and difficulties that had arisen in the state sector's management of these farms.

26. These figures were calculated from the figures shown for the occupation of harvest workers during the nonharvest months (Aznar, 1986:76–77). The categories for nonremunerated family members and those who were inactive during the nonharvest months were combined, as per Aznar's hypothesis, to reach this conclusion. I found the employment of relatives in the harvest to be the norm on many coffee cooperatives in the Carazo region as well.

27. This informant specifically mentioned Region IV (particularly Carazo) in this regard. I can confirm that many such mutual assistance arrangements do exist. They complement the UNAG's more formal organization of the Contingente, which responds to the needs of agroexport cooperatives in the regions affected by the war.

28. See Conroy (1990) and LASA (1990) for discussions of the factors that contributed to this surprising election outcome.

29. Unpublished campaign speeches by Violeta Barrios de Chamorro, UNO campaign rallies, Ciudad Darío and Sébaco, November 25, 1989.

30. See, in particular, UNO (1989) and *La Prensa* (1990a).

31. The first figure for the number of families still needing land was estimated by the Sandinista government before the elections (*Barricada Internacional*, 1990). Former Vice-Minister of MIDINRA Ivan Gutiérrez (1989:125) calculated that this figure could be as high as sixty thousand.

32. The case of Enrique Bolaños's refusal to accept a negotiated settlement (either in the form of monetary payment or the provision of land elsewhere in the country) when his company's land was affected by the agrarian reform in 1985 is a clear example of the problematic nature of this alternative.

Bibliography

AID (U.S. Agency for International Development)
1976a   *Health Sector Assessment for Nicaragua*. Managua.
1976b   *Nutrition Sector Assessment for Nicaragua*. Managua.
Alemán, M., Ortíz, R., Barreda, E., Chávez, M., García, L., Guerrero, L., Henríquez, S., Monterrey, N., Olivares, S., Guerrero, G., Sandino, J. L., and Torres, I.
1986   "La estrategia de sobrevivencia de los sectores populares de Managua y el impacto del Mensaje Económico Gubernamental." *Encuentro* 29 (September–December): 47–83.
Altimir, Oscar
1979   "La dimensión de la pobreza en América Latina." *Cuadernos de la CEPAL*, no. 27 (Santiago de Chile: CEPAL).
Americas Watch Committee
1985   *Human Rights in Nicaragua: Reagan, Rhetoric and Reality*. New York: Americas Watch Committee.
Arias, Eduardo
1977   *El algodón en Nicaragua*. Trabajo de Campo, no. 190, Instituto Centroamericano de Administración de Empresas (INCAE).
Ayón, Tomás
1977   *Historia de Nicaragua*. Managua: Colección Cultural, Banco de América, 3 vols.
Aznar, Pablo
1986   *El empleo en la caficultura de la Sexta Región*. Departamento de Economía Agrícola (DEA), Universidad Nacional Autónoma de Nicaragua (UNAN). Managua.
Banco Central de Nicaragua–Ministerio de Economía, Industria y Comercio
1974   *Censos Nacionales 1971: Población*. Vol. 1. Managua: República de Nicaragua.
Banco Nacional de Desarrollo
1984   "Información general, Crédito Rural, comparativo 1978–83." Managua. (Mimeographed.)
Barraclough, Solon
1982   *A Preliminary Analysis of the Nicaraguan Food System*. Geneva: United Nations Research Institute for Social Development (UNRISD).

Barricada (Managua)

1980a   "Cien estudiantes a los cortes de café." (December 6).

1980b   "1,100 estudiantes escogidos para cortes." (December 10).

1982   "A cortar café en Matagalpa: Se necesitan brazos." (December 9).

1983a   "Batalla por el algodón está al rojo vivo." (January 25).

1983b   "Conforman estado mayor de producción algodonera." (January 22).

1983c   "Cortes de café, un triunfo del pueblo: Emergencia casi superada." (January 22).

1983d   "La batalla por mercados y precios justos." (November 7).

1983e   "La victoria del pueblo." (February 10).

1983f   "Lunes socio-económico: La estrategia de desarrollo agropecuario para el mediano y largo plazo." (December 5).

1983g   "Lunes socio-económico: Reforma agraria: Esta es la democracia." (December 19).

1983h   "Problemas de la cosecha algodonera resueltos en Masaya." (January 19).

1983i   "Productores de algodón se reunen en oriente." (December 15).

1983j   "Sobrecumplimos meta en la batalla del café." (March 21).

1983k   "Urgen once mil cortadores." (January 13).

1984a   "A convertir Managua en una tumba de los interventores." (Speech by Cmdt. Wheelock, November 9).

1984b   "Cosecha algodonera fue muy buena a pesar de la agresión." (June 1).

1984c   "Emergencia en corte de café: Faltan siete mil cortadores." (January 13).

1984d   "Frente a todos los problemas la cosecha algodonera va adelante." (March 16).

1984e   "Hacen falta doce mil cortadores en Región VI." (January 23).

1984f   "Lunes socio-económico: Brigadas voluntarias y batallones estudiantiles de producción." (February 27).

1984g   "Lunes socio-económico: El nivel de vida: Prioridad de la revolución." (August 13).

1984h   "Lunes socio-económico: El Plan Contingente de Granos Básicos." (July 9).

1986a   "Reglamento de la Ley de Reforma Agraria." Acuerdo no. 22 (January 10).

1986b   "Todo listo para la cosecha de café." (November 21).

1986c   "Trece propuestas para mejorar cosecha de café." (March 23).

1986d   "Una nueva cosecha, pero el futuro?" Parts 1 and 2. (December 1).

1988a   "Caen dos brigadistas de la XXV Aniversario." (January 27).

1988b   "El avance de la reforma agraria." (January 2).

1988c   "Emergencia enérgetica: Agroexportación priorizada, trabajadores re-
         sponden." (February 2).
1988d   "Seguiremos defendiendo la paz." (Mensaje de fin de año del Pdte. de la
         República.) (January 2).
1988e   "Urge habilitar más cosechadores para el algodón." (January 9).
1990a   "Cambio de gobierno . . . y la revolución se queda." (February 28).
1990b   "Panchito amenaza a cooperativas y APP." (March 1).
Barricada Internacional
1990   "Elections 90: Manifestos of Destiny–Agrarian Reform." (February 17).
Baumeister, Eduardo
1982   "Capitalismo agrario, revolución y reforma agraria en Nicaragua: Un
         balance provisional." Paper presented at the Tenth World Congress of
         Sociology, Mexico City (August 16–20).
1984   "La importancia de los medianos productores en la agricultura nic-
         aragüense (Las raíces estructurales de su emergencia y consolidación)."
         Paper presented at a seminar organized by the Food and Agriculture
         Organization (UN) and the Latin American Studies Center, Cambridge
         University (September).
1985   "The Structure of Nicaraguan Agriculture and the Sandinista Agrarian
         Reform." In *Nicaragua: A Revolution under Siege*, edited by Richard Harris
         and Carlos M. Vilas, pp. 10–35. London: Zed Press.
1986   "Estado mundo agrícola: Una relación cambiante." *Pensamiento Propio*
         4, no. 34 (July): 18–22.
Baumeister, Eduardo, and Neira Cuadra, Oscar
N.d.   "Iniciativas de desarrollo y política en la transición Sandinista." Ma
         nagua. (Mimeographed.)
DCN (Banco Central de Nicaragua–Ministerio de Economía, Industria y Comercio)
1979   *Indicadores económicos* 5, nos. 1 and 2 (December).
Belli, Pedro
1968   "An Inquiry Concerning the Growth of Cotton Farming in Nicaragua."
         Ph.D. dissertation, University of California, Berkeley.
1975   "Prolegómeno para una historia económica de Nicaragua de 1905–
         1966." *Revista del Pensamiento Centroamericano* 146 (January–March):
         2–30.
Benjamin, Medea, Collins, Joseph, and Scott, Michael
1984   *No Free Lunch: Food and Revolution in Cuba Today*. San Francisco: In-
         stitute for Food and Development Policy.
BID (Banco Interamericano de Desarrollo)
N.d.   *Progreso económico y social en América Latina: Informe 1980–81*. Wash-
         ington, D.C.: BID.

Biderman, Jaime
1982   "Class Structure, the State and Capitalist Development in Nicaraguan
          Agriculture." Ph.D. dissertation, University of California, Berkeley.
Black, George
1981   *Triumph of the People: The Sandinista Revolution in Nicaragua*. London:
          Zed Press.
Black, George, and Butler, Judy
1982   "Target Nicaragua." *North American Congress on Latin America* (NACLA)
          16, no. 1 (January–February): 2–45.
Blandón, Alfonso
1962   "Land Tenure in Nicaragua." M.A. thesis, University of Florida.
BNN (Banco Nacional de Nicaragua)
1976   "Incidencia de INVIERNO en el Programa de Crédito Rural del BNN, en
          1976." Managua: Departamento de Programación y Control, BNN.
          (Mimeographed.)
Bossert, Thomas John
1981   "Health Care in Revolutionary Nicaragua." In *Nicaragua in Revolution*,
          edited by Thomas Walker, pp. 259–72. New York: Praeger.
Brader, L.
1979   "Integrated Pest Control in the Developing World." *Annual Review of
          Entomology* 24:225–54.
Browning, David
1971   *El Salvador: Landscape and Society*. London: Oxford University Press.
Brundenius, Claes
1987   "Industrial Development Strategies in Revolutionary Nicaragua." In *The
          Political Economy of Revolutionary Nicaragua*, edited by Rose J. Spalding,
          pp. 85–104. Winchester, Mass.: Allen & Unwin.
Buitelaar, Rudolf M.
1985   "La escasez de mano de obra en el café." Paper presented at the Fourth
          Congreso Nicaragüense de Ciencias Sociales, "Hans Gutiérrez Aven-
          daño," Managua (August 30–September 1).
Burbach, Roger
1986   "The Conflict at Home and Abroad: U.S. Imperialism vs. the New Revo-
          lutionary Societies." In *Transition and Development: Problems of Third
          World Socialism*, edited by Richard Fagen, Carmen Diana Deere, and José
          Luis Coraggio, pp. 79–96. New York: Monthly Review Press/Center for
          the Study of the Americas.
Cardoso, Fernando Henrique, and Faletto, Enzo
1979   *Dependency and Development in Latin America*. Berkeley: University of
          California Press.

Carter, Michael R.
1987   "Colectivos, cooperativas y parcelas: Un análisis económico de alternativas institucionales en la agricultura reformada." Paper presented at the Seminario Taller sobre Cooperativismo en Centroamérica, DEA, UNAN, Managua (June 10–12).

Casanova, Pablo González
1985   *Historia del movimiento obrero en América Latina: Centroamérica*, vol. 2. Mexico City: Siglo XXI.

Castro, Fidel
1985   *On Latin America's Unpayable Debt, Its Unforeseeable Consequences and Other Topics of Political and Historical Interest.* Havana: Editorial Política.

Centro de Investigación de la Realidad Nacional (CIRN)
1978   *Nicaragua: Reforma o Revolución.* Vol. 1. N.p.

CEPAL (Comisión Económica para América Latina)
1966   *El desarrollo económico de Nicaragua.* New York: United Nations.
1979a   *Nicaragua: Repercusiones económicas de los acontecimientos políticos recientes.* Mexico City: CEPAL.
1979b   *América Latina en el umbral de los años '80.* Santiago de Chile: CEPAL.
1983   *Notas para el estudio económico de América Latina, 1982: Nicaragua.* Mexico City: CEPAL.
1985   *Crisis y desarrollo en América Latina y el Caribe.* Mexico City: CEPAL.
1986a   *Balance preliminar de la economía Latinoamericana, 1986.* Santiago de Chile: CEPAL.
1986b   *Notas para el estudio de América Latina y el Caribe, 1985: Nicaragua.* Mexico City. CEPAL.
1987a   *Centroamérica: Notas sobre la evolución económica en 1986.* Mexico City: CEPAL.
1987b   *Notas para el estudio económico de América Latina y el Caribe, 1986: Nicaragua.* Mexico City: CEPAL.
1988   *Notas para el estudio económico de América Latina y el Caribe, 1987: Nicaragua.* Mexico City: CEPAL.
1989   *Notas para el estudio económico de América Latina y el Caribe, 1988: Nicaragua.* Mexico City: CEPAL.

CEPAL/FAO/OIT (CEPAL, Organización de las Naciones Unidas para la Agricultura y la Alimentación, and Organización Internacional del Trabajo)
1980   *Tenencia de la tierra y desarrollo rural en Centroamérica.* San José, Costa Rica: EDUCA.

CIERA (Centro de Investigación y Estudios de la Reforma Agraria)
1981   "Encuesta de trabajadores del campo." Managua. (Unpublished survey data.)

1982a   "El cortador del algodón, café y sus relaciones de clase." Managua.
           (Mimeographed.)
1982b   "Impacto del Crédito Rural sobre el nivel de vida del campesinado."
           Managua. (Mimeographed.)
1982c   "Nicaragua: Capitalismo y agricultura 1950–79." Managua. (Mimeo-
           graphed.)
1983a   *Distribución y consumo popular de alimentos en Managua.* Managua:
           CIERA.
1983b   *Informe del Primer Seminario sobre Estrategia Alimentaria.* Managua:
           CIERA (June).
1984a   "La escasez de fuerza de trabajo en el algodón." Managua (December).
           (Mimeographed.)
1984b   *La mujer en las cooperativas agropecuarias en Nicaragua.* Managua: CIERA.
1989   *La reforma agraria en Nicaragua: 1979–1989.* 10 vols. Managua: CIERA.
CIERA/ATC/CETRA (CIERA, Asociación de Trabajadores del Campo, and Centro de
Estudios del Trabajo)
1987   *Mujer y agroexportación en Nicaragua.* Edited by the Instituto de la Mujer.
           Managua: Editorial Unión.
CIERA/PAN/CIDA (CIERA, Programa Alimentario Nicaragüense, Canadian International Development Agency)
1984   *Informe final del Proyecto Estrategia Alimentaria: Directorio de Políticas Ali-
           mentarias.* Vol. 3. Managua: CIERA.
CNES (Consejo Nacional de la Educación Superior)
1984   "Sistema de ingreso a la educación superior." Published in *El Nuevo
           Diario, Barricada,* and *La Prensa,* (February).
CNPPDH (Comisión Nacional de Promoción y Protección de los Derechos Humanos)
1988   "Informe de la CNPPDH ante la X Asamblea Comisión Para la Defensa
           de los Derechos Humanos en Centroamérica (CODEHUCA)." San José,
           Costa Rica (27 May).
Colburn, Forrest D.
1984   "Rural Labor and the State in Post-Revolutionary Nicaragua." *Latin
           American Research Review* 19, no. 3:103–17.
Collins, Joseph
1982   *What Difference Could a Revolution Make? Food and Farming in the New
           Nicaragua.* San Francisco: Institute for Food and Development Policy.
CONAL (Comisión Nacional del Algodón)
1967   *Informe anual.* Managua: CONAL.
1973   *Estadísticas del algodón en Nicaragua, 1950–1972.* Managua: CONAL.
1975   *Memoria 1974/75.* Managua: CONAL.
1976   *Memoria 1975/76.* Managua: CONAL.

1977   *Algodón: Distribución de la mano de obra (numero y salario) permanente y temporal por intervalos de área sembrada: Cosecha 1976–77.* Managua: CONAL.

Conroy, Michael E.

1984   "False Polarization? Alternative Perspectives on the Economic Strategies of Post-Revolutionary Nicaragua." Paper presented at the Twenty-fifth Annual Convention of the International Studies Association, Atlanta (March 29).

1985   "External Dependence, External Assistance, and Economic Aggression against Nicaragua." *Latin American Perspectives* 12 (Spring 1985): 39–67.

1990   "The Political Economy of the 1990 Nicaraguan Elections." Paper presented at the "Coloquio sobre las Crisis Económicas del Siglo XX," Facultad de Ciencias Económicas y Empresariales, Universidad Complutense de Madrid (April 17–19).

Consejo Nacional de Economía

1965   *Cuadros estadísticos de desarrollo económico y social de Nicaragua, 1950–1964.* Oficina de Planificación. Managua.

Coraggio, José Luis

1984   "El sistema de acumulación en la transición." Paper presented at the PACCA/CRIES/SSRC conference, The Problems of Transition in Small Peripheral Economies, Managua (September 3–11).

1985   *Nicaragua: Revolución y democracia.* Mexico City: Editorial Línea.

1986   "Economics and Politics in the Transition to Socialism: Reflections on the Nicaraguan Experience." In *Transition and Development: Problems of Third World Socialism,* edited by Richard R. Fagen, Carmen Diana Deere, and José Luis Coraggio, pp. 143–70. New York: Monthly Review Press/Center for the Study of the Americas.

Crawley, Eduardo

1979   *Dictators Never Die.* New York: St. Martin's Press.

Cumberland, W. W.

1980   *Nicaragua: Investigación económica y financiera.* Managua: Colección Cultural, Banco de América.

DEA (Departamento de Economía Agrícola)

1987   *Estudios sobre cooperativismo: Disponibilidad de recursos y producción en 21 cooperativas CAS.* Equipo de Investigación de Cooperativismo, DEA, UNAN, Managua.

Deere, Carmen Diana

1982   "A Comparative Analysis of Agrarian Reform in El Salvador and Nicaragua, 1979–81." *Development and Change* 13 (Winter): 1–41.

1986   "Agrarian Reform, Peasant Participation, and the Organization of Production in the Transition to Socialism." In *Transition and Development: Problems of Third World Socialism*, edited by Richard R. Fagen, Carmen Diana Deere, and José Luis Coraggio, pp. 97–142. New York: Monthly Review Press/Center for the Study of the Americas.

Deere, Carmen Diana, and Marchetti, Peter, S.J.

1981   "The Worker-Peasant Alliance in the First Year of the Nicaraguan Agrarian Reform." *Latin American Perspectives* 8 (Spring): 40–73.

Deere, Carmen Diana, Marchetti, Peter, S.J., and Reinhardt, Nola

1985   "The Peasantry and the Development of Sandinista Agrarian Policy, 1979–1984." *Latin American Research Review* 20, no. 3:75–109.

DeFranco, Silvio

1979   "Employment and the Urban Informal Sector: The Case of Managua." Ph.D. dissertation, University of Wisconsin, Madison.

DeFranco, Silvio, and Cantarero, Rodrigo

1984   "Rural Nonfarm Employment and Rural Nonfarm Enterprises in Nicaragua." IDRA/INCAE Research Report (September). (Mimeographed).

de Janvry, Alain

1981   *The Agrarian Question and Reformism in Latin America*. Baltimore: Johns Hopkins University Press.

Dirección General de Estadísticas y Censos

1961   "El Café en Nicaragua." Managua.

Dorner, Peter, and Kanel, Don

1971   "The Economic Case for Land Reform: Employment, Income Distribution, and Productivity." In *Land Reform in Latin America: Issues and Cases*, edited by Peter Dorner, pp. 41–56. Madison: University of Wisconsin Press.

Dorner, Peter, and Quiros, Rodolfo

1973   "Institutional Dualism in Central America's Agricultural Development." *Journal of Latin American Studies* 5 (November): 217–32.

Eckstein, Susan

1981   "The Socialist Transformation of Cuban Agriculture: Domestic and International Constraints." *Social Problems* 29 (December): 178–96.

Eich, Dieter, and Rincón, Carlos

1985   *The Contras: Interviews with Anti-Sandinistas*. San Francisco: Synthesis Publications.

Enríquez, Laura J.

1989   "From Cotton to Corn: Popular Pressure Transforms a Region." Paper prepared for the Fifteenth International Congress of the Latin American Studies Association, San Juan, Puerto Rico (September 21–23), Congress canceled.

Enríquez, Laura J., and Llanes, Marlen I.

1988   "From Export Agriculture to Food Crop Production: The Transformation of Agriculture at the Regional Level." Paper presented at the Fourteenth International Congress of the Latin American Studies Association, New Orleans (March 17–19).

Enríquez, Laura J., and Spalding, Rose J.

1987   "Banking Systems and Revolutionary Change: The Politics of Agricultural Credit in Nicaragua." In *The Political Economy of Revolutionary Nicaragua*, edited by Rose J. Spalding, pp. 105–25. Winchester, Mass.: Allen & Unwin.

Evans, Peter

1979   *Dependent Development*. Princeton: Princeton University Press.

Fagen, Richard R.

1981   *The Nicaraguan Revolution: A Personal Report*. Washington, D.C.: Institute for Policy Studies.

1986   "The Politics of Transition." In *Transition and Development: Problems of Third World Socialism*, edited by Richard R. Fagen, Carmen Diana Deere, and José Luis Coraggio, pp. 249–63. New York: Monthly Review Press/Center for the Study of the Americas.

1987   *Forging Peace: The Challenge of Central America*. New York: Basil Blackwell.

Fagen, Richard R., Deere, Carmen Diana, and Coraggio, José Luis

1986   "Introduction." In *Transition and Development: Problems of Third World Socialism*, pp. 9–27. New York: Monthly Review Press/Center for the Study of the Americas.

FAO (United Nations Food and Agricultural Organization)

1972   *Production Yearbook, 1971*. Vol. 25. Statistics Division. Rome: FAO.

FIDA (Fondo Internacional de Desarrollo Agrícola)

1980   *Informe de la Misión Especial de Programación a Nicaragua*. Rome: FIDA.

FitzGerald, E. V. K.

1984a   "Acumulación planificada y distribución del ingreso en pequeñas economías socialistas periféricas." *Revolución y Desarrollo* 1 (April, May, and June): 30–37.

1984b   "Diez problemas para el análisis de la pequeña economía periférica en transición." Notes prepared for the PACCA/CRIES/SSRC conference, The Problems of Transition in Small Peripheral Economies, Managua (September 3–11).

1986   "Notes on the Analysis of the Small Underdeveloped Economy in Transition." In *Transition and Development: Problems of Third World Socialism*, edited by Richard R. Fagen, Carmen Diana Deere, and José Luis Coraggio, pp. 28–53. New York: Monthly Review Press/Center for the Study of the Americas.

1987   "An Evaluation of the Economic Costs to Nicaragua of U.S. Economic Aggression, 1980–84." In *The Political Economy of Revolutionary Nicaragua*, edited by Rose J. Spalding, pp. 195–213. Winchester, Mass.: Allen & Unwin.

FNI (Fondo Nacional de Inversiones)
1985   "Análisis del proceso inversionista nicaragüense, de 1979 a 1985." Managua (October). (Mimeographed.)

Fonseca, Carlos, ed.
1981   *Ideario Político de Augusto César Sandino*. Managua: Unidad Editorial.

Friedland, William H., and Barton, Amy
1975   *Destalking the Wily Tomato: A Case Study in Social Consequences in California Agricultural Research*. Davis: University of California, Department of Applied Behavioral Sciences Research, Monograph 15.

Furtado, Celso
1976   *Economic Development of Latin America*. Cambridge: Cambridge University Press.

La Gaceta—Diario Oficial
1979a   "Confiscación de bienes." 1:5.
1979b   "Aclaración y adición al Decreto 3." 6:42–43.
1980a   "Ley reguladora de los asentamientos de tierras destinadas al cultivo de algodón." 5:34–35.
1980b   "Ley reguladora de los arrendamientos de tierras destinadas al cultivo de granos básicos." 28:266–67.
1981   "Ley de Reforma Agraria." 188:1737–42.
1986   *Diario Oficial*, no. 8. Managua.

Galarza, Ernesto
1964   *Merchants of Labor: The Mexican Bracero Story*. Santa Barbara: McNally & Loftin.

García, Alan
1985   "Discurso ante el Congreso de la República de Perú." (July 28).

García Gallardo, Araceli
1987   "La productividad debe valorarse integralmente." *Boletín Socio-Económico* (INIES), no. 2 (April): 4–9.

García Gallardo, Araceli, and Delgado Silva, Félix
1987   "La productividad: Un concepto que se convierte en reto." *Cuadernos de Investigación* (INIES), no. 1 (April): 1–12.

Gariazzo, Alicia
1984   "El café en Nicaragua: Los pequeños productores de Matagalpa y

Carazo." *Cuadernos de Pensamiento Propio*, Serie Avances Dos (December).

Gereffi, Gary, and Evans, Peter

1981   "Transnational Corporations, Dependent Development, and State Policy in the Semiperiphery: A Comparison of Brazil and Mexico." *Latin American Research Review* 16, no. 3:31–64.

Gieskes, Thos, and Valkenet, Peter

1986   *De brigadistas en el corte de café: Un estudio de caso de dos brigadas en la Unidad de Producción Estatal "La Pintada."* DEA, UNAN, Managua (June).

Gorman, Stephen

1982   "The Role of the Revolutionary Armed Forces." In *Nicaragua in Revolution*, edited by Thomas Walker, pp. 115–32. New York: Praeger.

Gorman, Stephen, and Walker, Thomas W.

1985   "The Armed Forces." In *Nicaragua: The First Five Years*, edited by Thomas W. Walker, pp. 91–117. New York: Praeger.

Gorostiaga, Xabier, S.J.

1983   "Dilemmas of the Nicaraguan Revolution." In *The Future of Central America*, edited by Richard R. Fagen and Olga Pellicer, pp. 47–66. Stanford: Stanford University Press.

Government of National Reconstruction (GNR)

1982   *The Philosophy and Politics of the Government of Nicaragua.* Managua: Dirección de Divulgación y Prensa de la Junta de Gobierno de Reconstrucción Nacional.

Gutiérrez, Ivan

1989   "La política de tierras de la Reforma Agraria Sandinista." In *El debate sobre la reforma agraria en Nicaragua*, edited by Raul Ruben and Jan P. De Groot, pp. 113–28. Managua: Editorial Ciencias Sociales.

Gutman, Herbert G.

1966   *Work, Culture and Society in Industrializing America.* New York: Random House.

Haarer, A. E.

1969   *Producción moderna de café.* Havana: Edición Revolucionaria.

Hamilton, Nora

1982   *The Limits of State Autonomy: Post-Revolutionary Mexico.* Princeton: Princeton University Press.

Havens, A. Eugene, and Baumeister, Eduardo

1982   "Recruitment and Retention of Occasional Workers in the Export Sector of Agriculture in Nicaragua, 1981–82." Land Tenure Center, University of Wisconsin, Madison. (Mimeographed.)

Hightower, Jim
1973   *Hard Tomatoes, Hard Times: A Report of the Agribusiness Accountability Project on the Failure of America's Land Grant College Complex.* Cambridge, Mass.: Schenkman.

IAN (Instituto Agrario de Nicaragua)
1974a   *La Reforma Agraria de Nicaragua, 9 años de labor, 1964–1973.* Managua: IAN.

1974b   *Proyecto Rigoberto Cabezas.* Managua: IAN.

IHCA (Instituto Histórico Centroamericano)
1983   "Coffee and Cotton: Heart of the Economy, Symbol of Determination." *Envío* 3 (November): 1–10c.

INCAE (Instituto Centroamericano de Administración de Empresas)
1982a   "Nicaragua: Estudio de la situación del empleo, la absorción de la mano de obra y otros aspectos en fincas y productores de café y algodón." IDRC Rural Employment Project, INCAE (July). (Mimeographed.)

1982b   "Nicaragua: Estudio sobre la fuerza de trabajo familiar en recolectores de café y algodón." IDRC Rural Employment Project, INCAE (July). (Mimeographed.)

INCAP (Instituto de Nutrición de Centroamérica y Panamá)
1969   *Evaluación nutricional de la población de Centroamérica y Panamá: Nicaragua.* N.p.: INCAP.

INEC (Instituto Nacional de Estadísticas y Censos)
1983   *Anuario Estadístico.* Managua: INEC.

1989   *Nicaragua: Diez años en cifras.* Managua: INEC.

INIES (Instituto de Investigaciones Económicas y Sociales)
1987   *Plan Económico, 1987.* Managua: INIES.

INIES/CRIES (Coordinadora Regional de Investigaciones Económicas y Sociales)
1983a   "An Alternative Policy for Central America and the Caribbean." *Cuadernos de Pensamiento Propio* 2 (September).

1983b   "El subsistema de algodón en Nicaragua." Paper presented at the Second Seminar on Central America and the Caribbean, Managua (February 9–12).

1984   "CEPAL: Un cuadro dramático." *Pensamiento Propio* 2 (May–June): 19–24.

IRCT (Institut de Recherche Sur le Coton et Autres Fibres Textiles)
1982   *Informe de la misión tecnológica.* Director: Ing. Justin Gutknecht. N.p.: IRCT.

Jarquín C., Edmundo
1974   "Notas sobre el desarrollo del capitalismo en la agricultura." *Estudios Sociales Centroamericanos* 9 (September–December): 27–35.

1975   "Migraciones rurales y estructura agraria en Nicaragua." *Estudios Sociales Centroamericanos* 11 (May–August): 87–166.

Kaimowitz, David
1980   "The Nicaraguan Coffee Harvest, 1979–1980: Public Policy and the Private Sector." Paper presented at the Fifth World Congress for Rural Sociology, Mexico City (August 7–12).
1986   "Agrarian Structure in Nicaragua and Its Implications for Policies towards the Rural Poor." Ph.D. dissertation, University of Wisconsin, Madison.

Kaimowitz, David, and Thome, Joseph
1982   "Nicaragua's Agrarian Reform: The First Year (1979–1980)." In *Nicaragua in Revolution*, edited by Thomas Walker, pp. 223–40. New York: Praeger.

Karl, Terry
1975   "Work Incentives in Cuba." *Latin American Perspectives* 2, no. 4 (Supplementary Issue): 21–41.

Kinzer, Stephen
1984   "With Economic Woes Deepening, Managua Sees Years of Shortages," *New York Times* (October 22).

Kornbluh, Peter
1987   "The Covert War." In *Reagan versus the Sandinistas· The Undeclared War on Nicaragua*, edited by Thomas W. Walker, pp. 21–38. Boulder, Colo.: Westview Press.

LaFeber, Walter
1983   *Inevitable Revolutions: The United States in Central América*. New York: Norton.

Lanuza Matamoros, Alberto
1976   "Estructuras socioeconómicas, poder y estado en Nicaragua, de 1821 a 1875." Senior thesis, Programa Centroamericano de Ciencias Sociales, San José, Costa Rica.

LASA (Latin American Studies Association)
1990   "Electoral Democracy under International Pressure: The Report of the Latin American Studies Association Commission to Observe the 1990 Nicaraguan Election." Pittsburgh: LASA.

Las Casas, Fray Bartolomé de
1945   *Brevísima relación de la historia de las Indias*. Mexico City: Secretaría de Educación Pública.

Latin American Regional Reports
1981   (August 14) London.

Lehman, David
1983   "Gran empresa y pequeña producción: Aspectos de su articulación."
            Managua: MIPLAN. (Mimeographed.)

Levy, Pablo
1976   *Notas geográficas y económicas sobre la República de Nicaragua.* Managua:
            Colección Cultural, Banco de América.

Luciak, Ilja
1987   "Popular Hegemony and National Unity: The Dialectics of Sandinista
            Agrarian Reform Policies." *LASA Forum* 17 (Winter): 15–19.

Macaulay, Neill
1971   *The Sandino Affair.* Chicago: Quadrangle Books.

MacLeod, Murdo
1973   *Spanish Central America: A Socioeconomic History, 1520–1720.* Berkeley:
            University of California Press.

Majka, Theo
1978   "Regulating Farmworkers: The State and the Agricultural Labor Supply
            in California." *Contemporary Crisis* 2:141–55.

Marchetti, Peter, S.J.
1981   "Reforma agraria y la conversión difícil: Reubicación de recursos, re-
            distribución de poder y los explotados del campo en Chile y en Nic-
            aragua." *Estudios Rurales Latinoamericanos* 4 (January–April): 47–67.
1986   "War, Popular Participation, and Transition to Socialism: The Case of
            Nicaragua." In *Transition and Development: Problems of Third World Social-
            ism,* edited by Richard R. Fagen, Carmen Diana Deere, and José Luis
            Coraggio, pp. 303–30. New York: Monthly Review Press/Center for the
            Study of the Americas.

Marx, Karl
1959   "Excerpts from *The Eighteenth Brumaire of Louis Bonaparte.*" In *Basic
            Writings on Politics and Philosophy: Karl Marx and Friedrich Engels,* edited
            by Lewis S. Feuer, pp. 318–48. Garden City, N.Y.: Anchor Books.
1966   "The Communist Manifesto." In *Selected Works.* Moscow: Progress
            Publishers.

Maxfield, Sylvia, and Stahler-Sholk, Richard
1985   "External Constraints." In *Nicaragua: The First Five Years,* edited by
            Thomas Walker, pp. 245–64. New York: Praeger.

Mayorga, Salvador
1982   "La experiencia agraria de la Revolución Nicaragüense." In *Reforma
            Agraria y Revolución Popular en América Latina,* edited by CIERA, vol. 2.
            Managua: CIERA.

McWilliams, Carey
1971   *Factories in the Fields: The Story of Migratory Labor in California.* Santa
             Barbara: Peregrine.
MED (Ministerio de Educación)
1980   *La educación en el primer año de la Revolución Popular Sandinista.*
             Managua.
1983   *La educación en cuatro años de revolución.* Managua: MED.
Meislen, Richard J.
1983   "Nicaragua Reports an Attack by Insurgents on Major Port," *New York
             Times* (October 15).
MIDINRA (Ministerio de Desarrollo Agropecuario y Reforma Agraria)
1982   *Tres años de Reforma Agraria.* Managua: CIERA.
1983   *Informe de Nicaragua a la FAO.* Managua: CIERA.
1986a   "Los asentamientos en Nicaragua: Un nuevo modelo de desarrollo en el
             campo." *Informaciones Agropecuarias* 2 (June–July): 6–7.
1986b   *Plan de Trabajo: Balance y Perspectivas, 1986.* Managua: MIDINRA.
N.d.   "Las clases sociales en el agro." Managua. (Mimeographed.)
Millett, Richard
1977   *Guardians of the Dynasty: A History of the U.S.-Created Guardia Nacional de
             Nicaragua and the Somoza Family.* Maryknoll, N.Y.: Orbis Books.
Ministerio de Economía
1965   "Estudio sobre los problemas de la recolección del algodón." Dirección
             de Estudios Económicos. Managua. (Mimeographed.)
1966   *Censos nacionales: Agropecuarios.* Dirección General de Estadísticas y Cen-
             sos. Managua: Ministerio de Economía.
1971   *Censos nacionales agropecuarios: Cifras preliminares.* Oficina Ejecutiva de
             Censos. Managua: Banco Nacional de Nicaragua.
Ministerio de Salud Pública
N.d.   "Plan nacional de saneamiento básico rural (PLANSAR)." N.p. (Mim-
             eographed.) (ca. 1975).
MINVAH (Ministerio de Vivienda y Asentamientos Humanos)
1983   *Informe anual.* Managua: MINVAH.
MIPLAN (Ministerio de Planificación)
1980   *Programa de reactivación económica en beneficio del pueblo.* Managua: Sec-
             retaría Nacional de Propaganda y Educación Política del F.S.L.N.
1984   "Empleo y Reforma Agraria." Paper presented at a seminar organized
             by the Departamento de Empleo y Salario, MIPLAN, Managua (March
             13–16).
MITRAB (Ministerio de Trabajo)
1984   "Café: Fuerza de trabajo y salarios." Managua. (Mimeographed.)

Munslow, Barry
1983   "Is Socialism Possible on the Periphery?" *Monthly Review* 35 (May): 25–
            39.
Murray, Douglas L.
1984   "Social Problem-Solving in a Revolutionary Setting: Nicaragua's
            Pesticide Policy Reforms." *Policy Studies Review* 4 (November): 219–29.
Navas Mendoza, Azucena, Jímenez Alar, Adonaí, Cáceres Víchez, Luz Adilia, and
Montiel Castillo, Arnoldo
N.d.   "Algunos elementos para un análisis de los períodos críticos del algodón
            en Nicaragua." Paper presented by the Department of Social Sciences
            Research Team, UNAN, León.
Newson, Linda
1982   "The Depopulation of Nicaragua in the Sixteenth Century." *Journal of
            Latin American Studies* 14, pt. 2 (November): 253–86.
New York Times
1982   "Managua Suspends Individual Rights: U.S. Aggression Is Cited, 2
            Bridges Are Dynamited." (March 16).
1983a   "CIA Is Said to Supply the Rebels from Salvadoran Base." (October 2).
1983b   "Nicaragua Evacuates Port Raided by Rebels." (October 13).
1983c   "Rebel Aircraft Attack Managua, Bombing Airport and Residences."
            (September 9).
1983d   "U.S. Officials Say CIA Helped Nicaraguan Rebels Plan Attacks." (Octo-
            ber 16).
1985   "Coffee Futures Continue Drop as Harvest Nears" (February 14).
Nordland, Rod
1987   "The New Contras? Back in Battle, But Losing the War for People's
            Hearts and Minds," *Newsweek* (June 1).
Nuevo Diario (Managua)
1981   "Una ley que todo el pueblo debe conocer: La Reforma Agraria." (Au-
            gust 30).
1982   "Desocupados deben integrarse a brigadas de cortadores de café." (De-
            cember 4).
1983   "20 mil brigadistas para café y algodón." (September 24).
1984   "60% de cosecha de café cortada: Pero faltan brazos." (February 15).
1986a   "Café recolectado en 50 porciento." (January 27).
1986b   "MICOIN garantiza abastecimiento." (October 22).
Núñez Soto, Orlando
1981   *El somocismo y el modelo capitalista agroexportador*. Managua: Departa-
            mento de Ciencias Sociales, UNAN.
O'Connor, James
1984   *Accumulation Crisis*. New York: Basil Blackwell.

Offe, Claus

1974   "Structural Problems of the Capitalist State." *German Political Studies* 1:31–56.

1975   "The Theory of the Capitalist State and the Problem of Policy Formation." In *Stress and Contradiction in Modern Capitalism*, edited by Leon Lindberg, Robert Alford, Colin Crouch, and Claus Offe, pp. 125–44. Lexington, Mass.: D. C. Heath.

Oficina Ejecutiva de Encuestas y Censos

1978a   *Análisis demográfico de Nicaragua: Aspectos de la dinámica de la población relacionados con su dimensión económico social*. Part I. Boletín Demográfico 4. Managua: OEDEC.

1978b   *El algodón en Nicaragua*. Departamento Agropecuario. Managua: OEDEC.

Olivares, Sheila

1987   "La utopía popular Sandinista y el mensaje económico y gubernamental." Senior monograph, Escuela de Sociología, Universidad Centroamericana (UCA), Managua.

Ordóñez Centeno, Rigo

1976   "La política crediticia algodonera: El caso de Nicaragua." Senior monograph, Facultad de Ciencias Económicas, UNAN, Managua (August).

Ortega Saavedra, Daniel

1982   *Discursos pronunciados por el Comandante Daniel Ortega en las Naciones Unidas*. Managua: CIERA.

Peek, Peter

1982   "Agrarian Reform and Rural Development in Nicaragua (1979–1981)." General World Employment Programme Research, International Labor Organization (March).

Pensamiento Propio

1983   "La economía mixta en la tierra de Sandino," *Pensamiento Propio* 1 (July–August): 23–28.

Perdomo, Mario F.

1979   *Factores que afectan el cultivo del algodón en Nicaragua*. Trabajo de Campo, no. 238, INCAE.

Pizarro, Roberto

1987   "The New Economic Policy: A Necessary Readjustment." In *The Political Economy of Revolutionary Nicaragua*, edited by Rose J. Spalding, pp. 217–32. Winchester, Mass.: Allen & Unwin.

Pollitt, Brian H.

1982   "The Transition to Socialist Agriculture in Cuba: Some Salient Features." *Institute of Development Studies Bulletin* 3, no. 4:12–22.

Porras, Alonso
1987   "El movimiento cooperativo en Nicaragua." *Economía y Revolución* 1
            (October): 14–19.
Porras Mendieta, Nemesio
1962   "Tenencia de la tierra y algunos otros aspectos de la actividad agrope-
            cuaria en Nicaragua." Senior monograph, UNAN, Managua (Sep-
            tember).
Poulantzas, Nicos
1978   *State, Power, Socialism.* London: New Left Books.
PREALC (Programa Regional del Empleo para América Latina, Organización Internacional de Trabajo [OIT])
1981   *Informe de la Misión PREALC-OIT: Perspectiva del empleo agrícola para el
            ciclo 1981–82.* N.p.: United Nations.
La Prensa (Managua)
1982a   "Café genera $130 millones en divisas." (November 13).
1982b   "INRA explica marcha de Reforma Agraria." Interview with MIDINRA
            Vice-Minister Salvador Mayorga. (March 5).
1990a   "Agenda de Violeta Chamorro para el rescate de la economía nacional."
            (February 21).
1990b   "Se respetarán conquistas de la revolución." (March 3).
Programa Centroamericano de Ciencias de la Salud
1983   *Los trabajadores en la agricultura centroamericana (Condiciones de trabajo y
            de vida).* San José, Costa Rica: Universidad Nacional de Costa Rica
            (CSUCA).
Programa Centroamericano de Ciencias Sociales
1978   *Estructura agraria, dinámica de población y desarrollo capitalista en Centro-
            américa.* San José, Costa Rica: Editorial Universitaria Centroamericana.
Putterman, L.
1985   "Extrinsic versus Intrinsic Problems of Agricultural Production: Anti-
            Incentivism in Tanzania and China." *Journal of Development Studies*
            21:175–204.
Radell, David R.
1969   "A Historical Geography of Western Nicaragua: The Spheres of Influ-
            ence of León, Granada, and Managua, 1519–1965." Ph.D. dissertation,
            University of California, Berkeley.
Ramírez, Sergio
1981   *El pensamiento vivo de Augusto C. Sandino.* Vols. 1 and 2. Managua:
            Editorial Nueva Nicaragua.
Real Espinales, Blás A.
1974   "Dinámica de población y estructura agraria en Nicaragua." *Estudios
            Sociales Centroamericanos* 9 (September–December): 165–206.

Reinhardt, Nola
1987   "Agro-exports and the Peasantry in the Agrarian Reforms of El Salvador
          and Nicaragua." *World Development* 15 (July): 941–59.

República de Nicaragua
Memorias Aduaneras. Years consulted: 1935, 1936, 1937, 1938, 1939, 1940, 1941,
          1942, 1943, 1944, 1959, 1963, 1971.

Resnick, Idrian N.
1981   *The Long Transition: Building Socialism in Tanzania.* New York: Monthly
          Review Press.

Romero Vargas, Germán
1988   *Las estructuras sociales de Nicaragua en el siglo XVIII.* Managua: Editorial
          Vanguardia.

Rosengarten, Frederic, Jr.
1976   *Freebooters Must Die!* Wayne, Pa.: Haverford House.

Roxborough, Ian
1979   *Theories of Underdevelopment.* London: Macmillan.

Saul, John
1984   "Mozambique." Paper presented at the PACCA/CRIES/SSRC confer-
          ence, The Problems of Transition in Small Peripheral Economies, Ma-
          nagua (September 10).

Schmid, Lester
1967   *The Role of Migratory Labor in the Economic Development of Guatemala.*
          Research Paper 22. Madison: Land Tenure Center.

Scroggs, William O.
1969   *Filibusters and Financiers: The Story of William Walker and His Associates.*
          New York: Russell & Russell.

Selser, Gregorio
1979   *Sandino, general de hombres libres.* Ciudad Universitaria, Rodrigo Facio,
          Costa Rica: EDUCA.

Sholk, Richard
1983   "U.S. Economic Aggression against Nicaragua." Paper presented at the
          Eleventh International Congress of the Latin American Studies Associa-
          tion, Mexico City (September 29–October 1).

SIECA (Secretaría Permanente del Tratado General de Integración Económica
Centroamericana).
1975a   *La política de desarrollo social dentro de la integración económica.* Guate-
          mala: SIECA.
1975b   *VI Compendio Estadístico Centroamericano.* N.p.: SIECA.
1981   *VII Compendio Estadístico Centroamericano.* N.p.: SIECA.

Slutzky, Daniel

1982 "Movimiento campesino y Reforma Agraria en Nicaragua." Managua (September). (Mimeographed.)

Spalding, Rose J.

1983 "New Directions in Nicaragua's Agricultural Economy (1979–1982)." Paper presented at the Thirtieth Annual Meeting of the Southeastern Council of Latin American Studies, San Juan, Puerto Rico (April 7–9).

1985 "Food Politics and Agricultural Change in Revolutionary Nicaragua, 1979–82." In *Food Politics and Society in Latin America*, edited by John C. Super and Thomas C. Wright, pp. 199–227. Lincoln: University of Nebraska Press.

1987 "State–Private Sector Relations in Nicaragua: The Somoza Era." Paper presented at the Midwest Latin American Studies Association meeting, Chicago (November 6–7).

Spoor, Max

1987 *Datos macro-económicos de Nicaragua.* Departamento de Economía Agrícola, UNAN.

Squier, Ephraim George

1972 *Nicaragua, sus gentes y paisajes.* San José, Costa Rica: Editorial Universitaria Centroamericana (EDUCA).

Stahler-Sholk, Richard

1987 "Foreign Debt and Economic Stabilization Policies in Revolutionary Nicaragua." In *The Political Economy of Revolutionary Nicaragua*, edited by Rose J. Spalding, pp. 151–68. Winchester, Mass.: Allen & Unwin.

Stone, Katherine

1974 "The Origins of Job Structures in the Steel Industry." *Review of Radical Political Economy* 6 (Summer): 61–79.

Swezey, Sean, and Daxl, Rainer

1983 *Breaking the Circle of Poison: The Integrated Pest Management Revolution in Nicaragua.* San Francisco: Institute for Food and Development Policy.

Swezey, Sean, Daxl, Rainer, and Murray, Douglas L.

1984 "Getting Off the Pesticide Treadmill in the Developing World: Nicaragua's Revolution in Pesticide Policy." Managua. (Mimeographed.)

Thomas, Clive

1974 *Dependence and Transformation: The Economics of the Transition to Socialism.* New York: Monthly Review Press.

Tijerino Medrano, J. A.

1962 "Breves apuntes sobre mano de obra en el campo." Managua. (Mimeographed.)

Torres Rivas, Edelberto

1980a "The Central American Model of Growth: Crisis for Whom?" *Latin American Perspectives* 7 (Spring and Summer): 24–44.

1980b   *Interpretación del desarrollo social centroamericano*. San José, Costa Rica: EDUCA.

1982a   "La crisis económica centroamericana: Cuál crisis?" *Cuadernos de Pensamiento Propio*, Serie Avances (November).

1982b   "Quién destapó la caja de Pandora? Otras reflexiones sobre la crisis centroamericana." Paper presented at the Fifth Central American Sociology Conference "Roberto Castellanos Braña," San José, Costa Rica (November 22–26).

1983   "Central America Today." In *Trouble in Our Backyard*, edited by Martin Diskin, pp. 1–33. New York: Pantheon.

Torres Rivas, Edelberto, and Pinto, Julio César

1983   *Problemas en la formación del estado nacional en Centroamérica*. San José, Costa Rica: Instituto Centroamericano de Administración Pública (ICAP).

Tucker, Robert C.

1970   *The Marxian Revolutionary Idea*. New York: Norton.

UNAG/ATC/CIERA (Unión Nacional de Agricultores y Ganaderos, Asociación de Trabajadores del Campo, and Centro de Investigaciones y Estudios de la Reforma Agraria)

1982   *Producción y organización en el agro nicaragüense*. Managua: CIERA.

UNO (Unión Nacional Opositora)

1989   "Programa de Gobierno de la Unión Nacional Opositora." (Mimeographed.)

UNRISD (United Nations Research Institute for Social Development)

1986   *Food Systems and Society: Problems of Food Security in Selected Developing Countries*. Draft Overview Report. Geneva: UNRISD.

USDA (U.S. Department of Agriculture)

1974   *Agricultural Statistics, 1974*. Washington, D.C.: U.S. Government Printing Office.

Utting, Peter

1987   "Domestic Supply and Food Shortages." In *The Political Economy of Revolutionary Nicaragua*, edited by Rose J. Spalding, pp. 127–48. Winchester, Mass.: Allen & Unwin.

Velásquez, Julio

1977   *Sistema agroindustrial—El algodón en Nicaragua*. Trabajo de Campo, No. 117, INCAE.

Vilas, Carlos M.

1984   "Reforma agraria, agroexportación y empleo rural en Nicaragua." *Canadian Journal of Latin American and Caribbean Studies* 9, no. 18:111–32.

1986   *The Sandinista Revolution: National Liberation and Social Transformation in Central America*. New York: Monthly Review Press/Center for the Study of the Americas.

1987   "Troubles Everywhere: An Economic Perspective on the Sandinista Rev-
              olution." In *The Political Economy of Revolutionary Nicaragua*, edited by
              Rose J. Spalding, pp. 233–46. Winchester, Mass.: Allen & Unwin.
Warnken, Phillip F.
1975   *The Agricultural Development of Nicaragua: An Analysis of the Production
              Sector*. Special Report 168, Agricultural Experiment Station, University
              of Missouri, Columbia.
Washington Post
1982a   "Covert-Action Bar in Nicaragua Urged" (March 16).
1982b   "U.S. Approves Covert Plan in Nicaragua" (March 10).
Weber, Henri
1981   *Nicaragua: The Sandinist Revolution*. London: Verso Editions.
Weeks, John
1985a   *The Economies of Central America*. New York: Holmes & Meier.
1985b   "The Industrial Sector." In *Nicaragua: The First Five Years*, edited by
              Thomas W. Walker, pp. 281–95. New York: Praeger.
1987   "The Mixed Economy in Nicaragua: The Economic Battlefield." In *The
              Political Economy of Revolutionary Nicaragua*, edited by Rose J. Spalding,
              pp. 43–60. Winchester, Mass.: Allen & Unwin.
Wheelock Román, Jaime
1980   *Nicaragua: Imperialismo y dictadura*. Havana: Editorial de Ciencias So-
              ciales.
1984a   *Entre la crisis y la agresión: La Reforma Agraria Sandinista*. Managua:
              División de Comunicaciones, MIDINRA.
1984b   "Revolución y desarrollo: El sector agropecuario en la transformación
              revolucionaria." *Revolución y Desarrollo* 1, no. 1:5–14.
1986   "El trabajo: Un arma en la defensa de la patria." *Informaciones
              Agropecuarias* (MIDINRA, Managua) 2, no. 21, Special insert.
Williams, Robert G.
1986   *Export Agriculture and the Crisis in Central America*. Chapel Hill: Univer-
              sity of North Carolina Press.
Winson, Anthony
1978   "Class Structure and Agrarian Transition in Central America." *Latin
              American Perspectives* 5 (Fall): 27–48.
Wong, Carlos Iván
1978   *El algodón en la economía nacional, 1972–77*. Trabajo de Campo, No. 115,
              INCAE.
Woodward, Ralph L.
1976   *Central America: A Nation Divided*. New York: Oxford University Press.
Zalkin, Michael
1988   "Los olvidados: Campesinado medio," *Pensamiento Propio* 6 (Novem-
              ber): 8–14.

Index

Absenteeism, 126

Adult education programs, 139

Agrarian reform: Somocista, 13, 38, 50–52, 195 (n. 52); Sandino and, 32–33; Cuba, 210 (n. 4)

—Sandinista, xiv–xv, 17, 53, 54, 82, 86, 120, 125, 146; agroexport dependency and, xiii, 56–57, 83–85, 121, 156, 189 (n. 40); UNO government and, xiii–xiv, 174–77, 213 (n. 32); and labor shortages, 2, 57–58, 81, 87, 93–94, 106–12, 116, 119, 136, 145, 147, 156, 163–64, 173, 180–81; wage regulations, 84, 101–4, 106, 137–39, 140, 159–60, 203 (nn. 24, 26); agricultural credits, 87–88, 93–96, 98, 209 (n. 24); rent ceilings, 87, 88, 96–97, 98; guaranteed prices, 87–88, 98–100, 106–7, 111, 112; and campesinización, 87–88, 147, 163–64; land redistribution, 87–93, 98, 140, 156–58, 159–60, 201 (n. 7); colectivos de trabajo, 91–92, 142–43, 144, 145, 146, 209 (n. 26), 212 (n. 22); brigadas de producción, 141–42, 209 (n. 23); Plan Contingente, 143, 171, 209 (n. 27)

Agrarian Reform Law:

—1963, 195 (n. 52)

—1981, 89–90, 108; revisions in 1986, xiv–xv, 157–58

Agricultural communes, 88

Agriculture, 43, 180, 192 (n. 31), 193 (n. 37), 194 (n. 45), 209 (n. 30); revolutionary transformation, xiii, 7, 16–17, 53–54, 56–58, 143, 145, 146, 147, 156; Contra war and, xiv, 111, 113, 118–19, 120, 141, 160; food crop production, 2, 9, 46–47, 53, 84, 94, 96, 98, 120, 143, 170–71, 186 (n. 22); export production, 4–6, 7–8, 16, 18, 22, 45, 57, 121; production inputs, 6, 16, 36, 44, 133–34, 161, 162, 167–68, 197 (n. 8), 208 (n. 15); specialization, 8, 186 (n. 20); in Nicaraguan economy, 12, 17, 22, 45, 83, 196 (n. 2); latifundio-minifundio relationship, 21, 24, 29–31, 78–79, 80, 120, 191 (n. 20); Somoza and, 48–49, 50–52; civil war and, 74, 85–86, 87, 106, productivity, 113–14, 115

Agroexport capitalism, 10, 11–12, 34, 39

Agroexport production, 21, 39, 40–46, 47, 161, 193–94 (n. 42), 196 (nn. 2, 4, 5); agrarian reform conflict, xiii, xiv, 17, 56–58, 83–85, 86, 87, 90, 93, 104, 106–8, 120, 121, 122, 148, 163–64, 189 (n. 40); dependency, xiv, 2, 3, 4–6, 7, 11, 12, 16–17, 18–19, 29, 44, 45–46, 53, 120, 125, 139, 183 (n. 1); and peasant labor, xiv, 2, 8, 9, 11, 21, 47, 51–52, 57, 58, 77–79, 83, 84–85, 119–20, 191 (n. 18), 209 (n. 29); government and development of, 10–11, 26–28, 36, 41, 42; and social conditions, 11–13, 47–48, 49–50; and revolution, 14, 150;